Lying, Despair, Jealousy, Envy, Sex, Suicide, Drugs, and the Good Life

the text of this book is printed on 100% recycled paper

Lying, Despair, Jealousy, Envy, Sex, Suicide, Drugs, and the Good Life

---

LESLIE H. FARBER

HARPER COLOPHON BOOKS
Harper & Row, Publishers
New York, Hagerstown, San Francisco, London

For my sons

Steve, Luke, and Seth

and my daughter

Phoebe

A hardcover edition of this book is published by Basic Books, Inc. It is here reprinted by arrangement.

First HARPER COLOPHON edition published 1978

ISBN: 0–06–090604–9

Contents

Preface vii

I

1 *Thinking About Will* 3
2 *Will and Anxiety* 13
3 *Faces of Envy* 35
4 *Will and Willfulness in Hysteria* 46
5 *Despair and the Life of Suicide* 64
6 *Schizophrenia and the Mad Psychotherapist* 84
7 *Our Kindly Family Physician, Chief Crazy Horse* 106

II

8 *I'm Sorry, Dear* 123

9 *My Wife, the Naked Movie Star* 146

10 *He Said, She Said* 163

11 *On Jealousy* 180

III

12 *Lying on the Couch* 205

13 *Family Reunion* 221

Preface

THE ESSAYS in this book are of three kinds: earlier, later, and latest. The early ones belong to the period of my interest in the subject of will—the nature of will itself, its function as a category of psychological understanding, and its role in such forms of human distress as anxiety, envy, despair, etc. These essays, five of which appeared, with others, in my earlier collection, *The Ways of the Will,* appear here in Section I. "Thinking About Will" may serve as a brief introduction to this group, setting forth the basic structure of my understanding of the will as one of the authors of our lives.

Just as my absorption with will grew over me unawares (I had been tracking it for years before I knew its name), so it departed from the center of my attention stealthily too—at least it yielded to a new interest that did not announce itself thematically at once, either, but eventually—after several articles—was easily identified as men-and-women, natures-and-relation-of. I did not—have not—by any means abandoned my concern with will; it continues to inform my thinking on most subjects, as may readily be seen in these later (with one exception: "I'm Sorry, Dear" was written earlier and also appeared in *The Ways of the Will*) essays, which constitute Section II of this book.

The last section consists of my two most recent papers, which are addressed neither to will nor to the sexes, but which reflect in their own ways my continuing interest in both subjects.

Two of the essays in this book were addressed to topical issues: "I'm Sorry, Dear," written in 1965, and "Our Kindly Family Physician, Chief Crazy Horse" (then entitled "Ours is the Addicted Society") in 1966. At least I thought the issues were topical—I expected these articles to date rather quickly. In rereading them, however, it seems to me that we—as a society—have not rushed onward to new forms of these concerns—sex and addiction—with quite the speed we are reputed to be maintaining across the cultural board. Surprisingly, much that seemed true then still seems true now, justifying the inclusion of these pieces in this collection, "I'm Sorry, Dear" being my first real attempt to focus on the relations between men and women and "Chief Crazy Horse" an explicit application of my theories about will to a current issue.

It has often been remarked that my choice of subject matter is not upbeat: betrayal, despair, hysteria, deceit—what about trust, happiness, serenity, truthfulness—even love? What about them indeed—for they are, of course, in a sense, my ultimate subjects. But it is not my capacity or inclination to look upon such matters steadily or whole. Common items though they be in experience, I cannot confront them directly with my pen without falsifying or trivializing. Since it is my object to see these most precious and elusive concerns in their proper relation to our experience as a whole, I must pursue them in my own cautious, indirect way. I suspect many writers share this difficulty of mine, attempting to solve it in any number of ways. I look on the dark side (when I do—which is not always) in order to look both at and through the darkness.

While many friends have given help and support, there is really only one person who has been essential to this enterprise in every way. That is my wife Anne. Her contributions are so various, so crucially important, that I should properly devote a separate essay to express my gratitude. For the moment I shall withstand that temptation.

I

1

Thinking About Will

SYSTEMS OF PSYCHOLOGY, like the men who invent them, are lopsided affairs. In illuminating one aspect of the human situation, they neglect its other aspects. This is only to say that every psychology, like every man, has its strengths and weaknesses. Moreover, though each system will presume universal and perennial truth, the modest fact is that each psychology is, in its own way, a particular and contemporaneous response to the dilemma of a particular age. And why should it be otherwise? Though we may briefly transcend the contingency of history, we are historical creatures, unlike other forms of life, and therefore must acknowledge the perils of gainsaying our historicity. At this date few would dispute the fact that Freud's libido psychology, with its emphasis on sexuality as motive force, was nicely appropriate to the fussiness surrounding the subject at the turn of the century in Western Europe. The more recent inter-

This chapter originally appeared in the *Journal of the Otto Rank Association* 4, no. 1 (June 1969): 13–23.

personal psychologies, influenced by the social philosophies of Dewey and Mead, are peculiarly American in their insistence on the social nature of personality. And even more recently we have the fashionable example of the psychology of groups stemming from the dwindling sense of community in our times. As community fellowship disappears, a variety of arbitrary, even makeshift, communities are devised, in which we join together for reasons of therapy, drugs, alcohol, schizophrenia, old age, youth, integration, urban violence and urban renewal. In brief, group psychology appears at the same time that society erupts with its own solutions for the loss of community, just as the beginnings of psychoanalysis were accompanied by headstrong movements for sexual emancipation.

My remarks about the inescapable lopsidedness and, of course, the historical and social relevance of psychological systems apply equally to my own theoretical concerns. I have for a number of years been absorbed by the subject of will, attempting to develop both a psychology and psychopathology of will. As I have indicated above, I am convinced that it is the special nature of our age that has provoked me—as both witness and sinner—to focus upon—or become self-conscious about—a matter that for so long was in scholarly disrepute.

At this point, though, I believe it only fair that I explain, however sketchily, what I mean by will. Although the word has been used as a synonym for decision, choice, intention, passion, spirit, determination, control or volition, my use of the term is general enough to include all these qualities: I understand will to be the category through which we examine that portion of our life which is the mover of our life in a direction or toward an objective in time. In other words, through will I can arbitrarily raise my hand at this instant or prepare this essay over a period of time. Will, then, is the mover of actions both trivial and important. But now I must distinguish between what I call the two realms of will. So that the reader may have something concrete in mind as I describe the characteristics of these two realms, I suggest that he imagine some sports activity that interests him—tennis, for example. When our game is most fluid and effortless, we cannot really be said to be planning our shots and strategies: if we are thinking about the game, we are not aware of thinking; though will is involved in our shots and maneuvers, we cannot be said to be aware of will itself. We are, so to speak, of a piece—mind and body seamlessly and unselfconsciously joined in a totality. Will is so wedded to our faculties, our perceptions, our motor possibilities that it may be said to be unconscious in this first realm.[1] It is only after the fact, retrospectively, that we can infer the place of will, thought, footwork, and other components. Now let us assume that because of our opponent or ourselves, our game goes badly, requiring us to assess our failure. "It is the forehand that's at fault," we say. "Too slow and too much topspin." Will, clearly, has become conscious, for now we will ourselves to stroke the ball differently and are conscious of our willing. This ordinary state of affairs, in which will can be experienced consciously, I term the second realm of will.

Let me contrast these two realms of will a bit more. The first realm of will moves in a direction rather than toward a particular object. Our tennis playing has no particular object, such as a particular shot or point, but merely pursues its own direction, which is playing and winning and playing and winning and then going home. Direction, here, is to be understood not as an ideal goal toward which we press, however much we falter, but rather as a way in-

1 My use of "unconscious," whether as adjective or noun, derives from remarks by Martin Buber in a seminar in Washington, D.C., in 1957. The unconscious, as I understand him, is that state that precedes the split into psychical and physical, both being radically different modes of knowing that exist in consciousness. Buber would say, I think, that the unconscious is being itself, and that the physical and psychical are evolving out of it again and again at every moment. Seen in this way, the dream that I formulate on waking is a conscious psychical statement about dreaming itself, which was prior to the evolvement of the psychic and physical. In relation to will, the ruminations about the seriousness of decision and much of the associated bodily effort in the world are conscious psychical and physical aspects of the second realm of will. When Buber surveyed the vast history of philosophical speculation about the unconscious, he found nothing to improve on Plotinus, who wrote in the third century: "For it is very possible that even without being conscious of having something one has it in himself and even in a form more effective than if he knew it. . . . Consciousness seems to obscure the actions it perceives, and only when they occur without it are they purer, more effective, more vital" (Buber's translation; see equivalent passage in Plotinus, *The Enneads,* Stephen MacKenna, trans. [New York: Pantheon Books, 1957], p. 290).

terspersed with, yet not obstructed by, worldly detail and worldly objectives. Direction, therefore, is a way whose end cannot be known—a way open to possibility, including the possibility of failure. While this realm must, to some degree, remain impenetrable to inspection, its predominant experience is one of freedom—the freedom to think, speak, and act forthrightly and responsibly, without blinking the hazards such freedom entails. No human relation need occur within this first realm. Nevertheless, relation is always a dialogic potentiality.

In the second realm of will, will moves us toward a particular objective, all such movement being either conscious or potentially conscious. This could be said to be a utilitarian will, in that we do this to get that. We grasp the racket so that its face is more perpendicular, and as the serve arrives, rush to it and hit more energetically—all this willing in order to achieve a more effective forehand shot. Here the experience is not that of freedom, as in the first realm, but of conscious willing, successful or not. It goes without saying that in our utter absorption with this forehand we are less available to relation, should it arrive.

I would point out that I have not compared the quality of tennis in these two realms of will. Obviously there are tennis games which desperately cry for the will of the second realm, invoked by a competent teacher. And there are other games which suffer from hopeless self-consciousness in every movement. All of us, even tennis professionals, live our lives in both realms, trusting that the achievements of the second realm will correct the indulgences of the first, and that the freedom of the first realm will provide some direction and scope for the activity of the second.

There are, need I say, many feasible and relevant objects for the conscious utilitarian will. Much of our education has been accomplished under its dominion. Our day-to-day existence simply could not be gotten through without this will. Our burgeoning technology—that may destroy us all—owes everything to this realm of will. But I would call this the Age of the Disordered Will, and I would do so because it seems to me that increasingly we apply the will of the second realm to those portions of life that not only will not comply, but that become distorted—or even vanish—under such coercion.

Let me give a few examples: I can will knowledge, but not wisdom; going to bed, but not sleeping; eating, but not hunger; meekness, but not humility; scrupulosity, but not virtue; self-assertion or bravado, but not courage; lust, but not love; commiseration, but not sympathy; congratulations, but not admiration; religiosity, but not faith; reading, but not understanding. I would emphasize that the consequence of willing what cannot be willed is that we fall into the distress we call anxiety. And since anxiety, too, opposes such willing, should we, in our anxiety about anxiety, now try to will away that anxiety, our fate is still more anxiety. Within this impasse, meaning, reason, imagination, discrimination fail, so that the will is deprived of its supporting and tempering faculties. Under these reduced circumstances a man is, in a sense, all will. Or nothing but will. His disability is willfulness, meaning the state of being "governed by will, without yielding to reason," which is Webster's definition.

Day in, day out, every citizen is instructed by the public media that there is no portion of his life that is not wholly within his control or, in my vocabulary, wholly subject to his will. If life is difficult for you, an evening of television watching will teach you how to dispel your miseries through aspirin, deodorants, mouthwash, dance lessons, laxatives, vitamins, hair lotions, and edifying panel programs. And more professional sources can provide tranquillizers, stimulants, psychoanalysis, sleeping pills, religion, or instruction in sexual technique and business relations. I have no intention of surveying all the elixirs and panaceas that are offered us for the better life. Nor do I mean to suggest we all live like hayseeds at a county fair, at the mercy of every snake-oil salesman who happens to pass through town. After all, whoever *really* believed in the conjugal possibilities of Lavoris? The problem is less rational and at the same time more pathetic than that. The underlying presupposition for both the bombarders and the bombarded is that, in varying degree, everything and nothing is possible for our will. Simultaneously I have to believe that all that stands between me and my marriage is the latest mouthwash, and that a viable marriage being utterly impossible for me, I might as well distract myself with a new mouthwash. (For Lavoris you may substitute any other national product or technique advertised for the promotion of marital harmony.) I need hardly add that any marriage whose fate depends on technology is, at the very least, already a technological disaster. Compare the poignancy of believing we can will everything and nothing with the brasher optimism that prevailed not many years ago, before disillusionment set in. There must be others, beside me, who remember Henley's "Invictus," that was sung by the class baritone at every high school graduation. This callow young man, who happened to possess a deep voice, sang of his "unconquerable soul," of his head "bloody, but unbowed." And finally, to a mounting climax: "It matters not how strait the gate,/How charged with punishments the scroll,/I am the master of my fate;/I am the captain of my soul." It is not hard to imagine the pained incredulity on the faces of a senior class today, forced to listen to Henley's prideful sentiments. "What's he on?" would be one response, as they nudged each other. Or, more likely, "He's putting *us* on."

Certainly our decade, and perhaps our age, may come to be epitomized by our peculiar employment of such prepositions as "on," "off," "up," "out," "with." Being up-tight, and not with it, we can be turned on or off, be an up-head or down-head, drop out or freak out. When the incredulous student asks, "What's he on?" he suggests—somewhat enviously—that while being able to will everything is an attractive and even necessary belief for the baritone, it cannot be achieved except through self-induced or drug-induced rapture. In effect, he is saying, "How can we live unless we are captains of our soul," but since such a venture is futile, we must settle for the sovereignty of our will being merely a state of mind unrelated to the business of the world. And settling for a state of mind means, unhappily, turning our wills to ever new measures, devices, and chemicals which will bring us the willful intoxication we yearn for. I think I should mention that the prepositions with which we are infatuated are the language—if that's not too large a term—of technology. It is through these prepositions that we impose our will on the endless machines and appliances that facilitate the running of this world. As a young student put it, "Everything else in this world is being turned on and off—lights, television sets, refrigerators, stoves, freezers, fans, phonographs, vacuum cleaners, and so on—so why shouldn't we want to be turned on too?" Essentially his wish is not too different from scientific discussions I have heard where the scientists ask themselves and each other, "Is there anything human that can't be duplicated by an electronic computer?" They range over such human matters as choice, conflict, foresight, chess-playing, poetry, and even fornication, only to arrive at the answer that was already contained in their question. What they ask, in effect, is whether there is anything human that lies beyond their scientific will.

At this remove it is easy to be condescending about Henley's "Invictus," if only because it hardly qualifies as poetry. But even a bad poem can sometimes give a hint of the manner in which man views himself and his world. And I may as well confess here that at the time I was as thrilled by the song as the rest of my graduating class. In first referring to the song, I neglected to mention that the hero thanks "whatever gods there may be" for his "unconquerable soul." Such an admission, in religious terms at least, has to be judged a dubious expression of gratitude, inasmuch as it seems to be no more than a token gesture to a divinity no longer believed in. If there is gratitude in the hero's heart, it is really to himself for prevailing over all the obstacles in his path.

Nietzsche would have quickly recognized this exciting and desperate situation as a precise, if vulgar, Victorian description of the consequence of the death of God. "He who no longer finds what is great in God," Nietzsche wrote, "will find it nowhere—he must either deny it or create it." Or in Erich Heller's words, " 'The death of God' Nietzsche calls the greatest event in modern history and the cause of extreme danger. Note well the paradox contained in these words. He never said there was no God but that the Immortal suffered death at the hands of mortals: God is dead. It is like a cry mingled of despair and triumph. . . ."

It is of course easy for me to understand why I was flattered by Henley's heroic picture of me. But why, following Nietzsche in the matter, I was not also terrified by my lonely and arduous fate is harder to say. Partly, I suppose, I was too young, too naive to appreciate the painful nature of my life's course, as depicted by Henley and predicted by Nietzsche. But also, to give myself slight credit, I was not entirely persuaded. I am not a thorough Nietzschean today and many years ago I only half believed in Henley's desolate landscape. Like other young people of my generation, I accepted the fact that there was no higher power I could appeal to and that it was all up to me. If I was to make anything of myself, I could depend only on my own will. Since I assumed my friends shared my predicament, I saw humanity as a precarious affair indeed, every solitary mortal wrestling every other solitary mortal for the few rewards this desert terrain could provide. I am trying to say here that in behavior and attitude I carried on like a thin caricature, drawn many years ago by Nietzsche and later badly copied by Henley. And I cannot overestimate the degree to which these carryings-on robbed me of consolation even as I was persuaded of their brilliance. Nevertheless, not being an absolute simpleton, I had slowly to acknowledge there was a portion of my life not provided for by Nietzsche or Henley. There were occasions, for example, when I was valued in spite of my noisy strivings, i.e., my pathetic "unconquerable soul." There were times when the most perfunctory and public type of encounter gave way to a friendly and forthright moment which quite transcended what went before. There were gestures of kindness which I had neither earned nor anticipated. There were even times when my friends and I allowed a moment to develop in its own surprising ways without immediately twisting it to our own demands. Although we tend to believe, these days, that everything must be named, that unless it is named it will die, I note that in regard to these ordinary yet remarkable moments, I lived as a double agent, a respectable citizen of my times, a devoted Nietzschean. It was as though some prejudice or hunch or older wisdom had warned me that the vitality of these moments depended on not being named or categorized. Later I came to realize there were imposing terms from traditional religion and theology—terms like mystery and grace and revelation and faith and communion—that could conceivably be applied to my ordinary moments, but I was as wary of them as I was of the fashionable psychological barbarisms, with which I am more familiar. For one thing, as a practicing non-believer I had no right to appropriate the language of belief. But, more important, I was committed to secrecy, and even religious language would violate that commitment by naming what should not be named. I realize that on the basis of what I have said I could easily be convicted as a clandestine believer, or, worse yet, as a hardened secularist, exploiting the benefits of religion while denying its creed.

If a verdict on my condition may be momentarily withheld, let me attempt a defense of my habit of secrecy, on the possibility that my response to our contemporary dilemma is not untypical. As already suggested, I share Nietzsche's dour foreboding that the loss of the divine Will in our existence would have paradoxical consequences. In place of our relation to the Immortal, each of us must assume some of the prerogatives of Divinity. The tremendous advantages of such reliance on our own will are immediately apparent in our technological, scientific, and even social and political advances. On the other hand, the more ominous side of such willing would lie in our vainglorious attempt to impose this will on precious and private aspects of our lives that must wither under such coercion. I need hardly remind you of the extent to which ordinary and private relations between people have suffered from this imposition, sexuality being only one of the more conspicuous catastrophes resulting from this encroachment of will. My own failures repeatedly tell me I cannot will relation, any more than I can will not to will relation.

But if this is all there is, why should life be possible at all, no matter how intriguing Nietzsche's paradox may be? My answer is that I think it possible to grant whatever truth Nietzsche grasped about modern man and at the same time recognize that as a victim of the same historical dilemma he was interpreting, his own will led him to assert an absoluteness or certainty about our fate that was perhaps not entirely warranted by his own experience. In other words, his error or failure lay in his unwillingness to allow for his own willfulness in the exposition of his theories.

Whether God is dead, as Nietzsche said, or merely in eclipse, as Martin Buber would have it, I know I am granted occasional and surprising moments in my life, neither self-induced nor drug-induced, that lie outside the dominion of my conscious will. At such times my soul is indeed conquerable and I am more servant than captain of my fate. Yet even as these moments arise, I know my temptation to declare myself their master who must manipulate them into public certainties of knowledge or relationship. Since they are easy objects for my will, I stand ready to reduce them to nothingness out of my insistence on everything.

What then is left to me? On the one hand, I can subjectively note the extraordinary nature of these moments. "He who does not wish to see what is great in a man," Nietzsche wrote, "has the sharpest eye for that which is low and superficial in him, and so gives away—himself." This is to say that, in a spirit of some reverence, I can acknowledge the transcendent importance of these moments, without succumbing to sentimentality or mysticism or the other risks such acknowledgement entails. And if my wits allow me that degree of celebration, I can at least will myself to protect their privacy. In practice, this means that I can stubbornly will myself to shut up in the face of my own need or the world's demand to make them public. It goes without saying that I fail more than I succeed in this venture, but I personally know no other way. So, if I am asked, "Is this religion?" I must answer that I doubt it. Conversely, if I am asked, "Isn't this really an admission of your lack of faith?" my answer is the same: I doubt it. The verdict, it is my hope, will be indefinitely withheld.

2

Will and Anxiety

THE LAST HALF-CENTURY has been a propitious one for the development of psychological theory, particularly for that of the psychoanalytic variety. Without this development, our preoccupation with anxiety would be inconceivable, however impressed we might be by the peculiarly disruptive nature of our present human predicament. It is modern psychology that has given the term "anxiety" a categorical density it never previously carried. Perhaps there is an apprehensive quality characterizing our age that requires the term to be isolated and then weighted—or even exalted—in our vocabulary. Or it may be that we turn in a special way to such a theme as anxiety because our psychological theories, despite the many novel notions they have provided about man's character, deny us other approaches that might be more illuminating. A young movement often must be parochial and even shun traditional knowledge if it is to maintain the enthusiasm necessary for pursuing its inspirations. This is why we counsel the young writer to have his own full say before he resorts to bibliography. But youthful parochialism willfully extended beyond its natural time—that is, shunning every possibility of eventual reconciliation with previous thought—brings a premature senility to the movement, which now enshrines rather than extends its early achievements.

If some detachment is possible, now that our youth draws to a close, I think it can be said the psychological theories that support and derive from psychotherapy have proliferated without explicit recourse to the subject of will, with its vast philosophical and theological literature. Will has been the category through which we examine that portion of our life that is the mover of our life. Though man is ceaselessly subjected to a variety of forces, human and nonhuman, the traditional concept of will asserts that, alone among these many movers, man's power of volition—however frustrated, however often vanquished—is nonetheless accountable, both in achievement and intention. To speak plainly, it is a serious deficiency in our theories that they contain no notion of a responsible mover as it has been described, at its best, since the beginnings of Western history. But, at this point, it may be of historical interest to recall the manner in which Freud turned aside from the category of will in one of his first essays. When Dora—to Freud's great chagrin—unexpectedly terminated treatment after only a few weeks, at a point when his therapeutic ambitions were at their highest, he wrote, after his outrage had subsided, that he recognized one of the limits to psychotherapeutic influence to be the patient's own "will and understanding." [1] But, in the course of this essay, he had second thoughts about his therapeutic failure—thoughts about the nature of transference, which now seemed a more revealing way to understand Dora's interruption of treatment. With this step, Freud may be said to have abandoned the traditional will as a psychological consideration and

1. Sigmund Freud, "Fragment of an Analysis of a Case of Hysteria," *Collected Papers*, 5 vols. (New York: Basic Books, 1959), 3:131.

instead now found, not unlike Schopenhauer, his mover in the libido. Like many important theoretical principles, transference had both advantages and limitations. But, at this date, it should be possible, without demeaning the knowledge gained through transference theory, to consider the price we pay for excluding will from our psychologies.

One reason for that exclusion was that the pioneers in psychotherapy at the turn of the century came largely from the medical sciences, so it is understandable that they would be more taken by the scientific spirit of the time than by the subject of will, with its roots in philosophy and theology—occupations that Freud (and he was not untypical) regarded as, if not curable, at least arrestable once their pathology was identified. Far more exciting were the discoveries in chemistry, biology, physics, and anthropology. Still, this is only part of the story, and it really fails to explain not only why we have no psychology of will but also why the subject of will fell into general disrepute, even in philosophy, which had proudly fostered it for so many centuries. As could be expected, science and scientific philosophy were antagonistic to the tangled metaphysical speculations on will. And it must be admitted that the antagonism was to some extent earned; much that had been called will badly needed the psychological surgery that psychoanalysis was more than ready to offer. If this readiness seems brash or presumptuous today, we should recall the intoxicating conviction shared by the early leaders of the young movement that there was nothing in all of human history—and especially prehistory—which would not yield to the new psychoanalytic weapons. In this regard, the argument has been made, with considerable generosity, that will was not excluded; that is, by omission or *in absentia,* will *is* the principal, though invisible, actor in the psychoanalytic drama. In other words, will is the residue, like Leonardo da Vinci's genius, remaining after psychoanalytic reduction. Thus, so the argument goes, psychoanalysis serves the purpose of clearing away the brush overgrowing the subject of will these many years.

At least some of the responsibility for the will's disfavor, as suggested above, must be credited to the accumulated scholarship on the subject—scholarship which, with certain bright exceptions, is often so tedious as to be virtually unreadable. But tedium alone, I am afraid, would be an insufficient obstacle, to judge from the fashionable careers of other large issues. Even a cursory inspection of this scholarship will reveal that on the one hand, the topic of will has been endlessly exploited for all manner of self-serving moralizing, and on the other hand has come increasingly to be the speculative plaything of the academicians who tinkered with it so whimsically that it would be difficult for the reader to know that will had any relevance to human considerations.

Thus, either as an ingredient of moral coercion or as a fruitless venture in philosophical or theological academicism, the subject of will gradually lost its connection with existence itself. On this basis alone, it is understandable why the psychotherapists of the beginning of the century preferred to abandon—or rather bury—this bloodless category. They would have needed both patience and erudition to root out the exceptions to this dreariness—those extraordinary thinkers who grasped the anthropological necessity for the term "will." Whichever emphasis they gave the will—choice, decision, resolution, passion, intention, determination, or spirit—these exceptional men tried at best to preserve will's identity as responsible mover, whether that mover be individual, communal, or divine. And they had assistance here, for literature was spared the attrition born of academicism. Literature—in whose view the human condition is inevitably a drama of conflict—has always been interested in man as a creature with some capacity, even if only potential, for independent personal volition: the one human capacity above all others that gives both interest and meaning to the literary records of conflicts between man and man, man and the world, or within man himself. It can hardly surprise us to find that the subject of will—explicitly and literally—has engaged the interest of authors as diverse as Flaubert, Butler, Goncharov, Tolstoy, Dostoyevsky, Ibsen, and even such moderns as Allen Tate and Lionel Trilling.

Having acknowledged my sympathy for those who preferred to

abandon the matter of will, given its tedious, moralistic, and sterile expressions in the scholarship of the past, I should now like to consider the price—or, more precisely, the theoretical and practical consequences—of this abandonment. The problem may be briefly put in this manner: *without a clear and explicit conception of will as responsible mover, we tend to smuggle will into our psychological systems under other names–this contraband will being usually an irresponsible mover of our lives.* A corollary to this proposition is: *when particular aspects of our will-less systems are asked to become or include will, the existential or phenomenological relevance of these aspects is diminished.* Thus, when Freud shifted from will to libido, in the example mentioned earlier, he was forced to slight the phenomenological investigation of sexuality in favor of argument or polemics, insisting on the libido's distinction as prime mover. In his postscript to the case of Dora, he wrote: "I was further anxious to show that sexuality . . . provides the motive power for every single symptom, and for every manifestation of a symptom." [2] It could be said, I think, that every system, including my own, contains a polemic for its particular prime mover, such polemic being antithetical to the phenomenological illumination of the system's prime mover. In other words, when Freud insisted that sexuality be the will of his system, it was his and ultimately our understanding of the place of sexuality in existence that suffered from this double burden.

I shall do no more than list some of the categories that have been made to do the work of the will in various psychologies: unconscious, aggression, dependence, power, inferiority, sadomasochism, guilt, and, of course, anxiety. But, before I move to the matter of anxiety, I should like to say a word about the issue of psychological determinism itself, as it pertains to the will. Here I deal not with prime movers, but with myriad small movers that appear to the imagination of the psychotherapist as chains of explanation, the scrutiny of which may reveal to him the order he is intent on discovering in neurotic and psychotic disorder. A critical question

2. Freud, "A Case of Hysteria," p. 137.

here, or so it seems to me, is how motive may be distinguished from will. It would seem that in psychology when will was abandoned in our theories, motivation became an object of increasing concern. Motive and will have some superficial resemblance in that they both provoke movement or action. If I disparage my friend's achievements out of envy, envy is the motive of my disparagement. However, envy is not the same as will, even though my will to disparage may be incited by my motive of envy. In other words, a motive cannot be responsible for an action of will, even though it may provoke or prompt such action. This has been the usual distinction between will and motive. Obviously, a psychology of will would not preclude psychic determinism, even though it might deprive determinism of some of the ill-begotten prerogatives it has acquired in this century. It is when motive is used as cause that it begins to usurp the will's domain and at the same time defeat the phenomenological venture. If, out of envy, I will to disparage, I still have the option of willing not to disparage. So far as I know, no such option occurs in disparagement whose cause is envy. The determinism relevant to these considerations seems more a professional tic, peculiar to psychotherapists, and might more accurately be called the compulsion or will toward causality, that constructs, inventing in its own image, other wills called motives. If there is a motive provoking the will toward causality, it would not be causality itself, but rather the need for order or perhaps the intolerance of mystery. Such a will, when asked to explore the *what* of a situation, turns instead to the *why*. It is but another example of Yeats's "will trying to do the work of the imagination." The will toward causality, given its imaginative limitations, spawns prior wills, preceded by prior wills, and so on. Ideally, one hopes that principles may eventually arise out of the imaginative search of the situation itself, but here the principles arrive first, and any phenomena developed are at the mercy of these principles.

With these introductory remarks, I have tried to suggest the direction of my dissatisfaction with anxiety theory. To begin with, I am never entirely sure what the nature of the experience is that anxiety is meant to describe. It is unusually difficult to know whether anxiety signifies a particular shudder of being, common to us all, or whether anxiety is a general category, a blanket term meant to cover a range of painful states. Before the advent of modern psychology, it was one of many expressions we used to indicate distress; its meaning, according to *Webster's,* is "painful uneasiness of mind over an impending or anticipated ill." This meaning is, it seems to me, quite precise when compared to its present swollen and ambiguous condition whereby, depending on the whim of its user, it may indicate (or conceal) a host of distressing responses, with any number of subjective or objective shadings—emotional, cognitive, or physical. What we call "anxiety" today might in another time be more exactly rendered as "apprehension," "fear," "fright," "tremor," "uncertainty," "uneasiness," "dread," "restlessness," "worry," "shakiness," "trepidation," "desperation," "palpitations," "queasiness," "agitation," "anguish," "alienation," or "cowardice," according to which experience we wished to describe. It might be objected that theoretical speculation cannot, if only for the sake of brevity, afford such novelistic precision as it searches for hypothetical principles to govern its theory. After all, we have many items of theory that are not to be confused with experience—ego, projection, regression, identification, and the like. But it must be answered that the abstract nature of these terms was clear from the beginning, whereas with "anxiety" it was never clear whether the term indicated a particular experience or a way of theorizing about a variety of experiences. As a result, what was at first an abstraction now passes itself off as experience itself, rather than as a way of talking about experience. In our scientific age, it is always a danger that a psychological term may trespass its original scientific boundaries. Once the trespass becomes convention, experience itself is vulgarized, since theories about experience inevitably subvert experience, much as our experience corrects our theories.

Those psychological theories that have developed within the medical tradition have given a physical emphasis to anxiety so that the "painful uneasiness" of the older definition is now one of the body rather than of the mind. Even when no description of the experience is attempted, what is implied is a bodily response comparable to that of fright, whose predominant manifestations—subjectively and objectively—are such physical disturbances as rapid heartbeat, tremors, dry mouth, overbreathing, sweating, muscular incoordination, insomnia, and so on. In this view, it is the bodily commotion that is primary, other aspects of our distress being derivative of this disturbance. The seeming advantage of a physical theory of anxiety is that the similarity of objective manifestations in babies and lower mammals allows a biological or evolutionary continuity to be asserted about all mammalian life when endangered. Partly because the subjectivity of lower animals cannot be inspected and partly because human danger need not be of the literal order of the jungle, a distinction is usually made in these theories between fear and anxiety. Whatever theoretical virtue this distinction may have, in actuality it is usually rather difficult, if not impossible, to separate objective from subjective danger. Needless to say, it is this bodily view of anxiety that has found common cause with the drug industry.

To pursue further the ambiguity of the experience of anxiety, let us consider briefly several modern definitions whose emphasis is not so physical. Kurt Goldstein describes anxiety as, in part, the subjective experience of the organism in a catastrophic condition.[3] Despite the fact that Goldstein's contributions have been in the general area of the medical sciences, it will be noted that his description makes no mention of objective bodily disturbance, but instead refers to subjective experience. Yet anxiety is for Goldstein clearly a categorical abstraction intended to cover a range of experience accompanying catastrophe. In an effort to be more particular about the human experience, Rollo May defines anxiety as "the apprehension cued off by a threat to some value which the individual holds essential to his existence as a personality."[4] The word "apprehension" has the virtue of having both psychic and physical implications. In contrast, Sullivan's descriptions are indeed abstract, suggesting some sort of un-

3. Rollo May, *The Meaning of Anxiety* (New York: Ronald Press, 1950), p. 49.
4. May, *The Meaning of Anxiety*, p. 191.

pleasant state brought on by the apprehension of disapproval in interpersonal relations.[5] Perhaps the most exhaustive description of the experience is contained in Karen Horney's definition of "basic anxiety," namely, "the feeling of being small, insignificant, helpless, deserted, endangered, in a world that is out to abuse, cheat, attack, humiliate, betray, envy." [6] This picture of helplessness in the face of a threatening world has a more hysterical, even paranoid, quality, in that the anxious person feels put upon and persecuted by the will of others but lacks any corresponding will to defend himself.

In summary, then, it seems clear that anxiety is a painful state invoked by threat to human integrity. But, in the theories we have considered, the experience of anxiety has been relatively neglected in favor of its causes and especially its consequences.

If I may return to an earlier proposition, the phenomenological thinness or ambiguity of the term "anxiety" as it appears in the theories I have just mentioned is largely the consequence of the burden laid on it to do the work of the will; that is, though unequal to the task, anxiety has been required to supply force, shape, meaning, and intention to the matter of psychological development and/or disability. Unlike the will, which pushes actively toward its goal, whether appropriate or inappropriate, anxiety is an ache that helplessly cries for relief. We are told by these theories that its painful urgency is so compelling as to overpower our discriminations, forcing us to settle for familiar and childish ways that serve us poorly in our life in the world. In passing, however, it should be remarked that the notion of settling for old ways is an unwitting attempt to smuggle the traditional will into the system. Be that as it may, the inevitability of pathological consequence associated with anxiety assists the cause of psychic determinism almost too well, failing to account for those times when, in spite of present or future pain, we choose a course that seems right rather than soothing. In order to

5. May, *The Meaning of Anxiety*, p. 148.

6. Karen Horney, *The Neurotic Personality of Our Time* (New York: W. W. Norton, 1937), p. 92.

contain this eventuality, some theories devise two anxieties, one normal and the other neurotic—the former liberating, the latter constricting. In terms of experience, "normal" anxiety does not differ from neurotic anxiety, and therefore is not to be confused with an ontological meaning that "anxiety" has carried for centuries, namely, solicitous or earnest desire. An example of this meaning would be "I am anxious to rejoin my friend." Although the addition of "normal anxiety" to a system would seem to allow anxiety more of the prerogatives of will, in effect it undercuts the original notion of anxiety as an insistent anguish, compelling relief. Here a proposition could be made that whenever a psychological category is asked to do the work of the will in psychopathology, sooner or later a normative version of that category must be added to the theory.

In order to consider further the issue of will and anxiety, I shall now confine myself to the theories and practice of Harry Stack Sullivan. According to him, the self is born of anxiety, or, as he says, the self "comes into being as a dynamism to preserve the feeling of security." [7] Being an unpleasant feeling, anxiety requires relief. And the relief it finds is apt to be limiting to the development of the person. Whenever these limitations are overstepped, anxiety arises again and dissociates these new threats from awareness. Whatever existential content there may be to anxiety in Sullivan's theories, it is evident that his is a most hypochondriacal view of development of the self. Unlike the traditional will, anxiety permits no choice, sees no ends, cannot discriminate between one course and another. In fact, since anxiety is always limiting, it would seem it insists not only on immediate but also on inferior relief. As such, the self is a tangle of makeshift adjustments, all hastily and mistakenly contrived for the sake of allaying anxiety. The system has no room for accident, risk, surprise, mystery, or grace. In Sullivan's melancholy view, there seems no hope except through psychotherapy.

It may be interesting here to say something of how his theory shaped his practice. Since Sullivan was one of my teachers, I can be

7. Harry Stack Sullivan, *Concepts of Modern Psychiatry* (Washington, D.C.: William Alanson White Foundation, 1947), p. 21.

anecdotal about this issue. Some psychotherapists profess one theory, but in practice seem to pursue another. They may write about mankind as a jungle of destructive strife, in which survival is almost accidental, and yet in their office life be the most kind and considerate men. But I would say of Sullivan that he was one of the most painfully consistent human beings I have known: he not only wrote of anxiety as the center of his theories—he also practiced it. In this he resembled some of the more active Zen masters I have read about—men with devilish skill in inventing all manner of mental and physical devices for unsettling their pupils. In the interest of accuracy, I should here say that Sullivan was a mild man physically: he did not cudgel with sticks, he never raised his voice, and his harshest physical mannerism was a glance which never met my own. Believing psychotherapeutic ineptitude, as well as psychological disability in general, to stem from, and to consist of, our poor efforts to cope with anxiety, he thought that any psychotherapy or teaching worth its name must eventually provoke that anxiety, in the hope that within such an ambience something more satisfactory might at long last occur.

Our first meeting, which had taken several months to arrange, and required the intervention of a mutual friend, was, to put it mildly, distressing. As I described the three patients I was treating at the time, he looked quite discouraged by the supervisory prospect. Two of my patients, he wearily explained, were wholly unsuitable for supervision and, by inference, for psychotherapy too. As I was beginning to wonder what presumption had possessed me to seek supervision with this eminent man, he grudgingly agreed to hear about my third patient, although he made it quite clear he expected no good to come of it. This patient was a young man with severe ulcerative colitis, who spent much of his energy, when he was not hospitalized, in both inviting and defeating the possessive intrusions of his divorced parents. For two hours, Sullivan sat in silence as I nervously tried to depict this young man's struggles, hoping all the while that my portrayal, while remaining faithful to my patient on the one hand, would be intriguing enough on the other to justify Sullivan's continuing to spend time with me in supervision. But he was too scrupulous, or too unimpressed, to indicate, through gesture or word, the tiniest interest in my account. Once or twice, when my desperation verged on sheer panic, I turned helplessly to him for advice, but he refused these overtures with a tired wave of the hand, as though my solicitations were too flagrant or too gross to deign a verbal refusal. When I finally ground to a limp and chaotic halt in my story, and made ready to flee this unhappy occasion, Sullivan roused himself to offer what the Zen masters would call a *koan*. "I would suggest," he said, "that until our next appointment you try to imagine—mind you, not say, *imagine*—how your young man might respond if you were to ask him what he imagined his mother's reaction would be to his saying, 'Mother, since you insist you are so deeply attached to me, let us go to bed together and have it over with.' " If I may translate this rather involved imaginative exercise, Sullivan was suggesting that, out of my own anxiety, I was taking my patient's account of his parents' erotic attachment to him much too literally.

When I managed to drag myself to his study two weeks later for our second appointment, he immediately asked me if I had had any thoughts about our first session. I confessed I had not really been up to thought; in fact, my anguish had been so paralyzing that I had taken to my bed for most of the period. Deliberately I skipped the details of my anguish, the consuming self-disparagement that had led me to question even my choice of profession. His astonishing reply was, "Well, that's rather promising. I hadn't really expected so much." To this day I can still almost physically recall the relief and gratitude that came over me at having earned, in such an unexpected way, this man's approval through my suffering.

I trust I have conveyed in this vignette Sullivan's way of practicing what he preached. Unfortunately, what I have been forced to slight in this anecdote is his remarkable clinical shrewdness as well as his tactful, often compassionate, manner of dealing with disturbances such as mine. It should be noted that, according to his view, it was the anxiety over my patient that led me into gullibility; however, when Sullivan reinvoked that same anxiety, he provided me with the opportunity for new knowledge about myself and my work with the patient. In a way, this theory resembles a species of folk wisdom which occurs in several forms: anything really good comes hard, or nothing really good comes easy. At first, it would seem that Sullivan had inverted the logic implicit in this belief, with the resultant conclusion that whatever comes hard is necessarily good. But such an assumption would be a serious underestimation: he was too knowing a psychotherapist and too convinced of the crippling power of anxiety to subscribe to such a proposition. Anxiety requires psychotherapeutic assistance if the patient or student is not to return to old ways.

I should now like to re-examine the episode from the standpoint of will. Having already pressed the phenomenological question about anxiety as experience, I shall arbitrarily and perhaps mistakenly assume in what is to follow that anxiety in Sullivan's theories is a satisfactory rubric for the range of unhappiness which befell me. Somewhere in Sullivan's writings he has a footnote to the effect that he was one of those fortunate human beings without any anxiety to speak of. If this was so, and I have no reason to doubt it, our relationship—in this respect, at least—was somewhat uneven. True, I stood to gain more than he in this inequality, since he could not profit from old anxieties reinvoked, but at least he could be comforted by his trusting belief in his own unassailable acumen. To begin with the matter of my own will, I would have to postulate two forms that my will took, even as I made the long journey to my first appointment with him. On the one hand, there was the will to become a psychotherapist, which could be expressed as an enduring and wholehearted wish to become a capable member of the profession. This expression is more explicit than the fact that I pursued a goal or was pursued by it, without so baldly formulating this pursuit. Such will came and went, depending on discouragement, on my shifting estimation of what psychotherapy might be, my waverings as to the worldly ways in which best to find my professional career, and, of course, the doubts plaguing me from time to time as to whether "psychotherapist" described in any important way the man I wished to become. At any rate, it was this will that effected the intricate arrangements that culminated in my time with Sullivan. In referring to this will, I delete backslidings, hesitations, and confusions that were to give way to a more self-conscious and stubborn determination to trudge through the course of psychoanalytic apprenticeship regardless of how my mind and body lagged in the process, regardless of the fatigue and boredom associated with this tiring and tiresome program. On the one hand, I wished to have supervisory time with such a renowned teacher in order to become a psychotherapist, whatever that was; on the other hand, I wished to impress him in order to become a favored pupil on my way to a diploma—and I knew what *that* was.

Sullivan's strategy or technique during our first meeting was characterized by his will not to respond. Regardless of intention, his deliberate indifference opposed my own will in two ways. To the extent to which I gave myself wholeheartedly to my task, with all resources joined to my will to become a psychotherapist under his tutelage, there was a dialogic possibility open to us, whose rebuff no doubt led to the agonizing question of my suitability for the profession I had chosen. At a lower, more self-serving and self-seeking level, my determination to win his admiration was easily routed by his will not to respond. I could no more will to admire him than I could will him to admire me. If I try to will my admiration of another, all I can grasp is the visage or posture of admiration: its actuality will elude me. If I try to will another to admire me, I shall self-consciously select only those gestures which are coercive of my end: regardless of my powers, he would have to be gullible indeed to be won by such manipulation. Willing what cannot be willed is by necessity an uneasy, even frantic, misdirection of the will: no cunning is required on the part of an adversary to bring such distress into frank and painful prominence. My guess is that, as every overture of mine was repudiated, my distress or anxiety grew, and, moreover, I was increasingly deprived of the few intellectual powers that were available to me, so that toward the end of our first appointment my will to impress Sullivan stood in harsh contrast with the uninspired and labored account to which I had been reduced. Even when he was later encouraged by the anxiety he had aroused in me, my relief was tempered by an awareness that, although he could will anxiety in me, I could not will anxiety in myself. Only the mannerisms of anxiety would be accessible to me, and these would not only fool no one but would defeat our joint pedagogical and therapeutic goal.

Out of my particular miseries with Sullivan, I wish now to define the relation between will and anxiety. In my understanding, the word *anxiety* is a broad term for human distress that contains a range of psychic and physical manifestations. With the exception of one additional phrase, anxiety in my usage does not differ essentially from *Webster's* definition, namely, a painful uneasiness of mind and body respecting an impending or anticipated ill. At any given moment, depending on which manifestations are most pressing, the exprience of anxiety may be more exactly identified as uneasiness, trepidation, and the like (see page 19), without losing its tie to the parent category, anxiety. But, by whatever name it is called, *anxiety is that range of distress which attends willing what cannot be willed.* In other words, anxiety can be located in the ever-widening split between the will and the impossible object of the will. As the split widens, the bondage between the will and its object grows, so that one is compelled to pursue something that seems to wither or altogether vanish in the face of such pursuit.

Before considering the implications of this definition, I should like to stress that my formulation is intended to be a phenomenological definition. As such, it would supplement rather than contradict other definitions of anxiety mentioned earlier, which are concerned, for the most part, with the causes and/or consequences of anxiety. Thus, in regard to Kurt Goldstein's definition, mine would explore the nature of "the subjective experience," as well as something of the "catastrophic condition" into which the "organism" falls in anxiety. In regard to Rollo May's definition, my definition does not attempt to contend with the "threat" to values which causes anxiety, but rather with the experience itself which follows such a threat. My purpose is to extend phenomenologically what Rollo May calls "apprehension."

If my life in the world is threatened by loss, betrayal, failure, disapproval, or injury, I may respond in various ways, depending on who and where I am in my world and on the exact nature and relevance of the threat endangering me. Melancholy, grief, despair, remorse, and enlightenment are but a few of the possibilities open to me, even when the threat is to values I deem essential to my existence. But anxiety, I would emphasize, is not my lot until I resort to my will to counter such threat and now will what cannot be willed. The severity of my impairment will vary according to the degree to which the will, in bondage to its object, is isolated from such faculties as reason, imagination, and the like, and the degree to which the object being willed recedes and diminishes in the rush of will. It is important to stress that the disability is principally one of will, because a serious deficiency of anxiety theory has been the inability of anxiety itself to account for the human mishaps it would explain. We need no special clinical background to remind ourselves of those who are privately and visibly anxious, without any particular disorder in their lives as a result of anxiety. This must mean that, in the midst of anxiety, crucial faculties are still available. On the other hand, we should be equally familiar with those who neither have nor have had any great anxiety in their lives, yet their difficulties are enormous. Here, it is simply not enough for anxiety theory to invoke the "little-man-who-wasn't-there" psychologism, asserting that anxiety could be there if it weren't so immediately assuaged by defensive and inferior stratagems. Since this inference cannot be argued, demonstrated, nor—more important—confirmed in the experience of the placid ones, belief in it must remain an article of faith in the dogma of anxiety theory. It is but another instance of making anxiety do the work of the will, said work unfortunately being shoddy and unconscious. It is worth remarking, however, that when either the anxious ones or the placid ones are asked to investigate the circumstances surrounding their anxiety or placidity, the result may be salutary even though it may not prove the theory. Salutary, because in either case the will has been offered a suitable endeavor for its efforts which hopefully will help return the world which has been lost or acquire a world which never was.

It follows that to characterize the nature of my encounter with Sullivan as mere anxiety would do it phenomenological injustice. At the same time, to abstract anxiety for theoretical purposes as the psychological mover toward either constriction or enlightenment would be equally fallacious. Anxiety may be an ache which cries for relief, but whether or what relief will occur cannot be a result of anxiety's decision. Unlike the will, anxiety must be considered morally (or psychologically) *inert,* which is to say that, whether good or evil follows, anxiety will depend on forces other than anxiety. My will to become a psychotherapist, though seriously shaken, allowed me to contend with a more meretricious need to impress Sullivan. I doubt very much that the anxiety which accompanied my willing what could not be willed—given his will not to respond—was in itself generative of insight about myself or my patient. Recognizing my own gullibility in work with my patient was, as far as I can see, a response to Sullivan's clinical shrewdness—not because of, but *in spite of,* anxiety. Conceivably, I might have chosen another way through which, indicting the man as cruel, arrogant, and a poor teacher, I did not return. Such a conclusion could have been willed only by blinding myself to my discriminations of this remarkable man. Had that been my way, I should no doubt have told myself and a few close friends that I was forced to discontinue because of the anxiety he provoked in me.

As has already been suggested, the more stubborn the will's pursuit of its intractable goal, the sooner it will be separated from those faculties that might allow its bondage to be objectified, diverted, or dispelled. In isolation from such powers as intellect and imagination, the will can only will, reflection about its own adversities being beyond its capacity. The failure of meaning, which is said to be characteristic of anxiety, stems from the deprivation of resources and the withering of the will's goal in the face of the will's demands.

Because of this failure, the anxious person may eventually no longer be able to say what he is anxious about. However, his failure should not be attributed, as is the habit, to the fact that the cause of his anxiety has been repressed, but rather to the fact that those rational powers that might assist the will have fallen away and will not return until, for one reason or another, there is an end to willing what cannot be willed. This same failure in self-reflection has often been used to distinguish anxiety from fear, whose cause, or so it is assumed, is actual and exterior. According to this view, the danger in anxiety is "inner" and unknown, while the danger provoking fear is "outer" and known. Even if we try to preserve a legitimate distinction between anxiety and fear (although I believe psychology has misused this distinction), it can readily be seen that both experiences have their inner and outer dimensions. So far as the present definition is concerned, fear does not merge into anxiety until willing what cannot be willed takes over. If I am summoned to an interview with a superior who, I am warned, will be sharply critical of my performance, my troubled anticipation of this event will contain, in addition to my willing, a mingling of subjective and objective considerations, but I doubt that it is either useful or possible to disentangle that portion of my apprehension which may be inner anxiety and that portion which may be outer fear.

A burst of thunder in a darkening sky can frighten me with the possibility that the plane in which my family is flying home will be caught in the same impending storm. Again, the inner and outer features of my unhappy state seem less critical than the degree to which I now fall into willing what cannot be willed: clear skies, gifted pilot, indestructible plane. Untempered by imagination and reason, not to mention information from the weather bureau and airport, my isolated will *wills*—that is, it demands its object absolutely, however futile that demand may be. And, with each new crack of thunder, I shall no doubt swing from the willed certainty of safety to the certainty of disaster, so that now the storm battering that fragile plane is violent, and the pilot hopelessly inept. Both obsessive extremes, with their attendant anxiety, are products of my isolated will. Should I, still in the mood of disaster, muse about how to bury my family and take up my life alone, it must be construed that my musings are born of that same isolated will, rather than a hostile, if unacceptable, desire for their destruction. Even were I to assume that such a motive supported my will in its authorship of these melancholy reveries, my disorder would still lie in willing what cannot be willed—namely, the storm's destruction of plane and family. Moreover, for the sake of completeness, I should have to assume a more considerate motive to account for my insistence on their safety.

If only because of their extreme and uncommon character, the conventional illustrations of fear to be found in the usual anxiety theory tend to reveal the effort to rid the problem of contamination by subjectivity: the armed burglar in the night, the rabid bat in the bedroom, the car careening toward us on the wrong side of the road. Yet even these examples, so weighted on the objective side, would seem to fail in their purpose. Presumably, immediate overpowering fright will give way to anxiety at the point that we retrospectively resort to willing what cannot be willed. But even that very first fright, so far as we can penetrate the experience, carries no lesson in the epistemology of danger from without; little reflection is required to realize that it, too, must mingle both inner and outer aspects. Clearly, it is as hard to construct an anxiety that is only inner as it is to imagine a fear that is only outer.

In the disability of will that we have been considering, anxiety is not the only experience. As the will is increasingly stripped of supporting faculties, and as what is being willed recedes further from the will's impositions, the will itself comes to be experienced as impotent thrust. It is the very powerlessness of the power pressing toward its refractory goal that accounts for the helplessness and uncertainty that most writers believe to be essential characteristics of anxiety. As discernment fails, what can most painfully be discerned are those bodily manifestations of distress which have occupied the medical approach to the subject of anxiety. Thus, the split between the will and its object, if extended in time and severity, enforces finally another split between mind and body in which our world, already diminished by the bondage described, shrinks still further toward that cramped cell where all we can do is suffer and observe those painful commotions of our flesh. And these bodily discomforts again oppose, even as they invite, the activities of our isolated will. This is the arena, peculiarly modern, which can loosely be described as fear of fear or anxiety about anxiety. More accurately, it is the shrunken state in which, as actor and audience of our body's disabilities, we will not to have anxiety, such willing bringing more anxiety in its wake. This impasse may well be the existential source for the biological or medical views of the problem of anxiety.

This has been called the "Age of Anxiety." Considering the attention given the subject by psychology, theology, literature, and the pharmaceutical industry, not to mention the testimony from our own lives, we could fairly well conclude that there is more anxiety today, and, moreover, that there is definitely more anxiety about anxiety now than there has been in previous epochs of history. Nevertheless, I would hesitate to characterize this as an "Age of Anxiety," just as I would be loath to call this an "Age of Affluence," "Coronary Disease," "Mental Health," "Dieting," "Conformity," or "Sexual Freedom," my reason being that none of these labels, whatever fact or truth they may involve, goes to the heart of the matter. Much as I dislike this game of labels, my preference, which might be anticipated, would be to call this the "Age of the Disordered Will." It takes only a glance to see a few of the myriad varieties of willing what cannot be willed that enslave us: we will to sleep, will to read fast, will to have simultaneous orgasm, will to be creative and spontaneous, will to enjoy our old age, and, most urgently, will to will. If anxiety is more prominent in our time, such anxiety is the product of our particular modern disability of the will. To this disability, rather than to anxiety, I would attribute the ever-increasing dependence on drugs affecting all levels of our society. While drugs do offer relief from anxiety, their more important task is to offer the illusion of healing the split between the will and its refractory object. The resulting feeling of wholeness may not be a responsible one, but at least within that wholeness—no matter how willful the drugged state may appear to an outsider—there seems to be, briefly and subjectively, a responsible and vigorous will. This is the reason, I believe, that the addictive possibilities of our age are so enormous.

At the same time that our lives are occupied by deliberate efforts of will, toward both appropriate and inappropriate ends, with or without drugs we suffer a mounting hunger for a sovereign and irreducible will, so wedded to our reason, our emotions, our imagination, our intentions, and our bodies that only after a given enterprise has come to an end can we retrospectively infer that will was present at all. In other words, within such totality, will, being unconscious, would not be a matter of experience, even though we might later try to portray the essence of the enterprise as one in which we wished with our whole heart or willed with all our being. The predominant experience within this realm of will would be one of freedom, as opposed to the bondage of the isolated will. The goal of will within this realm would be one of direction, rather than of a specific objective or achievement, although naturally the course of this will would be dotted inconspicuously by such concrete items. Never a permanent state, and always limited in duration, it would give way over and over again to the more self-conscious will with which we are necessarily more familiar. Needless to say, utilitarian opportunities for this more self-conscious will are vast in our technological age; in fact, it could be said that our technology could not have been accomplished without it. To move my hand, add a column of figures, even earn a psychoanalytic diploma, are all discrete and feasible objects for this will. However, there is no activity I could mention, however trivial, which, in the service of the joined realm of will, would not lose its utilitarian countenance and become part of the flow in a particular direction. I may say I went to the library to look at a book that I thought might be interesting. By all standards, this is an ordinary statement about an ordinary errand, requiring no comment except that the errand and the statement about it are singularly unmuscular in nature and point merely in the direction of possible interest. If I am asked, on my return from the library, for the physical details of my trip, I shall probably—and fortunately—not remember them. However, when my utilitarian will engineers this errand, something ordinary is now splintered into many things arduous. *Book* now becomes the principal object of this expedition, but of course there are subsidiary objects, too: I must pick the proper time, choose the right route, park on a crowded street, deal with a difficult librarian, and so on. Once the book is found, *reading the book* can splinter into similar tedious efforts of will, all open to memory, should someone be foolish enough to inquire. Though tedious and arduous, these actions are still feasible and, in their difficulty, will not compare with the anxiety that arises when this same utilitarian will is asked to will what it cannot will.

Consideration of the historical origins of our present situation lies outside my purpose and competence. I would, however, ask this question: could it be that the disordered will, with its paradoxical privilege for technology and all manner of scientific fact, and the hunger from which we suffer for another will, are the consequence of the death of God proclaimed by Nietzsche in the last century? If so, few of us, I suspect, believers and nonbelievers alike, have been spared. Depending on which side of Nietzsche's divide we stand historically, the other side is almost unimaginable. For this reason, the contemporary issue is not of the order proposed by Kirillov in Dostoyevsky's *The Possessed:* "To recognize that there is no God and not to recognize at the same instant that one is God oneself is an absurdity, else one would certainly kill oneself." Kirillov's choice, springing from its apparent logical necessity, has the terrified, yet abstract, quality of one who, while still on the other side of the divide, has glimpsed the loss, but that loss has not yet penetrated and shaped his life in all those subtle and pedestrian ways that make Nietzsche's proclamation, for most of us, merely another old-fashioned theological generalization. With the disappearance of the divine Will from our lives, we have come to hunger not for His Will—neither in the sense of living in His Will nor usurping His Will for ourselves—but rather for our own sovereign will, which is our modern way, this side the omnipotence of suicide or madness. And all exhortations notwithstanding, this will we cannot will.

3

Faces of Envy

UNLIKE MOST WORDS having to do with the human condition, the definitions of envy I have seen are remarkably similar. Unlike other moral terms in the West, whose meanings shift with the temper of the times, the etymology of envy has stayed unusually constant. Envy had the same meaning for Plato that it had for Sullivan. When Horace wrote in the first century that "Sicilian tyrants never invented a greater torment than envy," he was concerned with the sheer and ubiquitous "pain of mind," expressed by Onasander, that caused Richard Sheridan to observe, in the eighteenth century, that "there is not a passion so strongly rooted in the human heart as envy." Dante devised for envy, which he counted as one of the seven deadly sins, a torment chillingly apt: in his Inferno the eyelids of the envious were sewn together. Such punishment

"Faces of Envy" reprinted from Leslie H. Farber, *The Ways of the Will: Essays toward a Psychology and Psychopathology of Will* (New York: Basic Books, 1966).

would have suited Onasander, who wrote in A.D. 49 that "envy is a pain of mind that successful men cause their neighbors." More recently, it might have seemed equally fitting to Max Beerbohm, when he suggested that "the dullard's envy of brilliant men is always assuaged by the suspicion that they will come to a bad end."

The usual definition of envy, stressing its subjective nature, is "chagrin or discontent at the excellence or good fortune of another." [1] Since such feelings are rarely suffered in silence, some definitions include an objective expression of ill-will, such as disparagement of the envied one (although disparagement is only one of the manifest paths envy may take). For more than two thousand years, this is the meaning envy has borne. My scholarship has perhaps been too casual, but I find it very odd that it is so difficult to discover a systematic treatment for so common and so painful a human experience as envy, whether one looks in the theological, philosophical, or psychological literature. References are scanty and fleeting, and often epigrammatic, suggesting that envy's origins in human history and its manifestations in human sensibility and conduct are not easily discoverable. My guess is that envy, by its very nature, is obstinate in its opposition to investigation.

The protean character of envy and its talent for disguise account, I believe, for the infrequency of studies on the subject. Because of the variety of forms it may take, it is often simply impossible to recognize. This is true, not only for the observer, who by definition must be more gullible about such a subjective state as envy, but also for the envious one himself, whose rational powers may lend almost unholy assistance to the need for self-deception. Therefore, anecdotal examples of envy are usually crude. For instance, I remember with some clarity the first time I heard Harry Stack Sullivan lecture. His subject matter escapes me now as it escaped me then, but how well I recall him fussing with the recording apparatus. As I later explained to a friend, I was appalled that such a respected figure in our profession could so nakedly address himself to posterity. Wanting, of course, to give my friend a wholly objective picture of the oc-

1. *Webster's International Dictionary*, 2nd ed., s.v. "envy."

casion, I went on to depict Sullivan's affectations of manner and phraseology, always careful to preface each objective statement with some generous remark such as: "Don't think me envious, because I know this man to be a genius in the field of psychiatry. So it is doubly unfortunate," and so on. The example is as crude as my envy was strong. Inasmuch as envy rendered me impervious to the content of his lecture, the object of my disparagement, it will be noted, was his personal style. What I clearly observed in that style was his egotism, his infatuation with self, his dramatic need to impress that self on both posterity and on his more immediate audience. In brief, I detested his self-assertion, which is not an uncommon focus when envy takes the form of disparagement. But what of my own self-assertion? Certainly, to my friend, I dissembled the degree to which I was at a loss at this particular lecture and concealed the misery and stupidity fostered by my envy, which prevented me from giving him any idea of what Sullivan had said. Instead I asserted myself brashly and authoritatively, if unhappily, representing a confidence in my own abilities that was, at that moment, as necessary as it was undeserved.

Two authors have thought self-assertion to be so crucial in envy that they might have punished the envious in the Inferno by sewing together their lips, instead of their eyelids. Kierkegaard, contrasting envy and admiration, wrote that envy was unhappy self-assertion, while admiration was happy self-surrender. And Alfred Adler, speaking of aggressive children, wrote that "when the desire for self-assertion becomes extraordinarily intense, it will always involve an element of envy." On a prescriptive basis, it would seem that self-assertion was the best way of diminishing another's importance, while at the same time redressing one's own limitations. But, in the more devious forms of envy, self-assertion may not be so apparent, even though it is implicit. Take an example of what could be called "self-assertion by proxy." Using an instance from his own day, Thomas Hobbes wrote that "the praise of ancient authors proceeds not from the reverence of the dead, but from . . . envy of the living." Or, to use our own idiom, we might say to a colleague, more envied than admired, "I thought your paper excellent. Incidentally, didn't you get your central idea from a letter Freud wrote to Ferenczi on his fiftieth birthday?" Seemingly, with such a disheartening compliment, we merely refer to Freud's priority and trust that our demeanor is properly self-effacing. On the other hand, if our colleague is one of those suspicious, thin-skinned fellows, he might very well think we were making a tiny claim for our own scholarship in psychoanalytic matters, while withholding any real praise for his own effort. Indeed, one of envy's favorite stratagems is the attempt to provoke envy in the envied one—in this case, either for Freud's priority and prestige, or for our encyclopedic acquaintance with the field, or for both. There is something about the insistent nature of envy's self-assertion that makes it almost impossible to down. And it is just as hard for the envier to admit his self-assertion as it is to admit envy itself.

Suppose, still envious, we had chosen to chasten our colleague in this manner: "I don't remember when I've been so moved, so impressed. You are simply marvelous on this subject. You have an absolute genius for throwing a new light on difficult questions." As an actor with many faces, envy may try to pass itself off as its exact opposite—namely, admiration. Yet, when envy is the motive, admiration loses its tie both to affection and to the occasion, becoming wholly subject to the will. Unlike true admiration, which, because it is free of conscious will, always has the option of silence, envy's imitation of admiration clamors for public acknowledgment; the more stinging his envy, the more ardently must the envious one dramatize himself as an admirer whose passion overshadows and shames the more reticent responses of others. However, since it is as futile to will admiration as it is to will affection, this attempt at praise, inevitably self-assertive, turns excessive, inappropriate, and even irrelevant. Whereas true admiration keeps its distance, respecting the discrepancy between the admirer and the admired one, envy's assault upon its object with a barrage of compliments serves not only its need to assert itself in the costume of admiration, but also the lust of the envier to possess the very quality that initially incited his envy.

To some extent, envy is always a divisive experience, alienating us not only from our fellows but also from our own rational powers. We tend to forget that praise, just as much as criticism, may become an *ad hominem* venture when envy divorces us from our subject matter. If envy can move us to disparage our colleague's life rather than his subject, so can it move us to exalt his life at the expense of his subject. We tend to assume, mistakenly, that praise of another's character is the highest compliment we can offer him, overlooking how conveniently we may employ such inevitably general and abstract expressions of approval in an effort to avoid making a direct and concrete response to what he has said, done, or produced, this being certainly the most relevant and satisfying praise for the subject himself. Undiscriminating praise may, in fact, have a harsher effect on the envied one than criticism: it may arouse his own envy toward the exalted image we impose on him and, in his awareness of the immense disparity between it and his own image of himself, remind him ever more sharply of his limitations.

The least differentiated, and perhaps most childish, form which envy may assume is that of greed. By ordinary greed I mean merely the craving to possess the world's goods, whether food, drink, flattery, sex, parents, money, or psychoanalysis. In its materialistic and undiscriminating fashion, greed will take little notice of the manner or distinction that permitted their owner to acquire these goods. Greed is not necessarily restricted to those objects I do not have: I can be just as greedy for those goods which I already have in abundance. On the other hand, if I envy you, I begrudge you some quality or qualities of being which I do not possess: your wisdom, your dignity, your courage, your humility. What characterizes such virtues is that, although I may perceive and admire—or envy—them in you, your possession of them lies outside your self-consciousness; they may become a matter of concern to you only insofar as you lack them, or when you, in turn, recognize them in others. Most accomplishments and some virtues do not have this paradoxical nature. Skill or tact or a capacity for honesty, for example, may be pursued directly; to acknowledge and enjoy possession of them does not contradict their nature. But, only the fool proclaims his wisdom, only the proud man, his humility, only the coward, his courage. Not only do these virtues make a liar of the man who claims them, they forever evade any effort to achieve them. I may seek knowledge; I may not seek to be wise. Sharing an essential freedom from self-concern (which also characterizes the capacity for admiration), such virtues are not accomplishments and cannot be learned. They must be deserved, but their possession is a matter of grace, and is given only to him who denies it. If I observe a skill of yours, or some virtue to which imitation *is* appropriate, admiration may move me to emulate you, to work for such skill, to practice that virtue myself. But, when I perceive in you a quality of being such as I have described, my admiration may not move in the direction of emulation: I cannot imitate or learn from you; the attainment of such qualities is as removed from will of the second realm as their possession must be from self-knowledge. I may merely behold your virtue—and acknowledge my own inferiority. This is the most generous, and the most difficult, gesture admiration is called on to make. If my generosity fails, my response turns envious. Posing as greed, my envy will blink the virtues that aroused it and fasten instead on some material possession that has perhaps come to you by virtue of your distinction. Whether I now ridicule or covet this possession is not so important as the seeming advantage I gain by reducing my envy to greed and you to your possession. There is some irony in the circumstance that we have an entire advertising industry deliberately exploiting envy-qua-greed by asserting the proposition that a man is what he owns. The irony is compounded when we remember that we have a sociology of class dedicated to precisely the same proposition. So long as I believe that you are your possessions and that my motive is greed, I can avoid any acknowledgment of the essential inequality between us. However, unless I am especially talented at self-deception, this advantage will reveal itself as illusory; certainly, if I manage to acquire your goods and to satisfy what I imagine to be my greed, the poor comfort this affords me will hasten the exposure of my real motive.

Unlike greed and jealousy, with which it is often confused, envy arises from a person's apprehension of another's superiority, and his consequent critical evaluation of himself. Indeed, it is just this aspect of envy that inspires the envier's zeal and inventiveness in denying it. Greed affords little pleasure, jealousy only pain. Neither, however, requires one to acknowledge a deficiency of quality in himself. Greed admits one's lack of some material object whose acquisition depends not at all on his worthiness of it, but simply on his luck or will in attaining it. Jealousy acknowledges a threat (which may or may not be real)—the possible loss of some possession greatly valued, usually someone's love. Jealousy does not depend, however, on knowledge of the agent of the threat, but merely on knowledge, or suspicion, that a rival exists. If the rival is known, he may invoke envy as well as jealousy in the threatened person. When both emotions are present, they almost inevitably lose their separate identities in the abundance and commotion of feeling; indeed, they often connive at their confusion with one another, each gaining some advantage from concealment and sharing, as they do, fear, resentment, and blindness toward the rival, who ceases to be known in any personal, detached way, becoming merely his effect upon the jealous-envious sufferer. (This reduction of another person is both an aim and an effect of envy and jealousy alike.) However, despite their kinship, their similarities, their attraction for each other, their eagerness to dress up in one another's clothes, jealousy and envy are, in fact, different and separate, notwithstanding the reluctance of committed victims, as well as disinterested students, to concern themselves with a distinction. Jealousy is a monothematic, romantic drama involving three characters, one of whom—the jealous person—doubles variously as author, director, stage-manager, critic, and audience, according to the needs of each plot. Despite the anguished subjectivity of most of the dialogue, the issues of the conflict—loss and gain—are external to character and even to self-esteem (what causes humiliation and the fall of self-esteem in the jealous person is not the wound of his loss, but his jealousy itself), and the three starring figures are required to sacrifice a large measure of individuality to the ritual of their roles. Envy, by contrast, displays itself dramatically only in disguise, and involves two instead of three people, one of whom, by virtue of his self-assertion, is clearly the star; in fact, the scene does not require the actual presence of the other at all (although if played in his company he must be given a line or two for the sake of form). While the envied one cannot be anonymous, as the rival in jealousy can be, he rarely represents any external threat to the person who envies him, so that the central conflict in envy is internal and subjective to the envier. Envy is essentially static rather than dramatic; it has very little movement and no dramatic continuity of its own; and, it shapes its expression to conditions rather than to plot. Jealousy, on the other hand, insists on a relentless continuity; it eats conditions and spews out plot; obsessively, it gathers more and more of the world onto its stage, urging the drama onward toward its feared and assured doom.

Where jealousy has a real cause, and the loss is either imminent or actual, the jealous person is enraged, both at his beloved and at his rival, and craves, or is even greedy for, what has been, or is about to be, taken away. However, unless envy has already entered the picture on its own, the jealous loser is not envious, for he infers no superiority in the winner from the fact of his success. It has always been one of the more mysterious aspects of jealousy that not only is it independent of envy, but that, often, the less respect—or potential envy—the jealous one feels for his rival, the more he is tortured by his jealousy. This oddity may be traceable in part to the unpredictable nature of love, which, unlike other desirable things that we are told life has in store for the deserving, refuses to be earned, discriminates arbitrarily and according to a private standard, and always precedes rather than rewards worthiness. Although jealousy does not provoke envy, envy can easily stimulate jealousy in a susceptible host. And it sometimes happens that envy initially authors the three-cornered drama of jealousy when, out of his envious lust to dispossess and his envious spite to torment his tormenter, the self-appointed rival calculatedly performs the gestures that set the play in motion.

Because of its specific and acutely painful nature and its addiction to homemade theatricals, jealousy is more readily identifiable than its stealthier sister, envy, and has consequently received more attention from both experts and amateurs. It may, as a result, be better understood; it has undoubtedly achieved a more imposing reputation. When Sullivan says, "Jealousy is much more poignant and devastating than envy," I am inclined to agree, insofar as jealousy, which tends toward greater and greater concentration, sucking all things into itself, is thus experienced. Envy, which tends toward diffusion, hiding and effacing itself behind all things, escapes identification and confounds experience. I suspect that envy, because of its talent for disguise, may promote greater mischief, and I am convinced that the envious man is miserable, even though what he knowingly feels is not envy but perplexing pain.

For reasons of space and competence, I shall make only a few general remarks about the beginnings of envy in childhood. In one way or another, as I have tried to indicate, envy is a limp and unhappy response to another's superiority—a response that precludes, by its very nature, such vigorous activities as rivalry, imitation, or emulation. Essentially, it asks something for nothing: by demeaning the envied one and aggrandizing the envier, envy attempts to redress inequality without the risk of intervening effort or development. In this way, envy opposes change, enforces the status quo, and is inimical to learning. Being a painfully estranging experience, envy alienates the envier from the envied one and, in this way, is inimical to what might be called mutuality, or relation. In childhood, even more than in adult life, learning and relation are—ideally, at least—reciprocal movements; neither can flourish very long without the other. (While life begins for the infant almost wholly in relation, the intrusions of self-consciousness soon bring the other pole of this dualism into being.) Learning the most ordinary physical skills in childhood occurs only in the context of relation. On the other hand, relation between a child and his parents cannot long exist of itself: inevitably, it requires learning for its perpetuation.

Envy, in its inhibition of both relation and learning, invariably feeds on itself. Out of envy, the child may abandon the acquisition of a given skill that might repair the imbalance between him and the envied person—whether it be a parent or another child—resorting instead to some uncomfortable display of self-assertion. The more skills envy forces him to relinquish, the harsher grows the discrepancy between himself and others, providing him, of course, with greater opportunity for envy.

In addition to feeding on itself, envy breeds itself. To some extent, envy in the parents will provide the conditions for envy in the child. I do not mean by this that envy itself is a learned response, although to some degree a child may learn the policy of derogation where superiority is involved, and certainly may learn that even the capacity for admiration can provoke his parents' envy. But where envy is habitual to the parents, it is more than likely to direct itself sooner or later toward the child, and, strangely enough, to fasten on those qualities and capacities of his that the parents most admire. The child will probably at first find the invidious comparisons to which his parents' envy subjects him bewildering, arbitrary, and jolting to his own wavering experience of himself. In a house where envy is in the air, however, the child need but look, listen, and breathe to be instructed in consolation and counterattack. If he submits to such instruction he will respond in kind to the envy that is aimed at him, by imitating its self-assertive gestures; in embracing that which is inimical to relation, he conspires with his parents to substitute a style, dramatizing and posing as relation, for relation; in imitating that which is inimical to learning he learns to substitute a style, impersonating competence and authority, for learning. *If* he accepts the conditions offered him and agrees to be instructed by the example of his elders, thus will their envy breed his own. There is always, of course, the possibility that by finding, or imagining, other teachers, he will undertake to choose in a different direction.

Since childhood is a time of vast and manifold inequalities, the opportunities for envy or admiration are myriad. If the qualities of being, mentioned earlier, are beyond the perceptual reach of the child, certainly the privileges and possessions and appearances of adulthood are not. Given his intellectual limitations at this stage in life, his apprehension—whether admiring or envious—of superiority in the adults around him will be remarkably literal, concrete, and physical, reminding us of the manifestations of envy-qua-greed. Such states as penis-envy or breast-envy, which have occupied much of the psychoanalytic literature on this subject, are of this literal variety, mistaking possession of the physical attribute for the various prerogatives of adulthood. I suspect, also, that whatever its aggregation, whatever its disguise, envy, which by nature is nourished on self-consciousness, can take root in the mind only when considerable differentiation has been achieved, making its appearance in early childhood unlikely. It is my guess, however, that because of its dependence on self-awareness and its imperious claims on the will, envy's origins, although of interest, are less crucial than its manifestations and effects. In fact, the attempt to expose and explain present envy by means of propositions concerning its earliest forms may render a service, not to the patient who seeks relief from the oppression of his envy, but to the very envy itself. Such propositions offer the envier a double temptation. Rather than contend, painfully, with his present envious feelings, which would require acknowledgment of another's excellence and his own limitation, he may fall to scrutinizing the history of his envy, contenting his conscience with an "acknowledgment" of some ancient state of mind, possibly fictional and certainly irrelevant to his immediate discomfort. Second, in his absorption with historical origins, he may find it all too easy to locate a "first cause" for his envy somewhere outside himself; this established, a few simple operations of logic can lead him to a deterministic reconstruction of the whole development of envy in him, guaranteeing his escape from the responsibility with which possible freedom of choice, past and present, would burden him. It seems to me that the most pressing concern, for the patient or for ourselves, in regard to so damaging and disturbing an affliction as envy, is not so much to ponder when, or even why, it may originally come into being, as to discover it now where it is, to outwit its distractions and disguises, to measure its fear of being called by name.

4

Will and Willfulness in Hysteria

EARLY IN FREUD'S CAREER as a psychoanalyst, he suffered a spell of rapture in which he boasted to Fliess that he could cure every case of hysteria. Though he was now in his middle years, this exuberance really belonged to his therapeutic youth, a time when his medical past still suffused and shaped his view of psychology. If, at this stage, the strategies of psychotherapy seemed as specific as a scalpel, hysteria was for him, literally, a hidden abscess bloated with the debris of sexual trauma—an abscess that must be located, then opened to consciousness, before the systemic symptoms of this malady would disappear. (It is my impression that most psychoanalysts have passed through this phase of development, although it must be

"Will and Willfulness in Hysteria" reprinted from Leslie H. Farber, *The Ways of the Will: Essays toward a Psychology and Psychopathology of Will* (New York: Basic Books, 1966).

admitted that a few have lingered here unconscionably long.) For Freud, at least, little time passed before he inflicted such drainage on an abscess of hysteria—only to discover that his patient shared neither his enthusiasm nor his optimism. In fact, after only a few weeks, she ended treatment, never to return. His account of this therapeutic disaster contains one of the most anguished statements in the literature of psychology, a *cri de coeur* which must have helped him to leave his medical youth behind:

> (She) had listened to me without any of her usual contradictions. She seemed to be moved; she said good-bye to me very warmly, with the heartiest wishes for the New Year, and—came no more. . . . I knew (she) would not come back again. Her breaking off so unexpectedly, just when my hopes of a successful termination of the treatment were at their highest, and her thus bringing those hopes to nothing—this was an unmistakable act of vengeance on her part. Her purpose of self-injury also profited by this action. No one who, like me, conjures up the most evil of those half-tamed demons that inhabit the human breast, and seeks to wrestle with them, can expect to come through the struggle unscathed. Might I perhaps have kept the girl under my treatment if I myself had acted a part, if I had exaggerated the importance to me of her staying on, and had shown a warm personal interest in her—a course which, even after allowing for my position as her physician, would have been tantamount to providing her with a substitute for the affection she longed for? I do not know. Since in every case a portion of the factors that are encountered under the form of resistance remains unknown, I have always avoided acting a part, and have contented myself with practising the humbler arts of psychology. In spite of every theoretical interest and of every endeavour to be of assistance as a physician, I keep the fact in mind that there must be some limits set to the extent to which psychological influence may be used, and I respect as one of these limits the patient's own *will and understanding* [italics mine].[1]

Within this outcry can be discerned the frantic flailings of spirit that would declare to the world the pain this perverse creature had inflicted on Freud and, at the same time, give rational form to his outrage. It is despair that demands that she be charged with both

1. Sigmund Freud, "Fragment of an Analysis of a Case of Hysteria" (1905), *Collected Papers*, 5 vols. (New York: Basic Books, 1959), 3: 131–132.

the cunning to know that his "hopes . . . were at their highest" as well as the meanness to shatter these hopes. Equally understandable is the simultaneous conviction, barely skirting the edges of self-pity and self-aggrandizement, that such catastrophes must be the penalty for ventures as heroic as his. At this point his pain subsides, the rhetorical scale diminishes, and he turns to reason for consolation and even instruction, seeking an order and detachment that so far have eluded him. As if he had now forgotten his violent description of her impact on him, he wonders, in his new mood, if he might not have deliberately "exaggerated" to her the importance of remaining in treatment. But he could not countenance such pretense on his part. Almost safely past the claims of indignation, he can now hope, in the teeth of what has just occurred, that he has always contented himself with "practising the humbler arts of psychology." He can acknowledge that there are limits to psychological influence. It is precisely at this point that he comes to a glimmering of the truth about his experience with Dora: "I respect as one of these limits [of psychological influence] the patient's own *will and understanding.*" In other words, regardless of the inventiveness and accuracy with which he and Dora have traced the origins and meanings of her disorder, there is a force in her that says "no" to this mutual creation. To this force he gave the name allotted to it by history, namely, will. At the same time, he simultaneously, and even paradoxically, ruled this traditional category out of bounds. But did this mean that henceforth the will, as it had been understood by the ages, was to be excluded from his psychological considerations? Not entirely. In his postscript to the case of Dora, his anguish had subsided to the extent that he could more calmly consider his therapeutic failure:

> I have been obliged to speak of transference, for it is only by means of this factor that I can elucidate the peculiarities of Dora's analysis. Its great merit, namely, the unusual clarity which makes it seem so suitable as a first introductory publication, is closely bound up with its great defect, which led to its being broken off prematurely. I did not succeed in mastering the transference in good time. . . . In this way the transference took me unaware, and, because of the unknown quantity in me

> which reminded Dora of Herr K., she took her revenge on me as she wanted to take her revenge on him. . . . If cruel impulses and revengeful motives, which have already been used in the patient's ordinary life for maintaining her symptoms, become transferred on to the physician during treatment, before he has had time to detach them from himself by tracing them back to their sources, then it is not to be wondered at if the patient's condition is unaffected by his therapeutic efforts.[2]

In other words, he no longer recognizes the "limits . . . to which psychological influence may be used"—i.e., will and understanding—and is instead elaborating his theories of transference, which were to prove so significant for therapy. However, "tracing . . . cruel impulses and revengeful motives . . . back to their sources" is not quite the same as considering the psychology of will itself. In fact, it could be said that Freud in his postscript chose to limit himself to a fragment of the problem of will: its motivations. And what he thought these motivations to be is clearly stated in the same postscript:

> I was further anxious to show that sexuality . . . provides the motive power for every single symptom, and for every single manifestation of a symptom. The symptoms of the disease are nothing else than *the patient's sexual activity.*[3]

Thus, as was so often the case with Freud, the problem of will was equated with the motive of sexuality. For every act, a variety of motives can be adduced—anxiety, sex, ambition, prestige, aggression, and so on, but even if we grant their validity as motives, their temporal priority cannot automatically endow them with ontological, nor psychological, superiority to the act itself. A motive cannot explain an act; the act must ultimately be judged on its own terms. Though we must be grateful for the second glance that permitted Freud to develop his theories of transference, I should like to suggest that his first impassioned outcry caught more of the truth about hysteria.

My thesis is that hysteria is a particular disorder of will whose

2. Freud, "A Case of Hysteria," pp. 141–144.
3. Freud, "A Case of Hysteria," p. 137.

principal expression is willfulness. By willfulness, I do not mean mere intention or determination, which are older definitions of the term. I am using here *Webster's* more contemporary definition, namely "governed by will, without yielding to reason; obstinate; perverse; stubborn; as a willful man or horse." This definition suggests that, in willfulness, the life of the will becomes distended, overweening, and obtrusive at the same time that its movements become increasingly separate, sovereign, and distinct from other aspects of spirit. And, with distention of will that is relatively unrelieved, intellect is bound to suffer. I mean, of course, intellect in the large sense, including not only will's usual adversary, which is reason, but also imagination, humor, discretion, and judgment. In willfulness, then, will pursues its own tyrannical course with reckless disdain for what we usually mean by content, unless that content be will itself.

In willfulness, the will does the work of the imagination. Though rather quaint and crude, no better example of this situation exists than that bizarre occasion called hypnosis, in which hysteric-as-hypnotist barters with hypnotist-as-hysteric, making it impossible to say at any given moment who is Trilby. It could be argued that hypnosis is one of hysteria's necessary and characteristic inventions. Even the persistence of its early nineteenth-century trappings (though the cloak and flowing tie have been replaced by a business suit) testifies to the intransigent, mindless quality of hysteria's inventiveness, which remains so indifferent to historical context. So little, really, has the form of hypnosis changed that it would seem to be lifted bodily from the pages of a Gothic novel of the period. Let us remember that at the same time Mesmer was discovering Nature's magnetic forces within himself, Shelley was augmenting his own powers by merging with the west wind. "Be thou, spirit fierce, my spirit!" he cried. "Be thou me, impetuous one!" [4] The prime quality of that romantic movement, according to Allen Tate, was "the momentary illusion of individual power." "The romantic,"

4. Percy Bysshe Shelley, "Ode to the West Wind," *Poets of the English Language* (New York: The Viking Press, 1950), 4: 332.

wrote Tate, "ranged over nature in the effort to impose his volitional ego as an absolute on the world." [5]

The illusions of absolute power and absolute compliance that occupy hypnosis are necessarily momentary and fragile, quickly dispelled by the intrusions of life or psychotherapy, which is why they seem reserved largely for hypnosis, and why hypnosis itself seems so unlike anything else in life. To maintain these illusions requires the unflagging will of both parties, "will" here meaning the "willing suspension of disbelief." The first events in hypnosis, which usually consist of the hypnotist's exploitation of such items as gravity, muscular fatigue, and inertia, are seldom questioned by the subject, but are arbitrarily attributed to the hypnotist's powers. And, a "good" hypnotist will initially resist, just as much as his subject, any rational formulation of these events, since his dramatic or hypnotic effectiveness hinges on his *own* belief in his powers. Qualities suggesting the "merely human," such as self-consciousness, doubt, and humor, in either the hypnotist or the subject, are inimical to the pact of hypnosis, which must be irrational and romantic to succeed. In Melville's sense, each participant should be a Confidence Man—i.e., a man who has confidence. It is thus understandable why, in terms of his development, hypnosis is apt to be an absorption of the youthful psychiatrist, embraced most passionately during the period when his skills are least formed. Hypnosis becomes one willful way of overriding the despair of the young psychiatrist not yet qualified by age or humanity to give counsel. At this stage in life, the romanticism of science urges him to dip into Nature for the verification of his own powers. But once the hypnotist begins to lose his belief, it will not be long before the spectacle strikes him as comic, for—retrospectively, at least—outbursts of will are apt to appear more comic than pathetic, because of the unadorned combination of presumption and ignorance.

Having once been isolated as willfulness, the will can no longer step outside itself, so that its inventiveness must be within its own

5. Allen Tate, "Three Types of Poetry," *On the Limits of Poetry* (New York: The Swallow Press & William Morris, 1948), pp. 100–101.

terms. While willfulness may seize other categories, under its dominion these categories lose their original substance, serving only as illusions of themselves. It has been said that hysteria and hypnosis have been used to prove every possible psychological theory, including psychoanalysis. But, of course, under the sway of the two parent illusions of hypnosis—absolute power and absolute compliance—what is apt to be proven is the power of hypnosis, rather than any particular theory of psychopathology. Although the theories contrived may be wildly different in form, they are invariably coercive in nature, describing how the will of the child is assaulted by the will of the parents. Thus, the will invents in its own image. It may be recalled that Freud at first took the tales of early seduction of his hysterical patients quite literally, only to discover that these episodes were more in the realm of fantasy. Eventually, he managed to reconcile this error with his previous theories about sexuality. But, what he failed to note was that, in either case, the will had contrived its own willful theory.

No phase of existence is so easily appropriated to the needs of the will as sexuality. But both erotic adventures that are invented, and those that are lived, must be read allegorically as episodes in willfulness, so that form will not be mistaken for content, or expression for cause. It is precisely this confusion that has led to several errors about hysteria that still persist today, even though our therapeutic experience refutes them. Because the hysteric is so absorbed with sexual drama, in fact and in fantasy, and because he brings this form of willfulness almost immediately into the therapeutic situation, it has been assumed that such sexual freedom entitled hysteria to a top position in the libidinal hierarchy. The fact of the matter, as most therapists will agree, is that hysteria deserves no such rank, remaining one of the most incorrigible states taxing the therapist. Another common assumption, equally mistaken, was the belief that with sexual emancipation, hysteria would disappear. In point of fact, sexual emancipation, and the spread of physiological and anatomical knowledge, have merely diminished the cruder conversion manifestations. It was often the case that the hysteric, in stress, might in a sense exert the same absolute dominion over his own body that he exerted over others'. What he would not move was paralyzed; what he would not hear deafened him; what he would not see blinded him. The hysteric's peremptory dealings with his own body would resemble the changes wrought by the hypnotist on the person of his subject; and, in both cases, the signals for these impositions could be as arbitrary as any number from one to ten.

Before sexual emancipation, willfulness in sex was restricted to whether the person would or would not. With emancipation, willfulness has shifted from the fact of participation to an absorption with the details of the sexual act itself. It is thus a larger arena we have built for the hysteric, and the rules are more complicated, now that sexual performance has been atomized, with each particle exploitable. When Freud called a spade a spade to Dora, giving the sexual functions their clinical appellations, he offered her a new range of metaphor, if her vocabulary was that of the usual woman of her class. Nor was fresh metaphor all he offered, for his theory of symbolism endowed even her ordinary expressions and activities with sexual importance. It may be asked, however, whether such exegesis constitutes emancipation, or whether, instead, the means of expression are merely extended. To put it another way, and possibly more exactly, what Freud may have achieved was a change from the method of concealment to that of disclosure, without necessarily altering the motivation.

The manner of hysteria, viewed critically from outside the experience of the beholder, will usually be described with adjectives derived more from theater than from psychology. "Dramatic" or "histrionic," used pejoratively, are the terms most commonly invoked to convey the hysteric's impact. They suggest a repertoire of personal decoration, gesture, intonation, and even vocabulary, whose flourish puts more modest or commonplace devices of expressiveness to shame and is disproportionate to the spoken or written message. If a choice can be made between the physical and psychic realms, this repertoire belongs more to the former, even though it uses psychic materials. When this dramatic insistence becomes too overpowering, whatever intellectual substance there may be is blurred for the listener, whose attention finds itself split in a manner not unlike the division in the hysteric. In such fragmentation, listening, in any honorable sense, is no longer possible. Instead, mannerisms of body and voice, formerly inconspicuous, acquire a new and crude existence, widely separated from what is said. As the beholder's attention hesitates between these two poles, the possibility of any fully imaginative response recedes: he must now choose between style and content, such choice necessarily involving his own will. Inevitably, now, he compels himself, whether in agreement or disagreement, to address himself to the hysteric's manner. Thus does it happen that will responds to will, and dialogue can be no more than illusion.

In an absolute, or dialogic, sense, in which manner and content can be separated only arbitrarily, hysterical drama may be said to be bad drama. Everyone has his own style of expression. Even the deadpan "objective" approach, in its seeming absence of style, intends to accord "scientific" or "sensible" or "unemotional" substantiation to a statement. Yet, for most people their dramatic style will have an intimate, though wavering, bearing on their thought, with sometimes one, and sometimes the other, being in the ascendancy—still without the connection being lost. However, it is quite possible for very little to be said extravagantly well, in which case the listener may be persuaded that he has heard more than he can later remember at a moment when the speaker's manner has faded from his recollection: "I can't remember what he said, but he had a most charming way of expressing himself." Here the important word, of course, is "himself," for when the disproportion between manner and message is great, when manner turns so top-heavy as to be called hysterical, personal style, in its self-assertiveness, would enhance not the idea so much as the brilliance and charm of its author.

"Flirtatious," "coquettish," or "seductive" would describe hysterical behavior where the drama is apparently sexual. Apparently—because were it clearly sexual, the adjectives would no longer apply. The seducer suggests his availability without quite acknowledging his intention. Thus, his manner will consist of persuasive or coercive nudgings, hardly overt enough for an overture, for extorting sexual commitment. Although these stratagems may be unacknowledged, it would be improper to call them "unconscious." Let us say that their recognition would impose a problem in morality which might diminish the excitement of the campaign. Recognition is postponed rather than repressed. The theory that the stratagems themselves are witless manifestations of dark sexual forces—puppets whose strings are pulled by the libido—is welcomed by the hysteric because it absolves him of willful intent. He is *acted upon* by Nature, who works her will on him. So long as both wills—his and Nature's—reside within his person, there can be no defeat; victory is his, whatever the outcome. Though the defeat of his will may, in reality, have brought him to treatment, this theory offers him a way of viewing that defeat as a victory for Nature's will, an outcome not too uncommon in the speculations of the nineteenth century. Returning to seduction, once the partner commits himself sexually, the will may find another goal in fending off that commitment. The will's nimbleness in shifting goals has been aptly called "teasing," the organ prefix depending on the sex of the partner.

With the idolatry of sex through sexology and psychoanalysis, opportunities for the will have increased, through the appropriation of the details of sexual union. In an age characterized to some extent by "the tyranny of the orgasm," the choice is no longer between sex or no sex; instead, the will joins itself to those particles of sexual behavior whose sum, it is hoped, will constitute the sexual act. When this particular absorption with the willful possibilities of sex occurs at the feverish beginnings of psychotherapy, it is apt to be called "positive transference," and to be mistakenly considered a good omen for cure. During this phase, before the two wills begin to oppose each other, the hysteric makes sexuality out of the therapist's science, while the therapist makes science out of his patient's sexuality. In this affair, the hysteric has the advantage, there being more sex to science than vice versa. The therapist's disadvantage, moreover, is increased by his habit—encouraged by psychoanalytic theory—of isolating the sexual function: whether his language is clinical or vernacular, he works on the brink of pornography. To serve pornography, sexuality must be torn from the larger human context and exalted into a life of its own.

What Tate has said of the romantic imagination applies equally to hysteria: "It has no insight into the total meanings of actual moral situations; it is concerned with fictitious alternatives to them, because they invariably mean frustration of the will." [6] If, at this precise moment in my writing, I fall into conflict about how best to develop the hysteric's incapacity for conflict; if now there seem several possible ways, all with their privileges and limitations, yet none leading in a conclusive direction, I may suddenly discover myself moving briskly away from my chair, possessed by the almost physical necessity to walk to the drugstore, where I shall case the paperback collection and purchase a second toothbrush. If I am harsher with myself than is my custom, I will wonder briefly what I am doing on this expedition, and my answers will probably have to do with fresh air and exercise. Should I be so foolish as to assure myself that this little trip allows me to think my way out of a writing dilemma, I shall have to confess that there have been no thoughts: only a trip and a purchase—a compulsive voyage, a quickly achieved, though irrelevant, goal, and, finally, a return to this same chair, to begin again. This example is a deliberately trivial instance of my will inventing a fictitious alternative for me at a time when conflict would be more suitable. Obviously, many activities that enjoy the name of distraction are actually fictitious alternatives the will devises for sidestepping possible moral conflict. To a great extent, the emotionality of hysteria, ranging from rage to tears, can be understood as the fictitious alternative to real conflict. And, in hysteria, much of what is called by such names as "impulsivity" or "acting out" are more serious, even catastrophic, adventures invented by the will, alcohol being one of its most faithful accomplices in these escapades: it performs the double service of inflating the will at the same time as it dulls discrimination.

6. Tate, "Three Types of Poetry," p. 102.

As Tate has suggested, a moral situation must involve "frustration of the will," and a fictitious alternative to this frustration can be, in hysteria, a new and feverish exertion of will. The advantage of this willful exertion is the illusion of wholeness, forcibly grasped rather than gained or granted. Unlike the first realm of will, not only is there no joined totality of the privileges of mind and body, but there is a serious diminution of ordinary capacities, although this may not be immediately apparent. What we are likely to experience in this state is not the freedom of the first realm, but rather the exhilaration that we are, at last and again, doing what we want to do. In such excitement, the self *is* the will, but it is no longer that shadowy, elusive creature, flickering over the surface of consciousness, that we traditionally call the self. Thanks to the work of the will, the self now emerges whole into the bright light of the world: suddenly it has acquired shape and dimension and substance: it has been concretized by the will. But the faint resemblance that this imposing apparition bears to the true nature of the self testifies both to the formidable powers of the will and to the urgency of the need we all share to experience wholeness. When wholeness eludes us in its proper setting—in dialogue—so vital is it to our lives that we turn wildly to will, ready to grasp at any illusion of wholeness, however mindless or grotesque. Caught in this illusion, and delirious with well-being, we are convinced of the extraordinary keenness and clarity of our intellect, but in point of fact, no state of mind so deadens and injures our faculties as our belief in this illusion of wholeness. The more dependent a person becomes on this illusion, the less he is able to experience true wholeness in dialogue, and at the point where he is no longer capable of dialogue, he can be said to be *addicted* to his will.

The absence of "insight into the total meanings of actual moral situations" should not be understood merely psychologically. Not only does possible frustration of will serve as a motive for blinking actual conflict as it arises in life, but more important, will's solitary and inflated sovereignty as willfulness actively opposes the acquisition of precisely those intellectual faculties with which we perceive the "total meanings of actual moral situations." For the severely hysterical person, there has been a cumulative failure in learning over the years, as he pitted his will against the will of his parent and teacher. Whether in compliance or opposition, with charm or with rancor, he could surrender himself neither to his teacher nor to his subject matter. The open admission of ignorance contained in the phrase "I don't know" is the essential precondition for learning. But for the hysteric, "I don't know," except when used as strategy, means a defeat of will. As the gaps in learning accumulate, "I don't know" is replaced by a manner of knowingness, which is an assortment of gestures, physical and verbal, implying not merely understanding, but also the possession of far more knowledge than can be expressed in words. The hysteric considers these gaps in his learning more shameful than sexual aberration and artfully hides them from the world, thus insuring their perfect isolation from the knowledge that might repair them. What was trouble with addition and subtraction in the second grade now causes the hysteric to keep his hands hidden as he counts on his fingers. But, more ominous than arithmetical insufficiency, is the probability that his failure with numbers is closely related to his present clumsiness in logic as it pertains to himself and to the world about him. What used to be his original problem with grammar in the third grade now exists as an impoverishment of language rendering him invulnerable to those syntactical discriminations which we call by such names as humor, irony, ambiguity, and paradox. Since we are all, to some extent, the language we speak, we cannot be surprised when an hysteric whom we have recently studied announces soberly, after reading the first chapter of *Huckleberry Finn,* that it is a sad story about an adopted child, neglected and intimidated by his foster parent. Such a reading is only in part an instance of a willful person discovering willfulness in a story where there is none: it also demonstrates his utter dependence, in making such a discovery, on his willful indifference to language itself. Though willfulness would seem accessible to psychotherapy, the hysteric's intellectual failure, which has accumulated over the years, will hardly respond to motive analysis, insight, or even relation therapy, although these may constitute a beginning for learning those discriminations that belong to the world of intelligence. When it is understood that hysteria consists of a double failure, in the realms of will and intelligence, it is no longer mysterious that its treatment is so arduous and time-consuming. Nor is it mysterious why such treatment, ideally, should combine psychotherapy and education in the best sense of both disciplines.

If ethical considerations lie beyond the capacities of hysteria, can any generalization be made about the nature of hysterical discourse? By and large, the hysteric's way of addressing and perceiving both his fellows and the world about him can be said to be aesthetic. It should be quickly noted, however, that the aestheticism of hysteria, since it is relatively uninformed by imagination and intelligence, is not of the honorable order that we often associate with the term. Moreover, the aestheticism of hysteria, being deprived of real subject matter, turns about the self, even about the body, of the hysteric. The question "What do I say and do?" becomes "How do I look when I say and do?" And not merely "How do I look?" but "How do you look?" As my friend talks to me I may be on the verge of a critical statement about what he has said, but because my attention has wandered and my intellectual powers are stunted for the moment, I simply cannot achieve the formulation I desire. At this instant, I am struck by the fact that he is not as interesting-looking as I had thought, nor for that matter has his way of expressing himself been particularly felicitous. Let me add that I could have been on the verge of an admiring statement, which eluded me, and at the same instant I could have been struck by how well he looked and how well he spoke. Both examples involve my being reduced to aesthetic comment. The aestheticism of hysteria concerns itself with many variations on two questions: "Am I pretty?" (or "Am I manly?") and "Am I bright?" Both questions may be asked separately, sequentially, or simultaneously. In combination, they may amount to the question "Am I interesting?" or "Do you like me?" Although these questions may be asked affirmatively when mutual endorsement is enthusiastic, when disenchantment comes, they will most probably be phrased, "You think me stupid. Or ugly. Or dull." Or, with more discouragement, "I'm a fool, a mess. How could anyone like me?" Psychoanalysis, with its theories of motivation, will extend, if not enrich, the vocabulary of the hysteric, for this aestheticism can subvert any of the categories of characterology. "Aren't you being hostile?" or "I am put off by your tone." In a sense the hysteric welcomes the motive-analysis of psychoanalysis, both as a criticism of his style and as an opportunity to improve his manner.

Because the willful, and aesthetic, nature of hysteria has not been understood, many psychologists, including Freud, have mistakenly believed hysteria to be an almost exclusively female disorder. In fact, convinced that hysteria biologically belonged to women, they have usually located male hysteria within those varieties of homosexuality in which "femaleness" is mimicked, if not parodied. However, according to the formulation I have described in this chapter, hysteria would belong equally to men, except that its style of discourse would revolve around the question "Am I manly?" An example of male hysteria would be the enforced masculinity of Hemingway, in his person and, to some degree, in his writing.

Such aestheticism is also characteristic of those hysterical suicidal gestures whose self-mutilations serve death only accidentally. These gestures resemble conversion symptoms in that the hysteric works his will on his own body. But, unlike the conversion symptom in which the function of the body is impaired, in the suicidal attempt the intactness of the body is disfigured. The gesture is an aesthetic rather than an ethical comment: despairing and bitter, it mocks the body that has failed its owner's romantic will. To the question "Am I pretty?", the gesture cries, "So be it! I *am* ugly!" or "If you think me ugly, I'll *be* ugly!" In an antiaesthetic way, ugliness, rather than death, would seem to be the object. And this same ugliness may spread, in its own perverse fashion, over the entire scene, affecting decor, dress, gesture, and even relationship: all may become as disheveled as the hysteric requires.

Philosophically, the distinction between will and intellect is an ideal one—an abstraction that, although useful in dissecting the human spirit, has, like other abstractions, done some disservice to the potentialities for totality in existence. And psychologically, if I attempt to describe the role of will in an unselfconscious activity, I cannot help but fragment that activity into psychic and physical aspects whose sum bears little resemblance to the original totality of the experience. In our most interesting moments—dialogic moments, if you will—will is unconscious and can only willfully be pried loose from the rest of life. It is when will becomes conscious that it exists separately, can be experienced separately, and can be discussed separately. As I indicated earlier, will as willfulness may not be acknowledged by the hysteric, but this does not mean that it is repressed or unconscious: awareness is merely postponed. Will as willfulness belongs to consciousness and, in varying degree, is an inescapable portion of our lives.

Subjectively, willfulness is experienced in a manner that reveals its kinship with the body. At the moment when will is preponderant it is felt almost physically, as a lunging of the body, a fact that may explain why Schopenhauer describes the body as the objectification of the will. Through will, consciousness of the physical self becomes as absorbing as physical pain. An unremitting pain, such as toothache, lands one squarely on the anterior side of the body-mind dualism: one *is* a body, one *is* mortal, and since, by definition, mortality is crumbling, its claims are imperious. In pain one observes the drama of his failing body, all thought centered on the aching part. On the other hand, when will is ascendant, no spectator-self observes the rush of the will; at the most, one may be aware of a breathless thrusting of self that may literally cause the body to lean forward. Will is now felt as personal weight with its own momentum, expressing itself in such questions as "Do you know what I mean?" or "Do you follow me?" With these questions, one reveals his awareness that the thought, or prethought, which lurched awkwardly through conversation, was fortified not so much by imagination as by personal emphasis, be it of body, pitch, or language. Like an idea that becomes too old too fast, its propulsive gait could not be healed, only affirmed. In willfulness, one is like a man who has lost his chance to tell his anecdote to the assembled party and now waits to seize the next opportunity. People seem to go on talking in what could be a foreign language. They look interested, knowing. They even seem to share in the allotted space in the air about them, much like a page of printed dialogue, indented every line or so, and seen for its typographical arrangement rather than for its meaning. Finally, there is or is not a pause, and our character says, "This has been reminding me of . . . ," and on with the story. The pathetic attempt to assert a relevance to his story stems from an awareness that will has dulled his responsiveness, isolating him from all that has gone before, yet still demanding to be heard.

This feverish figure, endlessly assaulting the company, seeking to wrench the moment to some pretense of dialogue, is the image of the eternal stranger: that condition of man in which he is forever separated from his fellows, unknown and unaddressed. It is the figure of man's separated will posing as his total self. Though always a stranger to those he moves among, this figure is no stranger to our imagination. Who is he but ourselves—you and I and everyman—as we have been over and over in the past and shall be again? This condition of willfulness, which at once drives us to grasp for wholeness and prevents out attainment of it, is no rare disease. Even by its harsher, clinical term, hysteria, it is, in varying degree, the lot of each of us. The temptations of will beset us all, because they belong inevitably to the human condition. That being the case, I should like to conclude with a word or two in defense of hysteria, but I am afraid that note of uplift is denied me. The most impressive claim made on behalf of hysteria is that the willful gestures characterizing it are often the necessary opening moves we make in overcoming the fear, despair, doubt, timidity, lethargy, or excessive rationality that may come upon us at the outset of any new venture, rendering our indispensable commitment impossible. This claim asserts that hysteria is a prelude to passion. But I would maintain that, far from being its prelude or preparation, hysteria is passion's deadly adversary; hysteria loathes passion as a potential usurper of its usurped domain. With similar shrewdness it abhors wit, discrimination, imagination, humor, and judgment—all those aspects of intelligence whose injury and impairment are its goal and result. It is true that we must live with hysteria, but we need not, I think, honor it. In fact, if we give it its rightful identification as the sworn enemy of our capacity to be fully human, we may give ourselves a crucial advantage in the struggle we must constantly engage in to transcend it.

5

Despair and the Life of Suicide

GABRIEL MARCEL has written: ". . . the fact that suicide is always possible is the essential starting point of any genuine metaphysical thought." [1] It might equally be said that the possibility of suicide will always oppose psychiatry's efforts to rid itself of metaphysical concern. For once that possibility disrupts the civilized and ordinary boundaries of psychotherapy, every technical category loses its ordered place in our thinking, and must be questioned with a new urgency, or exploited in a manner that robs it of whatever truthful meaning it may have earned. What I have chosen to discuss

---

1. Gabriel Marcel, *The Philosophy of Existentialism* (New York: The Citadel Press, 1961), p. 26.

here is—if I may be permitted this irony—the life of suicide, as distinguished from the act itself.

Martin Buber once remarked: "The act of suicide—it is a trapdoor which suddenly springs open. What else can one say?" Well, one can say a great deal, to judge from psychiatric literature. But it is my impression that while to the man who kills himself the act of suicide may be a trapdoor suddenly sprung, to the analyst it seems rather to resemble a psychological staircase, leading step by logical step to an inescapable culmination. And although I don't wish to force the image, I must remark that whether this staircase goes down or up, it must always be traveled backwards. Confronted with the fact of suicide, the analyst must construct his explanation in reverse, laying motive upon motive (hostility is favored here), and strategy upon strategy, until he reaches some final necessity. Having arrived at the end of his staircase, he may then retrace his steps forward, issuing those kitchen prescriptions for the heading-off of the act with which we are all familiar.

I would suggest that this staircase, though a far more reassuring and manageable structure than the suicide's own trapdoor, exists principally in the analyst's head, not in the real world. On the other hand, the world is full of trapdoors, even though the only ones we can be sure of are those which have already sprung open. The invention of the staircase is hardly surprising; a trapdoor offers very little to an investigator bent on explanation, and, by extension, recipes for prevention. But it is my suspicion that the staircase leads us, not to greater understanding, but merely away from the issue. It prevents us, after all, right at the outset, from even considering the possibility that the act of suicide is not the final move in a chain of causation—that perhaps it is not *caused* at all, in a psychological sense. Naturally, this is not an agreeable proposition to the psychologist, who tends, understandably, to feel somewhat panicked if suddenly robbed of his basic tenet and tool, causation. Be that as it may, I feel that there is a more fruitful approach, even for psychiatrists, to the issue of suicide than the construction of causes out of motives, and that is to leave aside, for the moment, the act itself, and to contemplate what I have called "the life of suicide"—which must be seen, not as that situation or state of mind which *leads to* the act, but that situation in which the act-as-possibility, quite apart from whether it eventually occurs or not, has a life of its own.

It is part of our most profound—or metaphysical—awareness of ourselves, as Marcel has pointed out, to acknowledge that the possibility of suicide belongs to the human condition. We know this and must live with it, in much the same way as we know and must live with the fact that sin and evil are no strangers to our nature. But the awareness that it is possible for us to kill ourselves does not lead us to embrace suicide, any more than does the awareness that we are sinners prompt us to go forth and sin. For the man who is caught up in what I have called "the life of suicide," however, the possibility of being the author of his own death exercises a demonic and seductive fascination over him. This fascination takes different forms. There is a certain kind of person for whom the idea of suicide is a secret and cherished solution to any difficulty life may throw across his path. Suicide is the ace up his sleeve (revealed to no one), the secret possession of which shapes his response to any and every problem. Such a man confronts his life whispering to himself, "If I can't find a better job, I'll kill myself. If my son won't confide in me, if my daughter flunks her final exams, if my wife forgets my birthday just one more time—I'll kill myself." This man, although caught up in one form of the life of suicide, is not, I think, in despair. Despair, which arises only in someone capable of some seriousness toward his life and himself, is literally beyond such a person. His secret scheming with the concealed trump of suicide altogether robs any event in his life—and quickly enough his entire life—of meaning, but without imposing upon him the necessity of acknowledging or dealing with meaninglessness. And, because concealment is so vital to his "advantage," as he conceives it, and therefore his deviousness and dishonesty so virtually impossible to penetrate, he is, I believe, the most difficult of all potential suicides to treat—or to help in any way. Though not suffering the estrangement of true despair, this man is actually more separated from the world and his fellows than the despairer in his worst agonies of despairing isolation. I will return to this question of estrangement, but at this point I would like to contrast the form of the life of suicide that I have described with a form that we more commonly encounter: the suicidal preoccupation of the man who *is* in despair.

Suicide finds no more fertile soil for its intrigues than despair—that "sickness unto death" in which, as Kierkegaard observed, we long to die and cannot. It is the middle years that are most vulnerable to the claims of this sickness of spirit, which now radically questions all we have been, at the same time scorning the solace formerly sought in the future, making who we are to become the most oppressive of questions. As both the workings and visages of the flesh falter and wither, all crude preconceptions of immortality are shattered, giving way to a brooding—and equally crude—apprehension of the finitude of our earthly stay. Gradually—or even suddenly—there emerges the realization, "For better or worse, that was it. There never was a second chance." Time past now isolates itself as an alien, often perverse accomplice, sometimes accepting, but more often refusing, memory's overtures. What cannot be remembered robs us of goods that seem rightfully ours, so that memory turns feverish and willful in its pursuit of the past—the past we thought we owned when it was the present, and assumed we would continue to own in the future. What we would remember eludes us, and what we would forget we now remember with a fresh and painful clarity we never before knew. All those cruelties, deceits, and betrayals which we inflicted on the human order disclose themselves as wounds that cannot heal. Of such real guilt Martin Buber wrote:

> A man stands before us who, through acting or failing to act, has burdened himself with a guilt or has taken part in a community guilt, and now, after years or decades, is again and again visited by the memory of his guilt. Nothing of the genesis of his illness is concealed from him if he is only willing no longer to conceal from himself the guilt character of that active or passive occurrence. What takes possession of him ever again has nothing to do with any parental or social reprimand, and if he does not have to fear an earthly retribution and does not believe in a heavenly one, no court, no punishing power exists that can make him anxious. Here there rules the one penetrating insight—the one insight

> capable of penetrating into the impossibility of recovering the original point of departure and the irreparability of what has been done, and that means the real insight into the irreversibility of lived time, a fact that shows itself unmistakably in the starkest of all human perspectives, that concerning one's own death. From no standpoint is time so perceived as a torrent as from the vision of the self in guilt. Swept along in this torrent, the bearer of guilt is visited by the shudder of identity with himself. I, he comes to know, I, who have become another, am the same.[2]

As despair deepens, what had meaning now seems meaningless; what seemed meaningless is fraught with meaning. There develops an ever-widening rift between the despairer and the person he was, between him and the world in which he lived. Though estranged both from the world and the self who formerly dwelt in that world, he is at the same time—out of his craving for reconciliation—now wholly absorbed with that world and that self. Envy and pride conspire to increase the rift. Strangers passing him on the street appear to him transfigured by their thoughtless possession of just what he has lost: the sheer, taken-for-granted ordinariness of life. In the misery of the envy they incite in him, he isolates and exalts that quality of life that can flourish only in disregard: a sense of belonging to whatever worlds one lives in, a sense that is both concrete and casual. Finding himself outside his own world, he discovers that he is unequal to it, and he yearns to sever whatever ties still bind him to this world to which he no longer belongs. Fitfully he contemplates other worlds—the simple job, the monastery, the tropical island, the sickroom. But he flinches as he imagines addressing himself to the machinery of preparation, explanation, and farewell that such a flight requires, and he realizes further that no haven offers a promise of honoring his passport on arrival. Though he may believe himself the most miserably humbled of men, it is not humility but pride that rules his imagination in this enterprise. His visions of escape from his tormenting world are apt to be rather grand in scope, and turn about such possibilities as remote lands and the monastic life. Taking a job as a shoe clerk does not occur to him—though it might be more in keeping with the humility he ascribes to

2. Martin Buber, "Guilt and Guilt Feelings," *Psychiatry* 20 (1957): 116.

himself. Within him, pride and despair, which since the earliest stages of his affliction have found themselves natural and powerful partners, each encouraging and supporting the claims and strategies of the other, now discover in the despairer's yearning for escape merely one more invitation to exercise their formidable collaborative gifts and assume command. Inspired by his despair, his pride now invents in its own image the possible alternatives to the world that surrounds him, excluding him. It may happen that he perseveres, and reaches his island, or the disturbed ward of some closer-by institution, thus shutting out the world that had shut the door on him. Yet what he cannot shut out, what accompanies him on any journey he makes, is his own despair. And, with his despair, his overweening pride. His despair is not in the possession of the world, nor can he abandon it as he can abandon a city, a job, or a marriage, and flee to some uncontaminated place. His despair is his alone; it travels with him and lives where he lives; and, whether he stays or flees, he must eventually discover that it responds—in any significant sense—as little to geographical as to stylistic change. Its indifference to maneuvers is absolute.

Because intercourse with his fellows now only reminds him of what he no longer has, he slowly loses the power to be with other human beings—even as their physical presence grows ever more essential. To some degree he is conscious that his mounting self-absorption is accompanied by a dwindling perception of others. What concern he manages he must will: thus does he leap from his reveries to arrange his features in some imitation of interest and animation, to open doors, light others' cigarettes, to "participate"—usually in some stilted, feverish way that constitutes the best performance to which his will alone can move him—in "the scene," in "a social situation," where his presence in a group of people seems to require certain ordinary capacities he finds he now suddenly and totally lacks. Dreading that others will recognize what he already knows and abandon him, he feels compelled to declare some disability that will legitimate his distracted self-absorption in the eyes of those about him, in the hope that they will extend the same tolerance toward him that any invalid may rightfully expect. Like the sinner in Camus' *The Fall,* the despairer knows that "the essential is being able to permit oneself everything, even if, from time to time, one has to profess vociferously one's own infamy." [3] In this state, he experiences an overwhelming longing to confess—but what he confesses is not his wickedness, which would be a proper subject for confession and which might involve him in some redeeming attitude toward both his confession and his life. Instead, what he wishes to confess is his worthlessness—his infirmity. Such a confession is spurious, of course; it does not touch on issues of forgiveness or repentance that are relevant to his condition. In "confessing" infirmity, what the despairer would coerce—and here his willfulness is quite brutal—is an acknowledgment of his disease in terms that are almost physical. I find no mystery in the eagerness of those in despair to secure a physical diagnosis—say depression—and then offer themselves to pills or electric shock or lobotomy—anything that will spare them real contrition. More mysterious to me is the willingness of those of our calling to accept the more demonic terms of despair, to conspire to relieve the despairer of his humanity through chemical, electrical, or surgical means.

Even in such a brief account of the landscape of despair, it must be clear that despair—potentially at least—is both destroying and renewing. With this double potentiality in mind, T. S. Eliot has addressed himself to the despairer in this manner:

I said to my soul, be still, and wait without hope
For hope would be hope for the wrong thing; wait without love
For love would be love of the wrong thing; there is yet faith
But the faith and the love and the hope are all in the waiting.
Wait without thought, for you are not ready for thought:
So the darkness shall be light, and the stillness the dancing.[4]

While we may not share the author's rather Eastern reliance on waiting itself as the way out of despair, still we must acknowledge

3. Albert Camus, *The Fall* (New York: Alfred A. Knopf, 1957), p. 141.

4. T. S. Eliot, "East Coker," *Four Quartets* (New York: Harcourt Brace Jovanovich, 1943), p. 15.

how difficult it is for the despairer to still his soul—or his mind. While despair means literally the loss of hope, the movements of despair are frantically directed toward hope; but the hope born of despair may turn to the prescriptions of the isolated will. Spurning the self-illumination arising from true humility, despairing hope concerns itself pridefully with certainties. Even the certainty of hopelessness may paradoxically appear as a form of hope, promising to make reasonable what is unreasonable, namely, hopelessness itself. The despairer may, at this opaque moment, be utterly convinced of the clarity of his vision, condemning the world that preceded his despair as no more than a sentimental insanity, a silly fabrication created by his own unwillingness to discern the harsh truth about this existence. It is as if his imagination, in its fullest sense, has abdicated, and now his will can apply itself to the task of reducing what is most human, to pursuing ever further the inevitability—and therefore the essential absurdity—of all that has been and all that will be. He now seems to himself, despite his melancholy, the most reasonable and forthright of men. Like Kirillov in Dostoyevsky's *The Possessed,* he proclaims, "I am just such a scoundrel as you, as all, not a decent man. There's never been a decent man anywhere . . . all the planet is a lie and rests on a lie and on mockery. So then, the very laws of the planet are a lie and the vaudeville of devils." [5] This is the realism of a truly macabre predictability. And a "vaudeville of devils" accurately describes the stale, repetitious, lifeless routines from which the despairer yearns to escape. Surprise and mystery have vanished from his view, if not from his experience. If he contemplates a visit with friends, he can no longer imagine the casual, the unexpected moment that might offer even momentary relief. No, instead he writes both scripts and concludes from his authorship that, since he knows what would happen, there is no reason for making such a visit. But, if life itself should provide a casual moment, even with a stranger, which quite cuts through his self-absorption, wholly transforming his mood, he has no capacity to celebrate this

5. Fyodor Dostoyevsky, *The Possessed* (New York: Modern Library, 1936), pp. 625–629.

moment. In fact, he will disown or conceal the moment, rather than allow it to question his dismal certainty; he thus learns cagily to protect his state from life's interventions. Even the rational or logical steps to his conclusions, which strike him as utterly convincing, may turn shabby if exposed to the light of discourse. So pride urges him to keep his own counsel, even though it mean his death. Thus does the despairer appear before us to ask that most extraordinary and truly diabolical question—especially when addressed to a psychotherapist—"Is there any good in talking?" After this, we may recover our composure and succeed in engaging him imaginatively, so that real talk, does, after all, begin to come about. Then, despite his absolute certainty of a few moments before that even momentary relief from the torment of despair was no longer possible, his despairing self-absorption may yield to forthright interest in the subject at hand, a yielding which goes beyond mere distraction. Relief has, in spite of everything, actually been granted him; his despairing certainty has been exposed to the real world of discourse and proved false. We might even say that a minor miracle has occurred. What are we to answer then, when, as the hour nears its end, our patient or friend, preparing to take his leave, turns to us and asks, "But haven't you something *useful* to say to me—something I can use after I leave here?" If there is an answer to this question, it has not occurred to me. I wish to comment only on one of its most curious aspects: the man who spoke these words was one who had recently been in despair and would, very likely, soon be in despair again. And yet, by this question, which could occur only to a despairing mind, despair reasserted its claim on him, still without forcing upon him the anguish that is its customary companion. Contained within his question is the reminder that such fleeting moments of relief are all very well, but after all truth is truth and logic is logic, and by truth of course he means despairing truth, and by logic he means despairing logic. This is to say that what he wishes to take with him to counter his despairing certainties are other certainties, maximlike morsels, prescriptive in nature, which, like pills, will offer him some comfort when the pain returns. Almost while still celebrating the wonder of his renewal, he has with his question submitted himself again to despair.

The fascination of suicide to a despairing mind lies in the fact that it offers a demonic solution for every anguished, humbling, and potentially renewing claim which despair may make. As Marcel has written, the possibility of suicide may provide the beginnings of metaphysical thought. However, when an absorption with suicide possesses the despairer, it becomes—as Marcel has said—"the expression of another much more profound and more hidden possibility, the possibility of a spiritual denial of self, or, what comes to the same thing, of an impious and demonic affirmation of self which amounts to a radical rejection of being." [6] We have, I think, no more desperate illustration of the manner in which suicide violates every human claim which may exist in despair than Kirillov's explanation of his suicide:

> Man has done nothing but invent God so as to go on living, and not kill himself . . . I can't understand how an atheist could know there is no God and not kill himself on the spot. To recognize that there is no God and not to recognize at the same instant that one is God oneself is an absurdity, else one would certainly kill oneself. If you recognize it you are sovereign, and then you won't kill yourself but will live in the greatest glory. But one, the first, must kill himself, for else who will begin and prove it? So I must certainly kill myself, to begin and prove it. Now I am only a god against my will and I am unhappy, because I am *bound* to assert my will. All are unhappy because all are afraid to express their will. Man has hitherto been so unhappy and so poor because he has been afraid to assert his will in the highest point and has shown his self-will only in little things, like a schoolboy. I am awfully unhappy, for I'm awfully afraid. Terror is the curse of man. . . . But I will assert my will, I am bound to believe that I don't believe. I will begin and will make an end of it and open the door, and will save. That's the only thing that will save mankind and will recreate the next generation physically; for with his present physical nature man can't get on without his former God, I believe. For three years I've been seeking for the attribute of my godhead and I've found it; the attribute of my godhead is self-will!

6. Gabriel Marcel, *The Mystery of Being,* vol. 2, *Faith & Reality* (Chicago: Henry Regnery, 1960), p. 194.

> That's all I can do to prove in the highest point my independence and my new terrible freedom. For it is very terrible. I am killing myself to prove my independence and my new terrible freedom.[7]

This quotation is a combination of two speeches of Kirillov's that occur close together in the course of a dialogue several pages long, a series of assertions that seem to me to constitute an excellent example of certain aspects of the suicidal despair I have been discussing. As I examine Kirillov's declarations, I will try to make clear my own understanding of what is happening in this passage, and what significance it may have for our consideration of despair and the life of suicide.

•

As Kirillov expounds on the purpose and necessity of his suicide, the voice we hear seems hardly to belong to a person. Or, if we can imagine a person to be present, it must strike us that this person's singular life as a human being is almost wholly submerged in a sea of generalizations about the human condition and the existence of God. Both the tone and the substance of these generalizations exhibit the certainty of a creature with godlike pretensions, while at the same time testifying, by the forced nature of the logic, that this certainty is constantly assailed by fear and doubt. Further, that uncertainty is unnaturally frightening to such a mind; in its fear of any sort of question, it leaps to answer the wrong questions. Again, Eliot's lines come to mind: Kirillov is precisely a man unable to still his soul—or his mind, which, indeed, has become merely the reasoning function (however impaired its power to reason) of his sovereign will. The very thing he cannot do is wait. Willfully he hopes, and inevitably his hope is hope for the wrong thing. Bereft of faith, yet lusting for faith, willfully he invents his own creed and embraces it with willful belief. He is indeed "not ready for thought," yet thought seems to be the only response his mind can imagine to the despair which overwhelms it.

We should note that at no point—in this passage or in the course

7. Dostoyevsky, *The Possessed,* pp. 629–630.

of the entire scene—does Kirillov admit, or indeed even begin to recognize, his own despair. This is the worst of all despairs in which, as Kierkegaard has written, the despairer does not know he is in despair. With that variety of logic that is born only in despair, he reasons that even though he might live on and on in "greatest glory" as God, he must be the first to kill himself in order to "prove" his divinity—or, more accurately, his immortality. Usually the despairer, as I mentioned earlier, learns to mask such demonic logic as this out of his prideful apprehension that any explicit exposure might reveal it as foolish, even absurd. But Kirillov, ignorant of his despair, fails to experience such apprehension; although not altogether confident of the truth of his assertions, neither his doubts nor his pain suggest to him the nature of his condition. What intervenes between the plentiful evidence of despair and his notice of such evidence is, of course, his will, which cunningly blocks his vision at every turn.

And, in this willed blindness toward his state of mind, he is incapable both of imagining, and certainly of contending with, such a real issue as guilt. There is little suggestion, in his discourse, of a human soul suspended in anguish and guilt over its own particular injuries to the human order. Being beyond remorse, all Kirillov can do is to call himself and all other men scoundrels, at the same time declaring the entire planet to be a mockery. That there might potentially be guilt, were he able to pursue real self-illumination, is suggested by his wish to save not himself but "mankind," even though all men be scoundrels. Out of his loss of faith, he perpetrates a familiar psychologism, strangely similar to Freud's view of religion: namely, that men have invented God in order to stay alive. Untroubled by any memory of other times when he must have deceived himself with other certainties, Kirillov now decrees without hesitation that if there is no God, then he must be God. Not only is there no suggestion of guilt in Kirillov's proclamations, neither is there any intimation that he may have wrestled with—or even acknowledged—the terror aroused in him by the idea of his own death. What we hear instead is the rather plaintive statement that he is unhappy and afraid. And, even the possibilities for self-illumination that might lie in this limited admission—were he able to hold himself still in the presence of such unhappiness and fear long enough to perceive some hint of their nature and meaning—are quickly dissipated in the generalization that "terror is the curse of man."

At only one point in this passage does Kirillov seem perilously close to an encounter with the real nature of his condition—an encounter which might force him to abandon his despairing logic. His abrupt assertion that his suicide is "the only thing that will save mankind and will recreate the next generation physically; for with his present physical nature man can't get on without his former God, I believe," contradicts the primary assumption on which his entire argument has rested up to this point: namely, that man could get on without God perfectly well, if it were only proven to him once and for all that God didn't exist. Here Kirillov seems suddenly to have stumbled upon an alarming and utterly unmanageable truth: man's need for God is contained in his very physical nature—his mortality, his helplessness to alter the absolute necessity of death. That such a truth could have penetrated the fortifications that will has erected on every side of his awareness must mean that Kirillov, despite his claims to omniscience, has failed to convince himself with his own despairing reasoning. In the moment of his realization of this failure, and faced with the truth he has just perceived, his despair would seem to be on the brink of a crisis of exposure and self-illumination. But his will, rather than accept such a defeat, commands avoidance of this crisis, and presses him instead to outwit the moment with the most extreme and bizarre assertion he has yet made: since man's "physical re-creation" is necessary to liberate him from his need for God, such "physical re-creation" is precisely what Kirillov's suicide is designed to achieve.

The principal attribute of his godhead, he has discovered, is "self-will," by which he means the naked will directed toward the self—an unconditional Nietzschean will, which we might term willfulness, or perhaps pride, and which suggests the "demonic affirmation of self" of which Marcel has spoken. But Kirillov will not entertain the possibility that such "self-will" might have landed him in his suicidal despair. Instead, he asserts the demonic principle that man has been unhappy because he has been afraid to be willful enough. Therefore, he will prove his independence and his "new terrible freedom" through the "supreme" act of "self-will," namely, suicide. This is to say that if, out of cowardice, he has failed himself and others, he will now prove his courage, not by contending in fear and trembling with the tumultuous questions of his existence and thus finding his life, but by ending his life. What never occurs to him is that by means of this very concept of "self-will" his whole argument has—perhaps not in terms of its own peculiar logic, but certainly in relation to truth—turned itself on its head. Instead of seeing "self-will" as his affliction, he conceives it as his godhead, and the instrument of his self-realization. Instead of seeing that his sovereign "self-will" enslaves every human aspect of his intelligence, he imagines it as the key to his "terrible freedom." Instead of recognizing "self-will" as the unmistakable clue to his demonic despair, he finds in it—by virtue of the extraordinary demands it imposes—the supreme heroism of his calling, justifying and explaining whatever fear, doubt, or pain may have threatened to shake his resolve. Instead of calling into question his manner—and, along with it, all his reasoning—the idea of "self-will" arrives in his mind as a sort of deus-ex-machina of logic, clarifying and confirming all that has gone before, setting upon the ordered whole its seal of authority and exaltation.

Having thus established the necessity of his suicide, Kirillov shoots himself. While perhaps a literary necessity, this is not really characteristic of the life of suicide, which may or may not terminate in the suicidal act itself.

Even before plots of suicide have begun to invade and absorb the despairer's subjectivity, his "self-will" may be exerted in destructive ways other than the "supreme" act of suicide. In an effort to breach his growing sense of estrangement, he may explode into a mania of self-assertive activity in which he would seem to be trying to overpower his anguish by exalting those more headstrong aspects of his nature which have brought him at last to despair. Alcohol or drugs may offer brutish assistance to this euphoric surge of personal motion, by means of which he tries to force his way back into the world. Of all the movements of despair, this clatter of the spirit is the most deafening and the most defeating, convincing no one, least of all himself. Deprived by this rush of will of the capacity for quieter moral discrimination, he now exposes himself to greater and greater opportunities for guilt, which must also be overridden. Desperately hungry for reconciliation, he becomes increasingly estranged from those loved ones who might conceivably offer him some relief, were it not being demanded of them. At this stage in his deprivation, he may turn unhappily to the task of documenting his estrangement by becoming a self-appointed, though miserable, expert on those deficiencies in his fellows that render them incapable of love—particularly the love toward him that would lighten his despair. While dimly conscious that his hectic state makes him unlovable, he maintains, in the midst of his fever, a wavering hope that the other will overwhelm his isolation with a burst of affection that will lighten his anguish and effectively dispute his despairing certainties. Naturally, he hesitates to reveal his perceptions of the manner in which the other has failed him, out of fear that he will make himself even more unlovable in the other's eyes. Nevertheless, his need may provoke him into an angry encounter in which, despite admissions of his own state, he still manages to list his charges. When love—or the inability to love—is examined in this objective manner as still another article of knowledge, every human being must acknowledge his failure. To defend one's capacity to love is a spiritual impossibility; it forces the loved one to objectify and therefore to lose that which cannot be objectified, namely, love itself. Often enough, the consequence of such an encounter is mutual despair. Even if the loved one manages not to fall into despair himself, he may still feel himself charged with the responsibility to love, so that in a self-conscious way he attempts to will what cannot be willed.

This phase of explosive activity will persist until the despairer's excesses become so outrageous to himself that a sudden—and shocking—perception of his own behavior plunges him into real self-loathing. In this state, he can no longer escape—or postpone—an acknowledgment of his despair, and, by virtue of this very acknowledgment, he may—still within despair—find his way toward the beginnings of self-illumination and renewal. But should the possibility of such renewal elude him, he will discover that this self-loathing has landed him in the bleakest, most naked realm of despair. The rush has subsided, leaving his despairing mind increasingly at the mercy of suicidal machinations. It is as though the will, which formerly asserted itself in activity, now turns to inventing the details of one's self-destruction. At this stage, the body grows heavy and alien, so that the most ordinary physical tasks seem like monstrous obstacles, making the despairer wonder how he could ever have taken these matters for granted. He experiences his body as a ponderous affliction to which he longs to put an end. Yet, at the same time, his physical vanity is offended by this new imposition, so that often, in the midst of his suicidal ruminations, he will leave his chair to inspect his face in the mirror for any new wrinkles that may have appeared. At one moment, he may have decided on the exact date for his demise, while in the next he finds himself considering the purchase of a new and fashionable jacket. Such an outlandish mixture of the profound and the trivial—so characteristic of the life of suicide—does some disservice to his view of himself as a tragic figure. Increasingly, he comes to charge himself with duplicity, shallowness, even frivolity, and now it appears that the act of suicide is necessary to prove his seriousness.

The absurdity and pathos of the life of suicide stem from the despairer's will to achieve—through suicide—his status as a moral human being. In a sense he asks, "How can I live decently in suicide?" Referring to the "radical rejection of being" that follows upon the "demonic affirmation of self" in the contemplation of suicide, Marcel adds, "that rejection is the final falsehood and absurdity; for it can exist only *through* someone who is; but, as it becomes enbodied it develops into perverted being." [8] As a demonically con-

8. Marcel, *Faith & Reality,* p. 194.

stitutive symbol, suicide invokes every human concern. Inevitably the issue of courage is raised—not the courage to live in spite of despair, but the courage suicidally to put an end to all those cowardly hesitations that prevent the despairer from consummating his death. Brooding over the manner of his suicide, he searches again and again for the considerate way—the way that will make manifest his continuing solicitude for those who would be most damaged by his death. Timing becomes a weighty problem: it would be cruel to spoil the Christmas season for his family, selfish to disturb office business at this particular moment. (Let us note that this intricate solicitude toward others is, in truth, merely an absurd imitation of—or substitute for—his real guilt toward them and toward the whole human order, a guilt he is incapable of contending with directly.) The suicide note, since it must justify what cannot be justified, becomes a formidable and frustrating document as it is composed and recomposed in the despairer's mind, each new version suggesting the possibility that perhaps no note would be preferable to an unconvincing one: particularly since any note, depending on its imaginative adequacy, may expose to the despairer the essential absurdity of all he seeks to prove.

Even the extent of the despairer's suffering must be witnessed and authenticated by suicide. Repeatedly, he announces to himself that his state is unbearable. But, should he be challenged on this score—that is, how is he to know what is and what is not bearable for himself, in other words, what gives him this godlike certainty?—his answer, to himself at least, is that it must be unbearable, otherwise he would not be thinking of suicide. In solitude, this answer appears unassailable to the despairer. In fact, it may happen that the act of suicide seems to have become necessary to demonstrate how unendurable his pain is, in which case he commits suicide in order to prove it unendurable. Here, the despairer takes his own life to prove that he is not responsible for taking his own life. By definition, what is unendurable cannot be endured; therefore his suicide is not a matter of choice but an externally determined response to a situation that has deprived him of choice. The flaw in this construct, of course, is that his definition of his condition as unendurable is very much a matter of choice, and thus, obviously, so is his suicide. What is interesting here is the despairer's effort to deny the true possibility of choice and, by extension, to deny responsibility for his suicidal act. He does not say: "I am in great pain; I do not know how much longer I can contend with it; I do not know if I will be permitted some relief, or how much, or how soon, or if it will afford me any more than momentary comfort. But I choose to bear these uncertainties no further. I prefer to end my life of my own will and by my own hand. I choose this act and accept full responsibility for it." Though such a declaration contains a fairly accurate description of his situation, the despairer goes to some trouble to avoid such an acknowledgment of choice and responsibility. He must believe his suicide to be an inescapable fate imposed on him from without. Why? Is it perhaps possible that, even in the grip of his despair, he has not lost contact with his more human self and with the human truths his despair strives to deny—has not lost contact to such a degree that he no longer conceives suicide as a demonic act? Indeed, it is because he *does* recognize its nature that he shrinks from confronting the actual role of choice in his act, for even his despair will not allow him such an unholy embrace of moral grotesquerie as suicide. Were he capable of acknowledging the nature of this unholy embrace, and his responsibility in submitting to it, his despair—and his despairing estrangement from the world of the human—would be complete. That his despair, instead of prompting this acknowledgment, labors to deny it altogether, to persuade him of his role as a helpless, and therefore blameless, victim suggests that in an important sense despair, by its very nature, is incapable of wholly fulfilling itself. As I remarked earlier, despair seems to afflict only those whose relation to life is a serious and potentially responsible one. It seems to me that those who are vulnerable to the worst torments of despair are also those who—because of what they were before falling into despair, and still, in the clutches of despair, potentially are—are seldom quite able to reach the demonic affirmation of self and the radical rejection of being toward which their despair strains. In some sense, the despairer moves hazardously, despite distractions and entrenchment, toward a tragic, often excessively tragic, position in regard to the inauthentic in his life and in his relations with others. In other words, through his objectifications he may arrive at an extreme and radical concern over the very center of his being, creating in this way an abyss too wide and too deep for easy bridging. The very strategies of despair, and especially the logical strategies involved in the contemplation of suicide, reveal that there is some connection still linking them to life-outside-despair—perhaps only imagined, but imagined still—that despair is unable to sever. Despair would not be so anguished a condition as it is were it as wholly and hopelessly estranged as it believes itself to be.

There is one last clause to the pact suicide makes with despair: suicide appears to offer a means of contending with the necessity and all the attending uncertainties of one's own death. What Buber has written of guilt applies equally to the person in despair: potentially he is permitted "the real insight into the irreversibility of lived time, a fact that shows itself unmistakably in the starkest of all human perspectives, that concerning one's own death." Opposing this insight, suicide promises, through an act of will, to resolve the terrors of mortality that, in despair, are so overwhelming. Death itself is certain; but how, when, where, in what manner, under what conditions, with what serenity or wild ravings, and *how soon*—this knowledge is not granted us. There is, however, one way in which a man may attain it, and by so doing "cheat" death—become its master by mastering its uncertainties—and that way is to stage and execute his own death, at the time, place, and in the manner of his own choosing. But once embarked on this enterprise—or its contemplation—he becomes absorbed in the scene itself. As though carelessly overlooking the inevitable climax of the action—death, *his* death—he focuses his attention upon the staging of the act; he reviews and evaluates the methods available to him; in his imagination he lives and relives the discovery scene—at which, in reality, he can hardly expect to be present. And yet in effect he must expect to be present, if through suicide he intends to master the terrors of death, because such terrors belong to life. Although the strategies involved in the attainment of this mastery can succeed only by luring his attention away from the real issue of his own death, their success is almost always incomplete and intermittent. Since his death is, after all, a detail of action inescapably necessary to his scenario—the single act about which his entire dramatic construction turns—its ultimate significance is not likely to remain safely hidden behind his busy concern with an endless variety of production problems; from time to time it rudely assaults his awareness, and in those moments he realizes all too clearly that the mastery that suicide seemed to offer him was a cheat and a fake. But, each time this dreadful moment arrives, he wrenches away from it and fastens his imagination again on the fictional representation of his death, in which what absorbs him is not his actual death but the possibility for self-expression that the drama affords. Why should an opportunity for self-expression—so strikingly, almost farcically, inappropriate to his particular situation—tempt him so? We need but briefly remind ourselves of his condition, and the extraordinary vulnerabilities common to it, to guess that the explanation for his response lies in what he believes is promised him in return for the cooperation he so wholeheartedly supplies. What can this promise be but that self-expression, given free rein in this exceptional enterprise, will produce for him the dramatic representation of some uniqueness, some singularity of self with which life has seemingly so far failed to provide him, and of which his natural—un-self-engineered—death threatens to rob him? In conclusion, what I wish to point out here is that all this is a dream of the will—a despairing attempt to affirm the self in a form in which the self has never been and can never be. The uncertainties—and even the terrors—of death belong, as Kirillov almost discovered, to life and to our nature. Living the life of suicide a man struggles to deny this truth, and should the trapdoor spring open beneath him, he will die proclaiming his denial. But it is a redeeming paradox of the life of suicide that it does not always—and need not—make its exit from life via the trapdoor. The despairing man can return to life—alive. Many have done so, and some have left their accounts of that treacherous passage to remind us that salvation is never wholly out of reach, even in the farthest country of despair.

6

Schizophrenia and the Mad Psychotherapist

DESPAIR ALSO, it seems to me, is more or less intrinsic to the therapeutic life as it involves schizophrenia. Such despair, moreover, if acknowledged rather than disowned, if contended with rather than evaded, *might* (the word is important) have a salutary effect on therapy.

My aim in this chapter is to examine what happens, especially to the therapist himself, when this despair is *not* acknowledged, not contended with.

Schizophrenia and the Mad Psychotherapist

Some time ago, I became aware that a number of younger therapists, each with several years' experience in treating schizophrenia, were seeking in one way or another to leave this area of psychiatry. The reasons they contrived for abandoning their work with schizophrenics were various, but I gradually began to suspect that underlying all their logic and detachment, their talk of the value of varied clinical experience, of opportunities elsewhere, and of a yearning for private practice was a vague, brooding, unspoken apprehension that their sanity was at stake. In this apprehension they were joined by their spouses, who also felt vaguely troubled by subtle changes in them. Although these wives or husbands had difficulty describing this alteration, they seemed to have no doubt that it constituted an unhappy development. Even when nagged or beseeched by their mates for reassurance, these spouses were unwilling or unable to consider the changes they observed as part of a decent maturation of character. (I am trying as carefully as possible to avoid being clinical; clinical categorizing here would be as inappropriate to our purposes of describing and understanding as clinical self-scrutiny was inadequate to the perplexing and ominous restlessness these younger therapists found themselves caught up in.) Neither the therapists nor their spouses worried that they might fall victim to a particular clinical disorder, least of all schizophrenia. If they feared for their sanity, it was in a private, unprofessional way; they wondered to what degree they were becoming what they were not, or—with equal relevance—to what degree they were not becoming what they were.

The uneasiness and concern of these younger practitioners have prompted me to reconsider my own experience in this area. For a period of over twenty years that includes working with schizophrenics, as well as with those young doctors who spend their days treating schizophrenic patients, I have also had the good fortune to know and be instructed by several great therapists, therapists with grave theoretical differences, but sharing nevertheless that power sometimes called "charisma," which the dictionary defines as: "a grace, as a miraculously given power of healing, or of speaking with tongues, or of prophesying, etc., attributed to some of the early Christians." Then, too, I have had a passing acquaintance with those occasional, ragged, even disreputable healers who seem to burst full-blown, apparently with little preparation, into the world of schizophrenia, brandishing their therapeutic powers with a flourish that far exceeds their theoretical accomplishments. Their period of therapeutic vitality is usually comparatively brief, and their subsequent course or fate disagreeable.

As I looked about me at these three different groups of therapists—the young, the old, and the vagabonds—I could not escape concluding (allowing for certain remarkable exceptions)—that the hazards are indeed serious for those who choose to devote their professional lives to the treatment of schizophrenia.

I sometimes wonder what impression the hospital world of schizophrenia—for example, a sanitarium devoted exclusively or primarily to schizophrenic patients—might make on someone who happened into it without advance explanation or preparation. His first thought, one he would quickly correct, would be that it was difficult to tell the doctors from the patients. But, as soon as he dismissed this notion—in spite of conceits to the contrary it is not a difficult distinction—I suspect that, as he observed the therapists in ordinary conversation and listened to them in meeting, it might strike him that no word but theatrical or histrionic could do descriptive justice to their extraordinary manner. He would have to conclude that, for reasons mysterious to himself, these therapists had apparently abandoned what must once have been their more usual habits of expression in favor of some more florid and declamatory style—a style that appeared to transcend style, elevating mere form or manner to substance itself.

At this point let me describe an incident from the therapeutic practice of a friend—one of the most distinguished therapists of schizophrenia in modern times. The incident is not especially unusual and may, therefore, suggest the flavor of life within an institution devoted to the treatment of schizophrenia, as it might appear to an outsider.

My friend had been treating a schizophrenic young man for about a year and a half. The therapy had had its ordinary portion of difficulty, impasse, silence, violence, and the like, but, at the time of this incident, seemed to be moving along satisfactorily. My friend owned a fountain pen of which he was very fond. It was an excellent pen, valuable, distinctive in appearance, and reliable. Not only did it give him pleasure on all these counts, but it also had personal significance for him, having been a birthday gift from his father. My friend used this pen constantly, carrying it with him in his breast pocket wherever he went. Somehow, in the course of a therapeutic session, the pen came to the attention of the patient, who seemed to admire it. He watched attentively as my friend used it to make notes, then hesitantly reached his own hand toward it. Noticing this gesture, the therapist, instead of returning the pen to his pocket, put it into the patient's hand and said, "Pretty, isn't it? Do you want to try it out?" The patient slowly fondled the pen, then suddenly unscrewed the cap and fell to making marks on a sheet of paper the therapist had placed before him. Totally absorbed, he hunched over his work, manipulating the pen with care and deliberation. Though solemn and silent, as was his custom, he seemed to be enjoying himself. Heartened by this responsiveness—if only to his fountain pen—and reluctant to ignore any opportunity for relation, my friend said, "Look, how would you like to keep the pen until tomorrow? Maybe you could write a letter with it tonight. You can bring it back to me at our hour tomorrow." The patient stopped marking the paper and gazed down at the pen, then up at the ceiling, then out the window, and finally into the therapist's face. "Thank you," he said. The remainder of the hour went very well.

The next therapeutic session came and went without mention of the pen. And the next. And the one after that. And then several more. At last, after some weeks had passed, my friend inquired politely about his pen and mentioned how convenient it would be to have it back again. The patient said nothing, but appeared to have heard the therapist's remarks. A few more therapeutic sessions passed with no sign or mention of the pen, and finally one day my friend said, "I don't want to press you about this, but the matter of my fountain pen is increasingly on my mind. I'm sure I didn't mention it to you at the time you borrowed it, but that pen means a great deal to me. I realize this may be sheer childishness on my part, but, you see, it was a present from my father, a little while before he died, as a matter of fact, and I'm very attached to it. Of course, I could easily just buy myself another pen, or use a pencil, and forget the whole thing. But, as I've explained, I'm especially fond of that particular pen. This may all seem quite silly to you, but surely you know how people sometimes become devoted to certain objects. . . . Well, maybe it *is* silly, but the fact remains that I *am* devoted to that pen, and I'd appreciate very much having it back. So, would you please bring it along with you next time?" There was no answer, but my friend assumed he had made his point and that it had registered. However, the fountain pen failed to appear at the next interview, or the next, or the next. A few sessions later my friend introduced the subject still another time. "About my pen. . . . You've had it six weeks now. Don't you think that's about long enough to keep a borrowed fountain pen? I've explained it all very carefully to you—why I'm anxious to have it back, and so forth. Now, please don't fail to bring the pen with you tomorrow."

And, two meetings later, "My patience is wearing thin. I mean to have that pen, and I don't want any more foolishness about it. Time after time I've asked you gently and politely to return it; I've explained how I feel about it, and why I insist on having it back, and all this has produced no result whatever. You don't return it, you won't discuss it. Now what the hell is all this about? Can you tell me that?" After a long silence the patient murmured, "It's lost." "It's *what?* What do you mean *lost?*" No answer. "Are you trying to tell me that you no longer have my fountain pen? You don't have it with you? It's not in your room? In other words it's *gone?*" Again the patient made no answer; in fact, he remained absolutely silent throughout the rest of the hour, while the therapist thundered at him and stomped about the office.

The interview concluded on this uncordial note, and the patient returned to his room. Immediately the therapist summoned two hospital attendants, and the three of them marched off toward the ward where the patient lived. When they reached his room, the therapist gave a curt order, and the attendants flung wide the door, bounded inside, and in a matter of seconds had the startled young man on his back, pinned to the floor. My friend then entered the room, and without taking the least notice of his gasping and astonished patient, made a rapid but efficient search for his pen. He found it in the drawer of the desk. He picked it up, regarded it a moment, glanced briefly at his pinioned patient while he jabbed the pen into his breast pocket, then wheeled about and stalked from the room. As he was making his exit the patient raised his head from the floor and shouted past the attendants toward his retreating therapist, "My God, what a madhouse! All this fuss about one little fountain pen!"

I am at pains to point out that my friend is a courteous, civilized person, whose normal manner—at least among friends—is gracious, reserved, and ironic. Ordinarily, he is simply not given to such carrying on as I have described. It would be more characteristic, in such a circumstance, for him to acknowledge that the problem of the borrowed-pen-gone-astray is the inevitable concern of anyone who has—and lends—cherished possessions, and, after polite efforts to retrieve some item had failed, he would, without undue commotion, replace it. This display over his patient's failure, or refusal, to return his pen is curiously uncharacteristic and might even be said to have been enacted somewhat larger than life. But we must be careful with our interpretations at this point. My friend is no method actor, who will facetiously describe to his wife during dinner the experimental situation he engaged in with his patient, reenacting his gestures and lines for her amusement. At no time, either while with his patient or while recounting the incident to his wife, does he imagine himself to be *acting* at all. In talking with his wife, he will declare, quite sincerely, that his exasperating patient provoked him beyond all human endurance, driving him to take the measures he took. The one thing about the incident that would surely strike an observer will just as surely escape the attention of my friend himself, namely, that this collision of wills has been shockingly naked, clothed by none of the artifices that usually conceal willfulness. If my friend has been theatrical, his theatricality has been effective enough to deceive himself. He may be ruthless in rooting out his motives for his violent action; he will call them "countertransference," which will enable him, by convicting himself of a vanity that led him to offer the pen in the first place, to seize full psychological responsibility for the whole encounter. Still, he will not be troubled by the quality and scope of his performance, nor is he likely to consider the possibility that the whole affair could be a fictitious alternative for some real moral dilemma confronting him and his patient. As a matter of fact, once he has thrashed out his motives—alone or, more commonly, with the assistance of his wife or a colleague—he may decide his handling of this incident has been direct, even courageous. Naturally, to come to this conclusion he will have to forget that the hospital situation stacks the deck in his favor; without a tremor, bravely, and in full view of the audience, he has shot the villain with a stage revolver loaded with blank cartridges.

Let me mention another incident, this one from the practice of the late Dr. Frieda Fromm-Reichmann, one of the most gifted people to work with schizophrenia.

Dr. Fromm-Reichmann was treating an extremely disabled young man who had been schizophrenic for years. He was habitually dirty and disheveled, rarely spoke, and even more rarely achieved much coherence in what little speech he did produce. Without question, therapeutic work with him was a grim business, affording scant hope, little satisfaction, and few of even those fleeting rewards so precious to the therapist specializing in the treatment of schizophrenia. One day, during a therapeutic hour, as this patient (mute, as usual) was sitting with Dr. Fromm-Reichmann in her office, she noticed that he was fingering his genitals with one hand that was crammed deep into the pocket of his trousers. It was also plain to her that he had an erection. She pondered this situation for a moment, then said to him, "If it will make you feel any better, please go ahead." Whereupon the young man unzipped his fly and proceeded to masturbate, while Dr. Fromm-Reichmann sat quietly across from him, her eyes down, her hands clasped in her lap.

Anyone who knew Dr. Fromm-Reichmann knew that she was a well-brought-up, refined, upper middle-class, German-Jewish lady. During Georg Groddeck's last years, prior to his commitment to an institution, she performed the offices of his hostess with fastidious skill. Once or twice a year, she helped Groddeck to assemble at his estate a group of distinguished European psychiatrists. It was her duty to arrange for food, wine, and cigars and in general to put these guests (many of whom did not know one another) at their ease, to ensure a comfortable social atmosphere out of which might come the sort of conversation Groddeck wished about matters psychoanalytic. Once the group had gathered, and following all her work of arrangement and preparation, she was required, as the only woman present, to assist in setting the scene and maintaining the appropriate tone to the occasion, but always without calling attention either to her assistance or to the novelty of her presence. Of course, it might happen that in the consideration of some question of feminine psychology, Groddeck would suddenly turn to her and say, "Frieda, we men cannot really know about these things. As a woman, Frieda, you must instruct us." At such moments, I am sure, she was more than rewarded for the physical and emotional labor of these occasions, not to mention the irritations involved in dealing with a person as crotchety and difficult as Groddeck became in his later years.

Dr. Fromm-Reichmann was always a marvelous hostess, and something of her quality as hostess appears in the incident I have recounted about her and the mute young man whom she encouraged to masturbate if it would help him to feel more comfortable. But I doubt that, as this man sat masturbating in her quiet office, full of tasteful mementoes of her European past, she found much resemblance to her life as Groddeck's hostess. To some extent a hostess resembles an actress, in that she plays a role (in this case, one of amiability toward a group she may not know); she is not required to believe that her role is anything more than a role. Believability is central to the effectiveness of the performance, but in order that it be achieved, actual personal sincerity—in regard to the scene itself—is unnecessary, if not irrelevant. In therapeutic encounters, on the other hand, the therapist's actual personal sincerity is considered absolutely essential to the occasion. I think that as Dr. Fromm-Reichmann described this incident with the mute and masturbating young man at a staff conference, she might well have blamed herself for some awkwardness in her invitation and would have been quick to acknowledge any erotic titillation she experienced. But she would have resisted the suggestion that there was anything unusual about her behavior, that while committed, in full sincerity, to her duties as psychotherapist she had suddenly found herself enacting the role of hostess. Her private conviction, I suspect, would have been, as in our previous example, that there was something real, something "down-to-earth" about this incident.

It does not actually matter if the part an actor plays is not really relevant to his life, because he knows (I am speaking ideally, of course) that he is playing a part. The therapist, however, is not granted such distance; he may be theatrical, but he is not playing a part. (Unlike the actor, he may believe what he will or will what he believes.) As he comes to believe in the reality of these overblown therapeutic encounters, so rich in the materials of strife and sexuality, it is his ordinary life outside the hospital that may come to appear artificial and pallid. It is not unusual for the therapist, as he settles into his work with schizophrenia, to begin to prefer the company of schizophrenics, even those who are mute. Given the extraordinary difficulty of treating schizophrenia, it might be expected that with experience, status, and income, the older therapist would try to restrict the hours he spends with such patients. But more often than not, the opposite is the case: he tends to fill more and more of his waking hours with such therapeutic work, and to feel quite bereft, impotent, and lonely, when, for reasons of illness, vacation, or grants, he is deprived of the schizophrenic's company. I shall return to this unusual preference later.

In telling the story about the therapist and the borrowed pen, I suggested that the whole incident had a quality of being somehow larger than life. But it is not merely the therapeutic encounter which is habitually writ large in this way; something of this quality passes over from the event to the man, and not infrequently gifted therapists themselves come to be writ large. They begin to resemble certain spectacular personalities—often, but by no means exclusively, actors and show people—in that no sooner do they enter a room than they fill it. Room after room after room, differences of setting and occasion mattering not at all, confronted with a room they fill it, in what becomes a characteristic style of their own, yet not predictable—as mere idiosyncrasy of manner is—and flexible enough to adapt itself to any particular situation. Just *how* they accomplish this, time after time, must to some extent remain a mystery; but what we have noted about their therapeutic life may give some clue to this quality of compelling social, or personal, presence, shared by a surprising number of those therapists who have spent years in the company of schizophrenics, a quality that seems gradually to unfold to full flower—quite a *large* flower, usually—in them over the years. Let me be quite clear here: filling a room is not merely—and sometimes not at all—a matter of talking long and loud; even silence may, on occasion, produce a unique resonance, affecting an entire scene. Nor can this capacity be attributed merely to physical manner. Manner is not unimportant, but it is more likely to be the vehicle (or perhaps only the packaging) of the effect than the key to its cause. It is true that *what* is said is usually less important than *how* it is said, but even here both the what and the how tend to vary with the therapist's dramatic feel of the occasion. There is, however, one general statement we can make about such a man and his manner: what he cannot or will not countenance is distance and—as a result—any real absorption in subject matter. His province is relation: not the relation that may slowly emerge out of content, nor even the relation that may come from a leisurely exchange of personal forthrightness, which always risks alienation as its culmination when two people strive (with success or without) to reveal themselves to each other. In one way or another, this room-filling therapist manipulates and forces the spell of relation, willfully exploiting whatever personal expedients come to mind.

In order to understand better this connection between will and relation—which I believe to be crucial to our subject—let us remind ourselves of the nature of the therapeutic life with schizophrenia. In an essay entitled "The Therapeutic Despair"[1] I attempted to portray something of the agony of the therapeutic life with schizophrenia that may end in what I have called "the therapeutic despair." But, as some of my older friends have reminded me, despair is not inevitable; in fact, they would prefer to believe that such despair is a morbid consequence of this work—as unhealthy, perhaps, as my own preoccupation with the subject.

I would like to suggest that avoiding despair by reducing it to a merely "morbid" or "unhealthy" state of mind—and thus refusing to conceive it as belonging inescapably in some measure to our lives as human beings—may be more malignant than despair itself. (It was Kierkegaard's belief that the worst of all despairs is that in which one does not know he is in despair.) It sometimes happens that despair itself provides the very condition of urgency that brings a man to ask those serious—we might call them tragic—questions about his life and the meaning and measure of his particular humanness. When despair is repudiated, these questions go unasked, and it may be exactly in the failure to confront these questions that there occurs a false turning in one's development.

Let us consider again the situation in which the therapist, knowing that even the wrong approach is better than none, may muse or soliloquize aloud to his silent partner. For most therapists who persist in this field, such soliloquizing becomes their principal refuge or solace—or, from their standpoint, the form in which their therapeutic powers find their most vigorous expression. While the schizophrenic may be largely unresponsive to the social event, every thera-

1. Leslie H. Farber, *The Ways of the Will: Essays toward a Psychology and Psychopathology of Will* (New York: Basic Books, 1966).

pist holds the premise that the patient hungers for relation even though he lacks the ordinary personal grace that might bring such relation about. Moreover, he fears that should he venture an overture he might, owing to his gross deficiency, increase his estrangement by revealing himself as even more unacceptable than he already appears. Given the schizophrenic's incapacities, not to mention his experience in hypocrisy and betrayal, the overtures of others will seem to him even more dubious than his own. Obviously, such a situation imposes a formidable constraint on what may be said.

How may we characterize this constraint? There is, of course, the fact of inequality between these two people: one is patient, the other, doctor; one is confined, the other, free; one mad, the other sane. And this essential inequality must be contended with—validly or invalidly. Equally important is the choice and treatment of subject matter. Of what shall the therapist speak? And in what manner, from what view, to what point? If he were to talk about the daily events of his own life, however scrupulously he stripped them of color and meaning and relevance, he would still imply a world in which he lived and worked, a world from which he himself was not estranged. And, aside from the effect on the patient, such a drab recital might very likely be dispiriting to the therapist, so eager himself to make some relational thrust into this seeming vacuum. (I am, of course, taking for granted that he will carefully avoid all those topics that might impinge on the patient's delusional propensities.)

Since we may assume with some safety that the therapist himself is not schizophrenic, we will expect that in addition to having a world he lives with*in* rather than with*out,* he is also blessed by affectionate connections with friends and, very possibly, a family as well—all of which, for our present purposes, can be called relation. However, unless he is sadistic, frantic, or simply stupid, he is hardly likely to expatiate to his schizophrenic patient over moments of intimacy with friends and family. If he chooses to speak of these people at all, it will probably be in order to emphasize whatever estrangement exists or has existed, seeking to appeal to his patient on the level of a fellow sufferer. The danger here, postponing momentarily the insidious effect this device may have on the therapist himself, is that often, to the patient, such talk about estrangement will serve to invoke intimations of those times when estrangement is (or was) either overcome or absent altogether. To forestall this danger, the therapist, almost without realizing it, may overstate and overgeneralize his case. Not deliberately, of course, since he is not being dishonest, but, in his need to join his patient, he may inventively overextend and exaggerate the oppressiveness of the situation he describes. And, since he is not an actor playing a part, and, more important still, since his own sincerity is essential to his convictions, as well as to the assurance with which he believes he must address his patient, he may succeed in persuading himself that through his work with his patient he has discovered patterns of pathology in himself and in his private life whose significance he had not heretofore appreciated, or perhaps even suspected. This is not the only way certainly, but it is an important way in which the therapist seeks, and often finds, kinship with his patient: discovering (or so he believes) his own schizophrenic possibilities.

As he pursues such objectifications of himself and his life and his past, the therapist comes to speak with a clarity about himself as a psychological dynamism that is not only excessive, but that may be quite false. But again, being no actor, he may, as the years roll by, begin to confuse this deterministic construct with himself. And the assembling of this construct is, of course, aided and abetted by the fact that it will seldom, if ever, be challenged or affirmed by the patient. Since determinism itself is not necessarily an evil affair—it may be appropriate or inappropriate, simple or complex—is there anything we can say about the nature of the construct that the therapist contrives to represent himself? By and large, so far as I have been able to tell, and regardless of the school of psychoanalysis to which he belongs, the therapist comes to view himself as victim, acted upon by forces of nature, society, or family in such a manner or at such an early age as to render him powerless. Whether he finds his victimization during the first six months of his life, when he failed to surpass the "paranoid position" postulated by Melanie Klein, or locates his trauma in the anxious mothering he received, according to Sullivanian theory, or—in modern fashion—discovers the "double bind" in which his parents trapped him; his story will be the familiar one of hero-as-victim irreversibly oppressed by the will of others. "I am this way because . . . ," he announces to his patient as casually as possible, implying that it *is* possible to live this life in spite of devastating victimization. Or, "The mood I inflicted on you yesterday has its explanation in a conflict I have been having with your ward administrator." Or, "My failure to hear you has always been provoked by withdrawal, whether yours or my mother's." Or, "Last Thursday night I had a dream in which I raped you. I tell you this so that you may understand my coolness these last few days." And so on.

Such remarks will be regarded, not as acknowledgments of moral limitation, but as manifestations of "countertransference," usually referring to personal attitudes acquired in the past and now inappropriate. We should notice here the easy and translucent clarity of these statements: in vain will we seek in them a hint of mystery, ambiguity, paradox, surprise, or uncertainty. And our visitor to the sanitarium, hearing several such therapists in conference (naturally they speak to one another about themselves in much the same way as to their patients), might, if he were impressionable, briefly believe that he had stumbled on a small band of medical monks, so brutally honest did their confessions seem. But, as he listened further, the utilitarian nature of this seeming candor might soon strike him; he would note that such "countertransference" explanations by and large gave whatever meaning seemed possible in a painfully chaotic situation. Of course, he could not help but observe also that these confessions were delivered, whether to patients or colleagues, rather cheerfully, unlike his own halting and anguished acknowledgments of weakness and evil. And finally, he might wonder whether *confession* was quite the proper word to describe such remarks as "I am this way because. . . ."

The realm of causation is treacherous ground for a man interested in the truth about himself. Although it is certainly probable that most phenomena of this world, human and otherwise, do have causes of one sort or another, an absorption with the role of causation in human affairs may lead to an habitual reduction of any human event to its postulated cause. It is apparent how such reduction promises refuge to a man beset by the necessity to "confess": once he turns his attention to cause, his personal responsibility (whether he acknowledges it or not) is diminished, along with any undue stress or discomfort he may have felt in facing what he believes to be his absolute worst. No matter what scandalous detail about himself he may reveal, he follows such revelation with "I am this way because . . . ," and everyone relaxes. Given the customary forms of psychology, and a close-knit society of colleagues, all trained to abide by these forms, and given in addition the harrowing, threatening, and chaotic environment of a sanitarium for schizophrenia, it is hardly any wonder that the solace of causation persistently tempts these therapists, appearing most seductive when they are speaking with one another about themselves and their lives with their patients. Even should a therapist's account of himself on such occasions include no direct reference to cause, his remarks are apt to lack that hesitant, hard-come-by quality that tends to characterize the statements of a man truly involved in making a moral confession.

As his stay in the sanitarium lengthened, our visitor might—depending on the degree of his disenchantment—soon find the atmosphere oppressive, sickly, somewhat like living in a hothouse where, in the midst of lush vegetation, the temperature was always too hot, the sunlight filtered and indirect, the humidity and fertility always controlled, with none of the accident of sudden cold or wind. Particularly as he listened to the therapists in conference, admonishing and even reassuring one another with countertransference interpretations, he might choose another image to describe the stifling effect on himself: a chamber of distorting mirrors, such as one finds in amusement parks, in which all that may be seen are reflections of reflections of reflections—of the psyches of the therapists. Failure, principally, but also the occasional therapeutic success, finds its cause and its meaning (by default of other sources of meaning) in the materials of countertransference, which constitutes a fashionable form of psychological determinism among those who treat schizophrenia.

Much of the responsibility for this absorption with countertransference lies in the nature of schizophrenia itself, which is a disorder consisting of a double failure in areas that might loosely be called meaning and relation. The intellectual defect, so strikingly displayed in the awkwardness with language, has been variously described in studies of schizophrenic thinking. Such civilized qualities as discretion, reticence, humor, judgment, and logic are poorly developed, if they are present at all. In the imaginative realm, what we usually call the capacity for metaphorical thinking is morbidly deficient, making the schizophrenic's understanding and perceptions, as well as his efforts to communicate, uncomfortably literal. This disability of imagination may be mistaken by the therapist for the workings of the bared unconscious—as though the unconscious were not subject to refinement. Here, the therapist is apt to regard as symbol either what properly is not symbol at all, or what could fairly be called only the rudiments of symbol. It is as though the therapist imagined the schizophrenic to contain within him a nonschizophrenic poet, who manipulated and molded his symbolic utterances and gestures, concealing in some inside pocket that texture of meaning that symbols may achieve. However, it is more likely that this nonschizophrenic poet, if he exists at all, resides not inside the patient but in the head of the therapist, who attributes to his patient's utterances a richness of meaning that is simply not deserved. There are, of course, certain desirable aspects to the therapist's attribution of meaning to the verbal or gestural productions of his schizophrenic patient, for not only does the patient need such imaginative assistance, if he is to recover, but such an exalted view of his capacities also incites an enthusiasm for this work on both sides that urges its continuance in the teeth of the discouragements that are intrinsic to the therapeutic situation.

Nevertheless, there is a hazard to this investiture; should the therapist forget the degree to which he has supplied meaning to a patient unable to provide any for himself, he may come to regard the schizophrenic as a sort of oracle with whom he sits each day—a truly ragged oracle, untutored, unverbal, and naturally unappreciated, who has the rare power to cut through the usual hypocrisies and pretentions of ordinary life, thereby arriving at some purely human meaning. His illness now appears as an appropriate response to the impurities in the therapist's heart, even to the deceits and contradictions of the world in which he lives.

Take the example of a schizophrenic young man whose disagreeable habit—in his family's home as well as in the ward—was a thunderous clearing of the throat, often followed by spitting on the floor. We may guess how disruptive this habit was to ordinary conversation, and how furious his father became when the young man chose the hour of the father's favorite television program for his most explosive performances. Some of us might even have commiserated with the father when, on one occasion, he angrily switched off the set and said, "One or the other, not both. Either I sit here and listen to you, or else you quiet down so that we can watch this program."

It is not entirely unreasonable, I think, to regard this young man's carrying-on as a contemptuous and willful bit of self-assertion. On the other hand, if we had been closeted with him for many months and had come to regard him as an oracle, we might see his behavior as an appropriate social protest against the bourgeois dishonesties of his family life, of which television represented only one. Hawking and spitting might appear to be the only valid or truthful event that ever occurred in this family. When approached as an oracle, the schizophrenic seems not only more perceptive, but more "real," which helps to explain the therapist's growing attraction, even addiction, to the companionship of schizophrenic patients.

Whatever may be the real "real" life that our oracular patient provides, language is not one of its virtues. Nor, for that matter, does it include those areas of knowledge or imagination that live through language: literature, history, philosophy, and so on. What tends to be celebrated is what is vaguely termed "the nonverbal," as though this were a department of gesticulation that need have no lively connection with language. Often accompanying the therapist's exaltation of the nonverbal may be an active intolerance toward, or even disparagement of, language. "Just words" will be a recurring phrase among those who share this view of language; it will suggest that words in general, any words, are crude and deceptive tools when compared to that superior, while at the same time more elemental, mode that dispenses with words altogether. Once the therapist embraces this view, not only does his own language, spoken or written, fail to develop, but he also finds it increasingly difficult to deal in a discriminating fashion with the spoken or written language of others. I have known several therapists who, after years with schizophrenic patients, gave up reading altogether—and not with shame, but proudly, as though they were glad to leave this brand of conformity behind them. What language they retained took on a pedantic, self-assertive quality that did little service to the development of their ideas, seeming increasingly to resemble physical gesture.

Let me mention one further consequence of endowing the schizophrenic with oracular powers—a consequence (for the therapist) that has been implicit in what I have already said. Partly because he has helped anoint this oracle by supplying meanings that the oracle did not possess, partly because the work itself has required him to assert meanings with an assurance he himself did not at first possess, and partly because his audience was both captive and unresponsive, the therapist, by virtue of the prolonged apprenticeship he has served in the most self-indulgent kind of self-expression, may gradually be led toward both the posture (and, ultimately, the belief) that he, too, is an oracle—well-dressed rather than ragged, affluent rather than impoverished, legally sane rather than clinically schizophrenic, yet possessed of the same charismatic power to grasp the truth in any situation, regardless of his intellectual or educational limitations. With the assumption of this toga, that dramatic room-filling quality to which I have referred will have reached full bloom. Though mad in that private sense in which he seems to have fallen away from his own particular direction in life and to have lost all relation to the shy, studious, thoughtful young man he may once have been, he will appear eminently wise, although possibly rather florid and eccentric, to those younger therapists whom he will train in the intricacies of the therapeutic life with schizophrenia.

We can now return to that most important aspect of our subject: the issue of the connection between relation and will. I believe that this unholy conspiracy characterizes, in an important sense, the behavior of both therapist and schizophrenic, not only in their relationship to each other, where it achieves its most dramatic form, but also, and equally important, in the relationship of each to his world, to all others, and to himself. In spite of the fact that the intellectual life of the schizophrenic is as fearfully impoverished as his capacities for relation with others, we must assume that he is still human enough to hunger for relation and, should it be even fleetingly achieved, to dread and to be enraged by its loss. In such an extreme state, much of his delusional and hallucinatory life will either reach for consummation, even glory, or else proclaim his repudiation of such a possibility through a web of corroborating though fantastic details. By his impoverishment, he is reduced in his attempts at relation, or in his repudiation of relation (and often the two are intermingled), to what I call his isolated will—or willfulness, if we define it as *Webster's* does (namely, that state in which one is governed by will without yielding to reason; obstinate; perverse; stubborn). It is a most important part of schizophrenia, and one that has been relatively neglected in the literature, though aspects of it have been considered under other categories. I would say that willfulness not only accounts for much of the schizophrenic's behavior, but authors a great deal of his delusional material. Without the assistance of the imagination, the will invents in its own image—it contrives plots in which will is pitted against will, its subject matter being, roughly, power. In delusion, the willful one may be an outside agent and the schizophrenic his victim. But, regardless of who is villain and who victim, the plot represents a crude example of what Yeats called "the will trying to do the work of the imagination." To some extent power *is* a real and ubiquitous motive in the world. And thus, if the therapist is adept at supplying texture and meaning to the plot, it is easy to see how he may come to endow his schizophrenic patient with an oracular vision of the way in which power controls and corrupts the affairs of all men.

Willfully, then, the schizophrenic grasps at, and withdraws from, relation—sometimes simultaneously. Sullivan once remarked that he thought that, with the exception of periods of panic, the schizophrenic's life with others was largely hysterical in character. Although my understanding of hysteria is quite different from Sullivan's, I think I know what led him to this observation. It was, I suspect, the violent, flamboyant, impulsive, often explosive and destructive quality of the schizophrenic's social movements that reminded him of hysteria. In this regard we should remind ourselves that one or two of the first hysterics Freud and Breuer studied would today be diagnosed as schizophrenic. To take but one example: the muteness of a particular schizophrenic may have originated in panic, when talk led him into such terrifying confusion about reality that his distress, instead of being relieved, was not only perpetuated but intensified. But as his panic subsides, the schizophrenic's muteness may become and remain a willful refusal to talk, in response to what he regards as the demand to talk being made on him by those about him. Reduced to his own will, the schizophrenic perceives himself as continually assailed by the willful demands of others. Examples of schizophrenic willfulness, whether or not they had their antecedents in panic, and despite the often confusing nature of their delusional elaboration or justification, are numerous: the refusal to eat, waxy inflexibility or the refusal to move, untidiness and nakedness, even smearing. All these may be willful responses to what seems to the schizophrenic to be willfulness on the part of those responsible for his care. Most of these examples are expressions of rejection of relation, but it should be said that the schizophrenic's sexual attempts to force intimacy can be equally willful, as with Dr. Fromm-Reichmann's masturbating patient, sometimes seeming almost assaultive in their grotesque lack of the nuances that usually assist the life of affection.

Not until the willfulness of the schizophrenic is recognized can it be understood why the therapeutic life with schizophrenia is such a bloodcurdling affair, its melodrama underscored by screaming invective, physical grappling of a brutal order, and all manner of obscenity. Even the mildest, most unassuming therapist, if he continues in this work, will soon find himself hurled into an arena where will is pitted bodily against will. Yet he may even come to count himself fortunate to have this semblance of relation, no matter how degraded, instead of none at all, which is his more frequent lot.

It is hardly surprising that the more violent forms of the therapy of schizophrenia should seem to be life in the raw, making all ordinary civilized existence trivial by comparison. But the problem for the therapist is more serious than this. Whether he is locked in frantic physical encounter with his patient, or else trying, through monologue, to breach the patient's muteness, he is thrown back on his own isolated will in his efforts to provoke relationship. Even in defeat, he may resort to a silence that is as willful as the silence of his patient. It can be said that both therapist and patient have a will to relation and a relationship of wills. But this is a rather reckless use of the word "relation." Relation, understood in any decent sense, cannot be willed: it happens or it doesn't happen, depending on what human qualities are brought to the event: honesty, imagination, tact, humor, and so on. By contrast, the willful encounter—a far cry from the chancy and fleeting mutuality that occurs from time to time between people, and that we designate by the honorable term "relation"—will have a special binge-like excitement, even though its center is hollow. Its intensity is of the moment; unlike friendship, when the moment vanishes little remains. This is the reason that the addictive possibilities of this therapeutic life are considerable. (In this regard it is no accident that two of the best-known therapists in the field have attempted to give ontological status to the experience of loneliness.)

As the therapist returns again and again to the excitements of this drama of wills that passes for relation, he becomes increasingly impatient of relation, although it is unlikely he will cease believing, and asserting, that the capacity for relation is his special power.

Gradually, but not casually, he becomes an apostle of relation who can no longer abide relation. It is an unhappy fact that when, through drugs or life-situation, one finds more and more scope for willfulness, those other human qualities I have mentioned are not merely held in abeyance, but fall into the atrophy of disuse. And, with such atrophy, the ordinary amenities of the world become not only no longer sustaining, but actually disturbing, making recourse to the drug ever more compelling. As the therapist continues to will what cannot be willed, those attributes of character that tend to expand and harden will be precisely those public, self-assertive gestures that are unfaithful to the person he might have become.

Schizophrenia, of course, is not contagious. In no way do I mean to suggest that the therapist, by virtue of prolonged exposure to schizophrenia and of the possibility of his eventual addiction to intimate association with its victims, actually succumbs to this particular malady and turns schizophrenic himself. He does not become schizophrenic; but, as I have said, he tends to become something other than the person he is, or was, or was meant to be. It has been my intention in this discussion to propose that the curious nature of the person he *does* become may best be understood as a particular, personal, and characteristic response to that particular disorder of human potentiality that is schizophrenia.

7

Our Kindly Family Physician, Chief Crazy Horse

THIS HAS BEEN CALLED the "Age of Anxiety," and if anxiety, as has been said over and over, is a predominant source of distress in our time, such anxiety is the product of our particular modern disability of will. To this disability, rather than to anxiety, I would attribute the ever-increasing dependence on drugs affecting all levels of our society. While drugs do offer relief from anxiety, their more important task is to offer the illusion of healing the split between the will and its refractory object. The resulting feeling of wholeness may not be a responsible one, but at least within that wholeness—no matter how perverse the drugged state may appear to an outsider—there seems to be, briefly and subjectively, a responsible and

This chapter originally appeared as "Ours Is the Addicted Society" in the *New York Times Magazine* 116 (December 11, 1966).

vigorous will. This is the reason, I believe, that the addictive possibilities of our age are so enormous.

Let me be more specific about the addictive consequence which, in varying degree, affects us all. Increasingly, I believe, we are addicted to addiction. This is to say that, with few exceptions, we subscribe to the premise—whether implicit or explicit—that this life cannot be lived without drugs. And those who would repudiate this unpleasant premise by living without drugs are still more or less captive to it, in that so much of their consciousness must be given over to withstanding the chemical temptations that beset them. Withstanding is a lesser evil than yielding, but it is no escape from the issue of addiction, so that I would have to characterize the predicament as one of being addicted to not being addicted. I do not mean to suggest that we choose one course or the other, but rather that both the premise and its negative variation exist in all of us. Even the most debilitated heroin addict retains his pride in the few items to which he has not become addicted.

Not many years ago, we had best remind ourselves, the problem of addiction seemed confined to a few chemicals—narcotics, alcohol, and, perhaps, barbiturates—and it was then possible to make fairly clear distinctions between addiction and habituation, based mainly on the presence or absence of physiological withdrawal symptoms. However, today, even the well-publicized and allegedly extreme agonies of heroin withdrawal have been disputed by the Lazaruses who came back. Recently, a member of Synanon expressed to a reporter his disagreement with the fictional clichés which have acquired the status of scientific fact, remarking: "Kicking the habit is easy. It's not like that Frank Sinatra movie, crawling all over the walls. Sure, it's tough for a couple of days, but it's more like getting over a bad cold." Fearing this view might be as extravagant in one direction as Nelson Algren's violent imaginings were in another, I checked with a friend who had been a staff member at Lexington. He thought the "bad-cold" analogy an accurate one, and added: "We had far more trouble with withdrawal symptoms in barbiturate users."

Our appropriation of the drug-user's vocabulary for our own purposes shows the extent to which the problem of addiction has invaded our daily existence. When our absorption with not only a chemical but a person, an activity, a distraction, an ideology seems to have more weight than is warranted, we say we are "hooked," meaning either that we wish we could be cured of our vice or else that we value the passion contained in our infatuation. If someone or something excites us pleasurably, we say he or it "turns us on," but if our response is indifference or boredom, we are "turned off." Our extension of these terms for our own purposes is, to some degree, a fashionable reaction to the notoriety drugs have earned in the mass media. However, my own belief is that we resort to the junkie vocabulary because it expresses a metaphysical or addictive shift in our existence that the older vocabulary did not quite account for—at least in ordinary usage.

Even if we try to restrict ourselves to drug-taking, statistics about the extent and degree of addiction are hard to come by. Certainly we are no longer surprised to learn of the growing proportion of college students who resort to such drugs as marijuana, amphetamines, barbiturates, LSD, tranquilizers. One expert is quoted in the *New York Times* to the effect that about 40 percent of the students at the University of California use drugs from time to time. This figure falls somewhat short of Timothy Leary's immoderate proclamation: "Today, in the molecular age, the issue is not what books you read or which symbols you use, but which chemicals are part of your life and your growth."

Numerical estimates notwithstanding, on the theory that convicts tend to riot for those privileges society deems essential, such as humane treatment, recreation, adequate food, civil rights, I am more persuaded by this news release:

> WALPOLE, Mass., Aug. 13 (AP)—Inmates rioted outside a medication dispensary at the Massachusetts State Prison in an attempt to steal drugs late last night, injuring nine guards. . . . Two guards were stabbed and five others beaten as the inmates pushed their way into the "pill" room, yelling, thrashing and literally gobbling down as many pills

> as they could at one time. . . . State Police Cpl. James Dunne, who led the squad equipped with 12-gauge shotguns, gas masks and crash helmets, said about 18 of the inmates were reeling "on Cloud Nine" when he arrived. . . .

And from industry, where access to drugs is sufficiently relaxed not to require riots, I offer this item:

> LOS ANGELES, Oct. 9 (Los Angeles Times)—Use of illegal drugs in industry, especially among production-line workers, is so common that to arrest everybody who sold or used them would mean some plants would have to hire whole new shifts of employes, according to a police narcotics specialist. The drugs most commonly used are amphetamine sulfate compounds and barbiturate derivatives, which keep workers awake, or put them to sleep. . . .

Since it is forbidden to peddle or "push" most drugs, including whisky, on television, Madison Avenue has responded to the double dilemma of addiction by advertising aspirin as though it were *the* drug for every tribulation we must undergo. On television we are shown scenes in which mothers snap at their children, employers lose their tempers with employes. With only an awkward swipe at the questionable ethics of permitting this poor old headache remedy to carry such a heavy burden, advertisers show these embattled and suffering creatures putting one hand to their heads while a kindly neighbor advises them that this new aspirin combination is the perfect cure for "tension." The happy scenes following their use of the drug are deliberate efforts to imitate the style in which the pharmaceutical companies persuade physicians of the virtues of their products.

Most touching are aspirin commercials in which an aging movie star, long past his prime and no longer regularly employed, sits thoughtfully in his well-appointed study, telling the television audience that movie-making is a hectic and demanding affair. To avoid tension and headache, intrinsic to such activity, he has always resorted to this particular remedy. Although probably unintentional, such a commercial goes to the heart of addiction, for we must contemplate the pathos of this formerly glamorous creature whose powers have so dwindled that he is reduced to doing headache commercials in which, fooling no one, he pretends nothing has changed. As he holds his bottle of pills to the audience, he seems to say life is really impossible without these pills. But we know, and he knows, that aspirin is not enough; for the vast restitution he demands of life, more powerful drugs are needed.

Should he seek them, he will not have to resort to any illicit drug traffic. He will have no trouble finding a physician who will prescribe amphetamines or psychic energizers to brighten his mood as he waits for calls from his agent. And if the phone refuses to ring, one or several of the many tranquilizers can be prescribed so that he can endure the waiting. Whatever insomnia may have originally been his lot will now be painfully exacerbated by his drug-taking so that other sedatives, fortified often by alcohol, will insure his sleeping. As he moves from one drug to another, mixing and testing the chemicals he believes his state requires and countering their disagreeable effects with still other chemicals, from time to time the sheer immodest scope of his undertaking will strike him; he has become a deranged chemist, his only laboratory his own poor body.

No matter how haggard that body becomes, he must unfortunately depend on it for fresh chemical inspiration. And, if everything else fails, there is LSD for instant revelation, if not wisdom, about the pretentious games that have brought him to this impasse, allowing him the death and rebirth that are now accepted pieties of the LSD mystique.

While it is true that the medical profession and the pharmaceutical industry together are the largest and most powerful group of pushers for the new drugs, I see no conspiracy on their part to make addicts of us all. It has long been common knowledge that physicians are the most devoted users of the drugs they prescribe, unlike the more disreputable pushers whose livelihood depends on abstaining from the drugs they peddle. The men who devise and merchandise these pills and the physicians who dispense them are, by and large, decent human beings who share the same disability of will that afflicts everyone.

Believing, as we do, that we should be able to will ourselves to be calm, cheerful, thin, industrious, creative—and, moreover, to have a good night's sleep—they simply provide the products to collaborate in such willing. If the satisfactions turn out to be short-lived and spurious, and if their cost in terms of emotion, intellect, and physical health is disagreeable, these scientists are ready to concoct new drugs to counter this discomfort. In other words, they offer us always new chances—virtually to the point of extinction—to will away the unhappiness that comes from willing ourselves to be happy.

Recently, Dr. Carroll L. Witten, president-elect of the American Academy of General Practice, was quoted in the press as being in agreement with a report issued this year by the United Nations Commission on Narcotics which expressed concern over "the alarming rise in the sale of barbiturates, tranquilizers and amphetamines." The report suggested further that the "explosive expansion of the use of drugs . . . was most likely a result of their being used less as medication than as agents for producing sleep, a sense of happiness and relaxation." Dr. Witten declared:

> I believe these drugs are not only used wrongly, to excess and without adequate indication, but that in many cases their indiscriminate use has led to dependency, habituation and addiction, with all of the consequent results thereof.

Dr. Witten said he was referring specifically to the non-narcotic drugs used as "psychic energizers, stimulators, activators, deactivators, depressants, alleviators, levelers, elevators or in whatever imaginative category one might place them. One must note with a great deal of alarm," he declared, "that the vast majority of cases first obtained their drugs through the prescription of a physician."

If willing what cannot be willed has led us to being addicted to addiction, it would seem that our addictive appetite will always be more than a match for the ever-mounting number of chemicals that are fashioned to gratify that appetite. And even if we eliminate actual drugs from our consideration, the addictive possibilities are endless: cigarettes, chocolate, detective and spy stories, football on television, psychoanalysis—to mention only a few of my own excesses, which I would unhesitatingly characterize as addictive. Everyone, I am convinced, has his own list, as well as another more prideful list of those objects and activities whose addictive claims he has successfully withstood.

If the term is not to be altogether meaningless, some distinction must now be made between one addiction and another. Concretely, when it comes to putting myself to sleep, how shall I distinguish between detective stories and sleeping pills? Or between watching football on TV and enduring my Sunday with tranquilizers? Or completing a tedious chore on amphetamines and procrastinating as usual?

The first generalization I would make about these sets of alternatives is that in an immediate sense drugs are clearly more effective. Detective stories, for me at least, are not entirely reliable as sedatives. If the story is so poor as to outrage or challenge my diminished sensibilities, I am in trouble, whereas I can always take another sleeping pill. Watching even an exciting, well-played football game on TV, I cannot entirely obliterate from my awareness the perception that there are other ways in which I could more profitably spend my time. And if the game is inept and boring and still I do not turn the set off, my view of my condition is grim indeed. On the other hand, with tranquilizers, I could achieve a state of not unpleasant relaxation, unruffled by the sort of nagging self-concern which interrupts my absorption with even a good football game.

It is the last set of alternatives that will prove the most troublesome. If I have a group of evaluations of psychoanalytic candidates to write, I am inclined to put it off. The reasons and/or rationalizations for my procrastination will be various: I don't feel well; such reports are too tedious to be endured; I resent the bureaucratic rule requiring these reports; I am reluctant to set myself up as a judge of the performance of these young men; I am convinced I am not equal to the imaginative discriminations that would do these human beings justice. With a dose of amphetamine, however, my self-concern, with its associated fatigue and hesitations and doubts, will vanish, so that in a single-minded way I shall vigorously engage my task. Within a few hours all the evaluations will be completed. Like a schoolboy who has at the last minute finished his term paper, I shall feel relieved and virtuous to have at long last done what my organization demands of me.

Reading over my reports after I have recovered from the drug, I may be chagrined to note a breathless, assertive and yet self-indulgent quality to my writing that did not trouble me at the time. But I can counter my dissatisfaction by assuring myself these deficiencies matter very little, since I have done all that was asked of me. It was my own sin of pride that initially led me to regard my task as such an intricate and demanding responsibility. Besides, I will tell myself, wasn't it a choice between doing nothing and doing something, however imperfectly? Thus will my mood of accomplishment prevail, helping me to disown my self-criticism and perhaps persuading me, since I won't have to read these reports again, that I had indeed been discriminating in preparing them. And my earlier doubts as to whether these evaluations should have been written at all can be postponed for another time.

The sensation of being a going, if unquestioning, member of society should not be slighted, because it is hard to come by these days. Nevertheless, we must concede that while the drugs in these sets of alternatives may be more effective, their effectiveness is largely dependent on the chemical deadening of important imaginative and critical capacities, whose privileges are admittedly problematic. Practically every drug invented, from opium to LSD, has had its champions in both science and the arts who insisted that their particular brew was not only not reductive but was actually heightening of human potentiality. The objective evidence for their claims, however, has always been depressing, and of the same order as my own reports, whether it be the music played under marijuana or heroin, the pictures painted and the poetry composed under LSD, the deadlines met by means of amphetamines, or even—perhaps especially—the perceptions and insights granted by drugs.

At this point, the question must be raised: aren't other addictions—nondrug addictions—also reductive? The answer has to be a qualified affirmative. The friend watching me glued for hours to the television set, isolated from all intelligible life, impervious to the claims of my children who have waited all week to have a few moments with me, has to find my human condition bizarre, to say the least. Far more seriously incapacitating, of course, are those nondrug addictions that involve ideas and habits of thought. Those who over the years develop an addiction to shopworn ideologies—religious, scientific, political, esthetic, psychological—in a sense forfeit, in willful dedication, the very capacities of spirit and intellect that might set them free.

Nevertheless, there is a difference between drugs and no drugs. While disdain and denial of these capacities will cause them to shrivel and grow ever more paralyzed as years go by, there remains the possibility of a response, however minimal at first, to some human claim. Chemical deadening, on the other hand, if pursued, will, by its very nature, render such capacities eventually heedless to any call.

But to return to my evaluations of those psychoanalytic candidates—my will, with the help of amphetamine, has had its undiscriminating way in my reports, without the reflective give-and-take between me and my writing that could be called dialogic, causing this enterprise to resemble other headstrong monologic sprees in which the speaker is deaf and blind to those about him at the same time that he is convinced of a singular openness and freedom and mutuality to the exchange.

The nonuser has a dispiriting effect on groups enthusiastically consolidated by such convictions, so that they would prefer him to find his own sober companions. And his response to them will be marked by his discouraged observation that, despite the cries of mutual congratulation, all he can hear are colliding monologues, breathlessly composed so that each participant gives in to his own worst headstrong and literal-minded inclinations. The person who ordinarily must guard against his habit of vast abstraction now becomes even more abstract in his theoretical pronouncements. The person top-heavy with esthetic sensibility becomes even more indulgent to that side of himself, abdicating his ability to temper such estheticism with moral and psychological discriminations.

The most blatant examples of the literal-minded aspect of the drugged state come from the public writings on LSD, but it is by no means restricted to this particular drug. Under LSD, it would seem one is at the mercy of any fancy that strikes him, much like the hypnotic subject responding to the commands of the hypnotist. Should he note that his hand is ugly, that hand becomes literally swollen and grotesque. Should the thought strike him that he is alone in the world, he will quickly and literally find himself as one small mortal in the midst of an endless desolate landscape. In each instance, what properly should be no more than a beginning metaphor has been exalted, at the behest of the will, into physical reality. Similarly, the death undergone with LSD can be regarded as more deathly than death itself. In a section, jarringly titled "Running Smack Into Your Essence," of "LSD: The Acid Test," published in Ramparts, one evangelist, Donavan Bess, wrote:

> The psychedelic death is especially lonely—lonelier, perhaps, than for the soldier who physically dies in a Vietnamese field hospital. He at least has the comfort of cuddling up in the image of his mother. Under LSD you have no such bourgeois comfort; you have no familial figure at all. You die grown up. If you can hang onto that, afterward, you can offer society some adult values. You came to this point in a rite of passage as explicit, as terrible and as meaningful as those rites used in aboriginal Australia.

In considering the addictive state which may result from drugs, narcotic and non-narcotic, I must of course neglect the specific effects each drug has or purports to have on the central nervous system. An unfortunate consequence of such neglect will be to give the false impression that my own addiction to nonaddiction has led me to advocate an impossibly ascetic life, requiring abstention from all chemical assistance, come what may. Let me quickly insist that all the drugs I have mentioned may be taken in nonaddictive ways for reasons that are appropriate to the effects of the particular drug. This is to say, there are times when prolonged sleeplessness can and should be interrupted by sedatives, just as there are painful occasions when morphine is the only answer. Even amphetamines may allow the completion of a low-level chore.

The difficulty, however, here, as indicated earlier, is that the mood of accomplishment may persuade us to disregard the quality, or lack of quality, of our performance, not to mention the disagreeable drug side-effects, so that we turn to the drug in situations that require more of our wits and equanimity than amphetamines will allow. Perhaps a greater danger, as the use of amphetamines becomes more widespread, is that the deadlines asked of us are increasingly determined by the amphetamine intoxications of those who ask. (Another illustration of the manner in which the drugged state influences social values is suggested by the aspirin commercials referred to in this article. The writers of these advertisements seem to be selling not only aspirin but also their conviction—possibly arrived at through their own experience with tranquilizers—that our ordinary difficulties, since they are only subjective and therefore not worth contending with, are best erased with drugs. Thus, an advertisement for meprobamate, addressed to physicians, shows a picture of an overwrought mother with a child, the caption reading: "Her kind of pressures last all day . . . shouldn't her tranquilizer?")

For the sake of completeness, alcohol and marijuana are two drugs whose object is explicitly pleasure, and which may be used nonaddictively. However, too much has been made recently by the younger generation of the nonaddictive properties of marijuana simply because its physical effects are less dramatic than those of alcohol and other drugs. More dramatic is its effect upon relation: the pleasures of monologue experienced as dialogue under the drug persist as a habit of tolerance for such illusion—which in a sense is the very issue of addiction.

Let us consider briefly the addictive course—from initial pleasure to ultimate disaster—that will result from prolonged and excessive use of any of the drugs I have mentioned, singly or in combination.

The first subjective experience of wholeness and the pleasure accompanying it will acquire its intensity partly through contrast with the discomfort which preceded the use of the drug and partly through the manner a particular drug answers a particular person's need at a particular time. Thus, users are labeled according to their preferences as "Up-Heads" or "Speed-Heads," "Down-Heads," "Acid-Heads," "Pot-Heads," "Lushes," "Junkies."

With further sophistication and availability, and the cooperation of the medical profession, drug-users already are specializing less and availing themselves more of other products and mixtures of products. But the initial feeling of well-being is difficult to duplicate precisely, regardless of the ingenuity of the user. As the drug and the state associated with it begin to wear off, the user returns to a world which has lost none of its oppressiveness and with which, in the midst of the drug hangover, he feels less able to cope.

The distance between himself and the wholeness he sought has grown somewhat, so that he is now vulnerable to the beginning belief that the relief the drug afforded is an extraordinary sort of transcendence which his usual life with others cannot provide, except in the occasional unpredictable and surprising manner in which such moments arise. In other words, he has been burned by the demonic and addictive notion that he need not wait on life for the transcendence he seeks, that he may invoke it whenever he so decrees or wills by returning to the drug or drugs which first allowed him this remarkable feeling.

With this seeming triumph of his will, he will be more impatient of the often frustrating give-and-take of life without drugs, willfully demanding his well-being of those about him and thereby suffering even more the penalties of such willing. In a sense he insists futilely that life now be his drug. Needless to say, his mounting impatience will be inimical to the exercise or development of such qualities as imagination, judgment, humor, tact. And should he glimpse, however dimly, his impoverishment, he may wish to believe these qualities at least can return with drugs, disowning the evidence accumulating to the contrary. However, without these qualities he is more and more confined to the exigencies of the moment, for he can no longer really remember his drug experience in the past, nor can he imagine what may follow. As his intolerance for life without drugs increases, his competence for such life diminishes, so that with every return to the drug he is, in the spirit of Heraclitus, a different and lesser person who attempts to cross the same stream twice.

What seemed the feeling of transcendence at the beginning has long since been abandoned as his drug goal in favor merely of getting from one moment to the next, in favor of mindlessly and minimally staying alive. What began with his will to decree well-being for himself without having to wait on life now culminates in almost a paralysis of will for every trivial action, even getting dressed or feeding himself. It is as though all the taken-for-granted stream of activity had disintegrated into a swarm of tiny yet insurmountable enterprises for his will, every one seeming to require further drugs for its accomplishment.

As a result of the bombardment of his body by such large dosages of drugs, his physical debilitation grows extreme. Yet even this bodily exhaustion and derangement offers a last resort to the will, which is now unequal to practically every small movement in his world. Unlike other depleting illnesses that mysteriously overtake us, this one has been induced by himself and seems to be within his control. That is, he may try to assuage his agonies with more chemicals or he can withdraw the noxious agent so that his body can slowly recover its strength.

All other dramas in which his will has been involved have given way now to the one small immediate drama of whether he shall live or die to this world. It is a far cry from the transcendence he sought originally, but every addict knows the drama of his failing body is the last plot his will must confront. Unlike the proponents of LSD, he is beyond metaphysical conceits about the meaning of dying to this world, nor will he glamorize recovery, to whatever degree it may occur, as spiritual rebirth.

Nietzsche, I believe, was not as interested in theological argument about the disappearance of the divine will in our lives as he was in the consequences of its disappearance. Today, the evidence is in. Out of disbelief we have impudently assumed that all of life is now subject to our own will. And the disasters that have come from willing what cannot be willed have not at all brought us to some modesty about our presumptions. Instead, we have turned to chemicals, which seem to enhance our willful strivings. It was only a question of time before man, in his desperation, would locate divinity in drugs and on that artificial rock build his church.

II

8

I'm Sorry, Dear

And the eyes of them both were opened, and they knew that they were naked; and they sewed fig leaves together, and made themselves aprons.

—GENESIS

Lust is more abstract than logic; it seeks (hope triumphing over experience) for some purely sexual, hence purely imaginary, conjunction of an impossible maleness with an impossible femaleness.

—C. S. LEWIS [1]

THE MODERN DIALOGUE that furnishes me my title is practiced throughout the Western world. As a theme with only a limited number of variations, it cannot sustain much repetition: familiarity breeds silence; and although never really abandoned, the script quickly becomes implicit. When reduced to a dumb show—or perhaps no more than a monosyllabic token—it still remains faithful to its pathetic premise. However, for the purposes of introduction, I

"I'm Sorry, Dear" reprinted from Leslie H. Farber, *The Ways of the Will: Essays toward a Psychology and Psychopathology of Will* (New York: Basic Books, 1966).

1. C. S. Lewis, *The Allegory of Love* (New York: Oxford University Press, 1958), p. 196.

shall try to represent its essence in a wholly explicit manner. The man speaks first.

"Did you?"

"Did *you?* You *did,* didn't you?"

"Yes, I'm afraid I—Oh, I'm sorry! I *am* sorry. I know how it makes you feel."

"Oh, don't worry about it. I'm sure I'll quiet down after a while."

"I'm *so* sorry, dearest. Let me help you."

"I'd rather you didn't."

"But, I . . ."

"What good is it when you're just—when you don't really want to? You know perfectly well, if you don't *really* want to, it doesn't work."

"But I *do really* want to! I *want* to! Believe me. It *will* work, you'll see. Only let me!"

"Please, couldn't we just forget it? For now the thing is done, finished. Besides, it's not really that important. My tension always wears off eventually. And anyhow—maybe next time it'll be different."

"Oh, it *will,* I *know* it will. Next time I won't be so tired or so eager. I'll make sure of that. Next time it's going to be *fine!* . . . But about tonight—I'm sorry, dear."

Unhappily, there is no end to talking and trying for our pathetic lovers. To deaden self-consciousness, they may turn to alcohol or sedatives, seeking that animal indifference that is unencumbered with hesitations, reservations, and grievances—in short, all those human tangles that create the sexual abyss they will themselves to bridge. To delay his moment, to quicken hers, they may try to assist the chemicals by thinking of other matters—football games and cocktail parties—in order finally to arrive at that mutual consummation that, hopefully, will prove their sufficiency unto each other, if not their love. All the strategies and prescriptions of sexology that have so often failed them in the past are not cast aside, but stubbornly returned to, if only because in such an impasse there is nothing else. Instead of alcohol or drugs or irrelevant reveries they may—in solitude or mutuality—resort to sex itself as their sedative, intending in their first try to spend their energies just enough to dull self-consciousness and thicken passion to that "spontaneity" necessary for their second and final attempt. Although normally truthful people, our lovers are continually tempted by deception and simulation: he may try to conceal his moment, she to simulate hers—as they stalk their equalitarian ideal. It can happen that they will achieve simultaneity by means of one or several or none of these devices. But their success—in the midst of their congratulations—will be as dispiriting as their failures. For one thing, the joy our lovers sought in this manner will be either absent or too fictitious to be believed. Furthermore, once the moment has subsided they must reckon with the extraordinary efforts that brought it about—efforts that appear too extraordinary for ordinary day-to-day existence. Thus does it happen that success may bring as much as, or more, pathos than failure. And, always lying between them will be the premise borrowed from romanticism: if they *really* loved each other, it would work. Small wonder, then, as self-pity and bitterness accumulate, that their musings—if not their actions—turn to adultery: a heightened situation that promises freedom from the impingements of ordinary sexual life. Or, pushed gradually past heightening, past hope, they may even come to abstinence, which can seem—with some irony—the least dishonorable course.

My conviction is that over the last fifty years sex has, for the most part, lost its viability as a human experience. I do not mean that there is any danger that it will cease to be practiced—that it will be put aside like other Victorian bric-a-brac. The hunger will remain, perhaps even increase, and human beings will continue to couple with as much fervor as they can provoke, while the human possibilities of sex will grow ever more elusive. Such couplings will be poultices after the fact: they will further extend the degradation of sex that has resulted from its ever-increasing bondage to the modern will. To those first pioneers at the turn of the century—sexologists, psychoanalysts, political champions of woman's suffrage—"sexual emancipation" seemed a stirring and optimistic cause. Who could have imagined then, as the battle was just beginning, how ironic victory would be: sex was emancipated, true, but emancipated from all of life—except the will—and subsequently exalted as the measure of existence.

At this point I think it only fair to commit myself, even if briefly, on how sex was, is, or could be a viable human experience. My view is not that of St. Augustine—that man, by reason of the Fall, is necessarily subject to the lust of concupiscence. Nor can I subscribe, at the other extreme, to the position of the Church of England, as reported at the Lambeth Conference in 1958: "The new freedom of sexuality in our time is . . . a gate to a new depth and joy in personal relationship between husband and wife." [2] Of the erotic life, Martin Buber has remarked that in no other realm are dialogue and monologue so mingled and opposed. I would agree that any attempt to offer a normative description would have to include precisely such mingling and opposition. Even if we place it optimally within an ongoing domestic world of affection, in which sex bears some relation, however slight, to procreation, our task is still the difficult one of maintaining that sex is both utterly important and utterly trivial. Sex may be a hallowing and renewing experience, but more often it will be distracting, coercive, playful, frivolous, discouraging, dutiful, and even boring. On the one hand, it tempts man to omnipotence, while on the other, it roughly reminds him of his mortality. Over and over again it mocks rationality, only to be mocked, in turn, at the very instant it insists its domain is solely within the senses. Though it promises the suspension of time, no other event so sharply advises us of the oppressiveness of time. Sex offers itself as an alternative world, but when the act is over and the immodesty of its offering is exposed, it is the sheer worldliness of the world we briefly relinquished and must now reenter that has to

2. Dorothea Krook, *Three Traditions of Moral Thought* (Cambridge, England: Cambridge University Press, 1959), p. 336.

be confronted anew. Residing no longer in the same room that first enclosed us, we lie now in another room with another topography—a room whose surfaces, textures, corners, and knobs have an otherness as absolute and formidable as the duties and promises that nag us with their temporal claims. What began as relief from worldly concern ends by returning us to the world with a metaphysical, if unsettling, clarity.

Though sex often seems to be morality's adversary, it more often brings sharply in its wake moral discriminations that previously had not been possible. Because the pleasure of sex is always vulnerable to a split into *pleasuring* and *being pleasured,* the nature of pleasure itself, as well as the relation between pleasure and power, are called into question. If pleasuring is the overpowering concern, intimations of the actual and immediate experience of slavery will appear. On the other hand, if being pleasured is the most compelling, tyranny and oppression will invade experience with some urgency. And, finally, should the lovers will equality between these two concerns in their effort to heal the split, they will suffer the problematic character of democratic forms. To some extent, our political past influences our sexual negotiations, but in equal measure sexual pleasure is itself a source of political practice and theory.

The list of oppositions and minglings could easily be extended, but such an extension would not change the fact that human sex inevitably partakes of human experience, for better or worse, and through its claim on the body simultaneously asserts its particular difference, for better or worse.

Its particular difference from everything else in this life lies in the possibility that sex offers man for regaining *his own* body through knowing the body of his loved one. Should he fail that *knowing* and *being known,* should he lapse into all those ways of *knowing about* which he has proudly learned to confuse with *knowing*—both bodies will again escape him. Increasingly, as D. H. Lawrence understood, man has become separated from his body, which he yearns to inhabit, such yearning understandably bringing sentimental and scientific prescriptions for the reunion eluding him. Yet it is through the brief reconciliation of his own and his loved one's body that he can now grasp—and endure—the bodily estrangement which has always been his lot, without succumbing to the blandishments that would betray the realities of both sides of this duality.

In order to develop more concretely my conviction that sex for the most part has lost its viability as a human experience, I wish to consider the now famous Sex Research Project directed by Dr. William H. Masters and Virginia Johnson at the Washington University School of Medicine. Through the use of women volunteers, Masters and Johnson endeavored "to separate a few basic anatomic and physiologic truths" about "the human female's response" to what they call "effective sexual stimulation." The subject, they believed, had been hopelessly beclouded by "literary fiction and fantasy," "pseudoscientific essays and pronouncements," and "an unbelievable hodgepodge of conjecture and falsehood." They acknowledged their "complete awe" for Kinsey's "time-consuming efforts" which had made their own research not only "plausible, but possible," but on the other hand, found that the work of their predecessors, including Kinsey, had unfortunately been "the result of individual introspection, of expressed personal opinion, or of limited clinical observation"—rather than "a basic-science approach to the sexual response cycle." [3] Therefore, they did what was indeed inevitable: they moved the whole investigation into the laboratory.

I should make clear that this project itself has always interested me far more than its exact findings. It strikes me as one of those occasional yet remarkable enterprises that, despite their creators' intentions, quite transcend their original and modest scientific boundaries, so as to become vivid allegories of our present dilemma, containing their own images of man—while at the same time charting a New Jerusalem for our future. Such an enterprise, when constitutive, is apt to be more relevant and revealing than deliberate art. Because no actual artist is involved, it is not particularly rewarding to ask how this matter acquires its revelatory, even po-

3. William H. Masters, "The Sexual Response Cycle of the Human Female," *Western Journal of Surgery, Obstetrics & Gynecology* 68 (January–February 1960): 57.

etic, power; often its director merely pursues the prevailing inclination in his field. Yet the pursuit is so single-minded, so fanatical and literal, that part of the power of the enterprise as constitutive symbol must be credited to the director's unflagging lack of imagination and his passionate naiveté, which stay undeterred by all the proprieties, traditions, and accumulated wisdom that would only complicate his course.

I shall not linger over the anatomical and physiological findings in Masters' and Johnson's several books; that subject could hardly bear any further discussion now. But there is one aspect of the research which still seems to me fresh, and even urgent, to talk about. And that is Dr. Masters' celebrated movie. For of all the mechanical, electrical, and electronic devices at his command in this research, it was movie-making which seemed to give Dr. Masters the clearest edge over the subjective distortions of his predecessors. Since the integrity of human observation of specific detail varies significantly, regardless of the observer's training or good intent, colored motion-picture photography was used to record in absolute detail all phases of the human sexual response cycle. The movie which resulted is a silent one. Wisely, I think, the director omitted a sound track, for the tiny events of the flesh he wished to depict are not audible. Moreover, had there been sound equipment, all that would have been heard would have been those adventitious rustlings of any well-equipped laboratory, and perhaps the quickened breathing and gasping of the subjects.

The movie opens quite abruptly with a middle-distance shot of a naked woman, standing, her head and lower legs deliberately outside the movie-frame. One arm hangs at her side, the other is stretched toward her genitals in an Eve-like posture, except that it is immediately apparent that she is caressing, rather than covering, her parts. More in the service of decorum than science, there are no close-ups of her hand. This opening scene of a faceless woman silently playing with herself against a neutral antiseptic laboratory background quickly sets the tone for what is to follow. The naked yet faceless body informs us this is a "human female" we are observing. The other bodies that will subsequently appear in the film will also be faceless; the viewer may momentarily wonder, as cuts are made from one body to another, if it is the same body he is looking at, until he becomes used to distinguishing one body from another by differences in shape of breasts, distribution of pubic hair, and the like. At no time do any scientists or technicians appear; they may be presumed to be standing fully clothed behind the camera. In any large dramatic sense, the arm manipulating the body's private parts furnishes the only real movement and cinematically asserts, even when not in view, that it will continue to fondle during the filming of more microscopic and glandular events. Since what is to follow will focus on relatively small and minute areas of flesh that ordinarily would not be cinematic, the first shot of the moving hand heightens the dramatic effect of the oozings, engorgements, and contractions this flesh will undergo as climax approaches.

Following this middle-distance shot—extended a bit in time to give the illusion of mounting excitement—the camera moves in on the skin of the abdomen and back, so that the film can record the first fine rash beginning to appear over the lower body.

Through the use of cuts, several bodies exhibit their rashes until the phenomenon is safely established. Now the camera moves to the breasts to portray distention, venous engorgement, and changes in the nipples. As these changes are repeated on a number of breasts, we must remind ourselves that the initial arm or arms are continuing their work, although it is obvious that views of such action must be suspended from time to time to allow for certain close-ups. Up to this point, all that occurs in the movie could take place on that lonely, upright body that appeared in the opening scene. Now, quite suddenly and without preparation, that body is no longer upright but supine, and the scene is a brilliantly lit close-up of the opening of the vagina. At this point, something of an operating-room atmosphere intrudes, largely because a speculum spreads the lips of the vagina apart to permit an unobstructed view of all that will occur during orgasm.

It is obvious from this portion of the movie that the source of vaginal lubrication is of special interest to the project, as evidenced by a series of ingenious shots of the wall of the vagina showing the formation of individual drops of secretion. The movie then proceeds with a rush to the point that has been imminent since the beginning—namely, orgasm—objective orgasm, displayed visually in the contractions around, and the dilations within, the vagina. The film ends, as might be anticipated, with a succession of photographs of other bodies undergoing similar spasms. With some shrewdness, the director has withstood the tempting aesthetic impulse to conclude his movie with a final shot of the upright naked body with both arms now hanging limply down.

This movie was often referred to in Dr. Masters' early writings and, I am told, was exhibited at a number of scientific institutes throughout the country. So fond is he of the film medium that there seem to be occasions when his scientific prose seeks, however incompletely, to emulate not only the objectivity but the aesthetic brilliance of his movie sequences:

> If the bright pink of the excitement phase changes to a brilliant primiparous scarlet-red, or the multiparous burgundy color, a satisfactory plateau phase has been achieved.[4]

There is even a point at which the film medium itself becomes the inventor: like the accidental solution or the contaminated culture, which have heroic roles in older scientific romances, movie-making has allowed Dr. Masters to uncover "the vascular flush reaction to effective sexual stimulation" that had not been previously described in the scientific literature:

> With the aid of artificially increased skin surface temperature, such as that necessary for successful motion-picture photography, the wide distribution of this flush becomes quite apparent. . . . With orgasm imminent, this measle-like rash has been observed to spread over the anterior-lateral borders of the thighs, the buttocks, and the whole body.[5]

4. Masters, "The Sexual Response Cycle," p. 63.
5. Masters, "The Sexual Response Cycle," p. 61.

Probably it was this discovery of the "measle-like rash" that inspired a more Pavlovian venture which, if read slowly, will be seen to have quite eerie dimensions:

> One observed subject, undergoing electroencephalographic evaluation, had been trained for four months to attain orgasm without producing concomitant muscle tension in order to provide significance for her tracing pattern. Yet, this patient repeatedly showed a marked flush phenomenon over the entire body during plateau and orgasm, and during resolution was completely covered with a filmy, fine perspiration.[6]

If movie-making was his main laboratory device, "automanipulative techniques" constituted his "fundamental investigative approach" to "the sexual response cycle of the human female." His frankness here is to be commended, particularly since some scientists might feel that such automanipulation was inadequate to the verisimilitude necessary for laboratory demonstration. Dr. Masters himself does not discuss the issue, but his obvious preference for this approach over coitus does not appear to have been ascribable to decorum. To some degree, I imagine, it was the laboratory procedures and devices—particularly motion-picture photography—which determined the approach, automanipulation being clearly more accessible to scientific inspection than coition. But, more important, Dr. Masters seems to have regarded automanipulation as more reliable [7]—that is, a more predictable—technique than "heterosexual activity" in the pursuit of "the more intense, well-developed, orgasmic response" cycle.

6. Masters, "The Sexual Response Cycle," p. 61.

7. In a later investigation of contraceptive devices, Dr. Masters was led to develop a research technique of "artificial coitus." (See William H. Masters and Virginia E. Johnson, "Intravaginal Contraceptive Study," *West. J. Surg., Obst. & Gynec.*, 70 [July–August 1962], particularly pp. 202–203.) Since it is not described in any detail, we cannot know whether the old limerick was its inspiration. (The one that goes, "There was a young man from Racine, Who invented a f——— machine," ending with "And was terribly easy to clean.") However, it does seem to involve an "artificial penis," whose principal virtue is that it "affords direct observation of the vaginal barrel during the entire female sexual response cycle." Its disadvantage, admittedly surmountable, lay in the fact that his volunteers did not immediately take to the method. "The technique of artificial coitus necessitates conditioning of these individuals to assure definitive research results. In every instance, all thirty members of the subject population . . . underwent three separate sessions to establish familiarity with, and effective response to, the artificial coital technique." Once again, the problem of verisimilitude is presented: how much threat of impregnation can this machine pose?

> This type of total pelvic reaction is particularly true for an orgasmic phase elicited by manual manipulation, but it also occurs, although less frequently, with coition.[8]

Yet even this approach, so admirably suited to laboratory research, must share part of the blame for Dr. Masters' inability to measure the "clitoral body" during sexual excitement.

> The attempts to measure increases in clitoral size objectively have been generally unsatisfactory due to the marked variation in size and positioning of the normal clitoral body, and the multiplicity of automanipulative techniques employed by the various subjects under observation.[9]

Little in the end has actually been told us about the volunteers in this research. Apparently the project began with prostitutes. But when objections were made that such a profession might not yield the best "normal" sample, subjects were chosen among medical students and medical students' wives who volunteered and were paid a modest fee for their activities. Naturally no studies could be made on those who, for whatever reason, would not volunteer. And presumably quickly eliminated were those young women who offered themselves out of their enthusiastic wish to contribute to science, only to discover they could not sustain their sexual excitement in the setting of the laboratory, with the paraphernalia, cameras, technicians, and bright lights. Even more quickly eliminated were those women who on initial interview were not sure whether or not they had had climax. "Our rule of thumb is if they're not sure about it, they probably haven't had it."

Other circumstances surrounding the study can only be guessed at. Like much scientific research, this particular project must have been an orderly affair. It can be assumed that the investigators did not wait on the whim of their volunteers; that is, they were not subject to call day or night whenever the volunteer felt in the mood. No, the women were given regular appointments during the working day when the entire research crew was available. Doubtless, too,

8. William H. Masters and Virginia E. Johnson, "The Artificial Vagina: Anatomic, Physiologic, Psychosexual Function," *Western Journal of Surgery, Obstetrics & Gynecology* 69 (May–June 1961): 202.

9. Masters, "The Sexual Response Cycle," p. 62.

the directors of the project considered it scientifically unseemly to encourage sexual titillation in their volunteers—certainly out of the question would have been anything resembling a physical overture. Should suggestive reading matter be required in the research—as it indeed occasionally was—it would have to be offered the volunteers in a spirit of detachment; not even the hint of a smirk could be allowed to disrupt the sobriety of the occasion. On the whole, the erotic basis would have to be provided by the scientific situation itself, in addition to the actual manipulation: that is, the prospect of arriving at the laboratory at 10:00 A.M., disrobing, stretching out on the table, and going to work in a somewhat businesslike manner while being measured and photographed would have to provide its own peculiar excitement. (Thank you, Miss Brown, see you same time next week. Stop at the cashier's for your fee.) So, back to one's ordinary existence.

If these speculations have any truth, what can be said about the qualities that the ideal subject for such experiments would have? In a general way, her sexuality would have to be autonomous, separate from, and unaffected by her ordinary world. "World" here would have to include not only affection but all those exigencies of human existence which tend to shape our erotic possibilities. Objectively, her sexuality would be mechanically accessible or "on call"—under circumstances which would be, if not intimidating, at least distracting to most bodies; hers would have to be indifferent to the entire range of experiences, pleasant and unpleasant, whose claim is not only not salacious but makes us forget there is such a thing as sexuality. Her lust would lie to hand, ready to be invoked and consummated, in sickness or in health, in coitus or "automanipulation," in homosexuality or heterosexuality, in exasperation or calm, hesitancy or certainty, playfulness or despair. (This would be the other side of that older, though not unrelated, romanticism which just as willfully insisted on soft lights, Brahms, incense, and poetical talk.)

In other words, her sexuality would be wholly subject to her will:

whenever she determined—or the project determined—that she should reach a climax, she would willingly begin those gestures that would lead to one. To use the modern idiom, all that would be unavailable to her sexological dexterity would be frigidity. Or, to speak more clearly, all that would be unavailable to her would be a real response to the laboratory situation. Insofar as her sexuality was under the dominion of her will, she would resemble those odd creatures on the old television quiz programs—also ideal subjects in their own way—who were led from boarding houses to stand in a hot soundproof isolation booth, and when the fateful question was delivered from the vault, answered correctly and without a tremor how many words there were in *Moby Dick*—answered correctly in a loud clear voice under circumstances in which most of us could not even mumble our name. The popularity of these programs (at least until skulduggery was revealed) suggests that the audience looked with envy and/or admiration at this caricature of knowledge—a knowledge uniformly responsive to its owner's will, regardless of contingency or trapping.

A truly constitutive symbol should embody both an accurate rendering of contemporary life and a clear indication of what that life should be. Taking, for the moment, only the ideal contained in my description of the volunteer in these experiments, I would say that she is a latter-day Queen of Courtly Love, a veritable Queen Guinevere. For most modern men and women, who grow ever more discouraged by their bodies' stubborn refusal to obey their owners' will, this Lady of the Laboratory has long been the woman of their dreams: men long to channel or claim this creature's prompt and unspecific response for their own specific overtures, while women dream of rivaling her capacity to serve her body's need whenever she so wills.

And what of those self-effacing scientists behind the camera who conceived and guided this project? Do they too reflect who we are and who we would become? We know as little about this research team as we know about the volunteers. How the scientific boundaries were staked out and protected against trespass is not described in the reports. Once again, we can only surmise, but that there was difficulty is suggested by a remark Dr. Masters made in one of his lectures—namely, that he preferred to have a woman scientist alongside him in these investigations because she helped to make or keep him more "objective." I assume he meant that having a real woman present, fully clad in the white coat of science, reminded him not only of the point of the matter at hand but of the more hazardous life to be lived with women outside the laboratory—of the difference between the ideal and the actual.

A ticklish problem would be how to maintain the proper detachment to protect the scientists without simultaneously inhibiting the volunteers. Here, the equipment and rituals of research would help. And, very possibly, there would be a deliberate effort to eliminate even the ordinary frivolity that sometimes overcomes a surgical team in the midst of the most delicate operation, because frivolity in this sort of research might be only a way-station en route to the lubricious. Any falling-away into the most ordinary locker-room talk, in or out of the laboratory, would have to be regarded as a danger signal. I imagine that each scientist, with all the resolution at his command, would remind himself continually that it was just an ordinary day's work in the laboratory, no different from the work next door with the diabetic rats. At the end of the day, when his wife asked, "How were things at the lab today?" he would reply, "Oh nothing, just the same old grind." And, if she pressed him in a jealous fashion, his justifications might resemble those of a young artist explaining his necessity to sketch nude models. Of course, there would be strict rules forbidding dalliance between scientist and volunteer after hours. But, should they happen to run into one another in the cafeteria, each would keep his conversation casual, trying not to allude to those more cataclysmic events of a few hours before. Mindful of his professional integrity, the scientist would have to guard against prideful thoughts that he knew her, if not better, at least more microscopically than those nearest her. Most troublesome of his self-appointed tasks, it seems to me, would be his effort to prevent his research from invading his own ordinary erotic life, particularly if it were worried by the usual frustrations. In this regard, he would indeed be heroic to withstand the temptation of comparing his mate's response to those unspecific, yet perfectly formed, consummations of the laboratory.

Again, if these imaginings have any truth, how may we characterize the ideal scientist in research of this immediate order? First of all, he would have to believe, far more than his volunteers, in a "basic science" approach to sex. This is not to say that he would consider the practice of sex a possible science, even though his practice might eventually be informed by his scientific theories. But it would have to be an article of faith for him that the visible, palpable reactions of the organs themselves, regardless of whatever human or inhuman context they might occur in, would speak a clear, unambiguous truth to all who cared to heed. In his hierarchy of beliefs, these reactions would take precedence in every sense. The questions we are apt to ask about human affairs, not excluding lust, ordinarily have to do with appropriateness, affection, and the like—in other words, with right or wrong, good or bad, judged in human terms. On the other hand, the Ideal Sexologist, as he presses his eye to his research, finds another variety of drama—inordinately complicated in its comings and goings, crises and resolutions—with its own requirements of right and wrong, good and bad, all writ very small in terms of "droplets," "engorgements," and "contractions."

The will of the Ideal Sexologist seems different from the will of the Lady of the Laboratory, but it may be that the contrast is more illusory than actual. The latter wills orgasm through physical manipulation. Certainly the sexologist supports and approves her willing, such sexual promptness being ideal for laboratory study. However, while his approval may be invented by his will, it is by no means the most important expression of his will. As a scientist, his will must be given to the systematic inspection of the sexual response of the "human female," literally portrayed. To this end he persists in his gadgetry, always at the expense of any imaginative grasp of the occasion. His will to be a scientist requires his further commitment to any number of willful enterprises; for instance, in the present circumstance he finds it necessary to will his own body to be unresponsive—not merely to the events on the laboratory table, but to any fictional construction of these events his imagination might contrive, because imagination, at least in this arena, is his opponent in his pursuit of science.

On the surface this dilemma of the Ideal Sexologist may seem a familiar one, being comparable to older ascetic ventures, particularly of the Eastern yogic variety. But the sexologist's task is actually more difficult: asceticism is not his goal—the very nature of his enterprise points in an opposite direction. He wishes indifference which he can invoke at will: it may be the project that demands his not responding, but—as we shall see later—it may be other moments, unofficial and unscientific, which also seem to call forth his willed lack of response. The will not to respond and the will to respond are related possibilities of the will. In this sense, the Lady of the Laboratory and the Ideal Sexologist are collaborators rather than opponents. Of course, I speak in ideal terms—whether these ideals can be achieved is another matter. But, if the Lady of the Laboratory is a latter-day Queen of Courtly Love, then our Ideal Sexologist is the modern Sir Galahad, and together—separately or commingled—they rule our dreams of what should be.

Let us remind ourselves that most of us could not hope to qualify for this research—either as volunteers or as scientists. But this does not mean the differences are great between us and them. True, compared to ours, their lives have an oversized quality, and true, they are in the vanguard. But, in a real sense our fleshly home is that laboratory. Whatever room we choose for our lovemaking we shall make into our own poor laboratory, and nothing that is observed or undergone in the real laboratory of science is likely to escape us. At this stage, is there any bit of sexology that is not in the public domain, or at least potentially so for those who can read? Whatever detail the scientific will appropriates about sex rapidly becomes an injunction to be imposed on our bodies. But, it is not long before these impositions lose their arbitrary and alien character and begin to change the way we actually experience our bodies. Unfortunately, our vision of the ideal experience tends to be crudely derived from the failure of our bodies to meet these imperatives.

Our residence in the laboratory is recent: really only since the turn of the century has the act of sex been interviewed, witnessed, probed, measured, timed, taped, photographed, and judged. Before the age of sexology, objectifications of the sexual act were to be found in pornography and the brothel, both illicit, both pleasurable in purpose, both suggesting the relatively limited manner in which will—given absolute dominion—could be joined to sexual pleasure. However else the Marquis de Sade may be read, he at least offered the most exhaustive inventory yet seen of techniques for exploiting the pleasure of the body's several parts, if one wholeheartedly put one's will to it. As a moralist, he seemed to say, "Why our particular rules? What if there were no limits?" More recently, but still before sexology, it was possible for shy erotomaniacs, disguised as greengrocers, to visit brothels, there to peek at the antics of the inmates. The bolder ones could join the sport. When the performance reached its final gasp our tradesmen, now satiated, would slink back to the propriety and privacy of their own quarters, convinced that their ordinary domestic world was discreetly separate from the world of the peephole they paid to enter. In fact, or so it seemed, the separateness of these two worlds heightened the erotic possibilities of each. The emancipation which sexology enforced gradually blurred this distinction, making it unclear whether each home had become its own brothel, or whether every brothel had become more like home. The truth is that sexology eventually not only blurred the distinction, but by housing us all in laboratories, made both the brothel and pornography less exciting dwellings for our erotic investigations.

When last we left our pathetic lovers, I suggested that as their self-pity and bitterness mounted, they might—in desperation—turn to adultery. Yet even for the person who believes himself to be without scruples, adultery—in fact or fantasy—is difficult to arrange, exhausting to maintain. Requiring, as it does, at least two persons and two wills, this illicit encounter risks the danger of further pathos. But, if we heed our laboratory drama carefully, we can see that there is another possibility preferable to adultery. According to the lesson of the laboratory, there is only one perfect orgasm, if by "perfect" we mean wholly subject to its owner's will, wholly indifferent to human contingency or context. Clearly, this perfect orgasm is the orgasm achieved on one's own. No other consummation offers such certainty and, moreover, avoids the messiness that attends most human affairs. The onanist may choose the partner of his dreams, who very probably will be the Lady of the Laboratory, or he may have his orgasm without any imagined partner. In either case, he is both scientist and experimental subject, science and sex now being nicely joined. In his laboratory room, he may now abstract his sexual parts from his whole person, inspect their anatomic particularities, and observe and enjoy the small physiologic events he knows best how to control. True, this solitary experience may leave him empty and ashamed. But, as a citizen of his times, he will try to counter this discomfort by reminding himself that sexology and psychoanalysis have assured him that masturbation is a morally indifferent matter. As a true modern, he tells himself that it is not as good as what two people have, but that does not make it bad. Superstitious people of other ages thought it drove one crazy, but he knows better; he knows that the real threat to *his* sanity is unrelieved sexual tension. In fact—he may decide—were it not for certain neurotic Victorian traces he has not managed to expunge from his psyche, that he could treat the matter as any other bodily event and get on with his business. So we must not be too harsh with our pathetic lovers if they take refuge in solitary pleasures—and even if they come to prefer them to the frustrations of sexual life together. Nor should we be too surprised if such solitary pleasure becomes the ideal by which all mutual sex is measured—and found wanting.

Let us now turn to the phenomenon being inspected and celebrated in our laboratory—the phenomenon which contributes most of all to our lovers' impasse. Of all the discoveries sexology has made, the female orgasm remains the most imposing in its consequences. De Tocqueville's prediction of life between the sexes in America [10] might not have been so sanguine, could he have anticipated, first, the discovery of sexology and psychoanalysis, and, in turn, their discovery of the female orgasm.

In the second half of the nineteenth century, Western man began to see nature in a new and utilitarian way as a variety of energies, hitherto unharnessed, which could now be tamed and transformed into industrial servants and which, in turn, would fashion never-ending progress and prosperity. The health of the machine, powered by steam and electricity, and the sickness of the machine, if those energies were misdirected or obstructed, were obsessive considerations of the period. It was entirely appropriate to regard the human body as still another natural object with many of the vicissitudes of the machine: this had always been medicine's privilege. But, for the first time, scientists, in their intoxication, could forget the duality previous centuries knew: namely, that the body is and is not a natural object. And once it was decided that the dominant energy of the human machine was sex, the new science of sexology was born. With the suppression of the second half of the dialectic, sexology and psychoanalysis could—with the assistance of the Romantics—claim the erotic life as their exclusive province, removing it from all the traditional disciplines, such as religion, philosophy, and literature, which had always concerned themselves with sex as human experience. Such qualities as modesty, privacy, reticence, abstinence, chastity, fidelity, and shame could now be questioned as rather arbitrary matters that interfered with the health of the sexual parts. In their place came an increasing assortment of objective terms like *ejaculatio praecox,* foreplay, forepleasure, and frigidity—all intended

10. ". . . I never observed that the women of America consider conjugal authority as an unfortunate usurpation of their rights, or that they thought themselves degraded by submitting to it. It appeared to me, on the contrary, that they attach a sort of pride to the voluntary surrender of their will. . . . Though their lot is different, they consider both of them as beings of equal value. . . . If I were asked . . . to what the singular prosperity and growing strength of that people ought mainly to be attributed, I should reply: To the superiority of their women." Alexis de Tocqueville, *Democracy in America,* 2 vols. (New York: Alfred A. Knopf, 1945), 2: 212–214.

to describe not human experience but the behavior of the sexual parts. The quite preposterous situation arose in which the patient sought treatment for *ejaculatio praecox* or impotence, and the healer sought to find out whether he liked his partner.

If the Victorians found sex unspeakable for the wrong reasons, the Victorian sexologists found it wrongly speakable. (To what extent Victorian prudery was actually modesty or reticence, I cannot say. It has become habitual for us to regard Victorian lovemaking as an obscenity.) Science is usually democratic, and since sex now belonged to science, whatever facts or assumptions were assembled had immediately to be transmitted to the people, there to invade their daily life. Writing of the Kinsey Report, Lionel Trilling found—correctly, I believe—a democratic motive for the study:

> In speaking of its motives, I have in mind chiefly its impulse toward acceptance and liberation, its broad and generous desire for others that they be not harshly judged. . . . The Report has the intention of habituating its readers to sexuality in all its manifestations; it wants to establish, as it were, a democratic pluralism of sexuality. . . . This generosity of mind . . . goes with a nearly conscious aversion from making intellectual distinctions, almost as if out of the belief that an intellectual distinction must inevitably lead to a social discrimination or exclusion.[11]

If we disregard Kinsey's scientific pretensions, we still must recognize his eminence as an arbiter of sexual etiquette. Like the lexicographer who finds his sanction in usage, Kinsey discovers his authority in practice: his democratic message is that we all do—or should do—more or less the same things in bed. And any notion lovers may retain from an older tradition that what they have together is private and unique is effectively disproved by his cataloguing of sexual matters, providing that the lovers join him in equating behavior with experience. As a fitting disciple of Kinsey, Masters actualizes the "pluralism of sexuality" within the demo-

11. Lionel Trilling, "The Kinsey Report," in *The Liberal Imagination* (New York: Doubleday, Anchor Books, 1954), pp. 232–233.

cratic unit of the laboratory and enlarges behavior to include the more minute physiological developments which, too, should belong to every citizen.

The political clamor for equal rights for the woman at the turn of the century could not fail to join with sexology to endow her with an orgasm equal in every sense to the male orgasm. It was agreed that, just as she was entitled to the vote, she was entitled to her orgasm. Moreover, if she were deprived of such release, her perturbation would be as unsettling to her nervous system as the frustration of orgasm was thought to be for the man. Equal rights were to be erotically consummated in simultaneous orgasm. On the one hand, it was unhealthful for her to be deprived of orgasm, and, on the other hand, psychoanalysis decreed that an important sign of her maturity as a woman was her ability to achieve orgasm. In other words, without orgasm she was neurotic to begin with, or neurotic to end with.

Though the achievement of simultaneous orgasm seemed to be a necessary consequence of equal rights, the problem remained that, in matters of lust, more than a decree or amendment was required for such an achievement. True, the sexologists were most generous with instruction, but each citizen has had to discover, over and over again, the degree to which he is caught in the futile struggle to will what cannot be willed—at the same time that he senses the real absurdity of the whole willful enterprise. The lover learns, as his indoctrination progresses, to observe uneasily and even to resist his rush of pleasure, if it seems he is to be premature. When no amount of resolution can force his pleasure to recede, he learns to suffer his release and then quickly prod himself to an activity his body's exhaustion opposes. In other words, he learns to take his moment in stride, so to speak, omitting the deference such moments usually call forth, and without breaking stride get to his self-appointed, and often fatiguing, task of tinkering with his mate—always hopeful that his ministrations will have the appearance of affection. While she is not likely to be deceived by such dutiful manipulation, she nevertheless wishes for both their sakes that her body, at least, will be deluded into fulfilling its franchise. Still, it cannot be easy for her to ignore the irony that her right to orgasm may perhaps depend for its realization upon her willingness to be diddled like a perverse underwater edible whose shell refuses to be pried open.

As far as I know, little attention was paid to the female orgasm before the era of sexology. Where did the sexologists find it? Did they discover it or invent it? Or both? I realize it may seem absurd to raise such questions about events as unmistakable as those witnessed in our laboratory. But I cannot believe that previous centuries were not up to our modern delights; nor can I believe that it was the censorship imposed by religion which suppressed the supreme importance of the female orgasm. My guess—which is not subject to laboratory proof—is that the female orgasm was always an occasional, though not essential, part of woman's whole sexual experience. I also supect that it appeared with regularity or predictability only during masturbation, when the more human qualities of her life with her mate were absent. Further, her perturbation was unremarkable and certainly bearable when orgasm did not arrive, for our lovers had not yet been enlightened as to the disturbances resulting from the obstruction or distortion of sexual energies. At this stage, her orgasm had not yet been abstracted and isolated from the totality of her pleasures, and enshrined as the meaning and measure of her erotic life. She was content with the mystery and variety of her difference from man and, in fact, would not have had it otherwise. Much that I have said, if we leave aside the erotomanias that have always been with us, applies to the male of previous centuries. For him, too, the moment of orgasm was not abstracted in its objective form from the whole of his erotic life and then idealized. He, too, preferred the mystery of difference, the impact of human contingency, becoming obsessed with the sheer anatomy and mechanics of orgasm only when all else was missing, as in masturbation.

Theological parallelism is a treacherous hobby, especially when we deal with flagrantly secular movements. Nevertheless, the manner in which lovers now pursue their careers as copulating mammals, adopting whatever new refinements sexology devises, covering their faces yet exposing their genitals, may remind us of older heresies which, through chastity or libertinism, have pressed toward similar goals; one heretical cult went so far as to worship the serpent in the Garden of Eden. But the difference between these older heresies and modern science—and there is a large one—must be attributed to the nature of science itself, which, by means of its claims to objectivity—if we accept such evidence as the Lambeth Conference—can invade religion and ultimately all of life to a degree denied the older heresies. So, with the abstraction, objectification, and idealization of the female orgasm, we have come to the last and perhaps most important clause in the contract which binds our lovers to their laboratory home, there to will the perfection on earth that cannot be willed, there to suffer the pathos that follows all such strivings toward heaven on earth.

9

My Wife, the Naked Movie Star

BERGMAN-ULLMAN, Bogdanovich-Shepherd, Newman-Woodward, Ponti-Loren, Cassavetes-Rowlands, Dassin-Mercouri: these are but a few of the romantic, or connubial, associations between director or producer and star. In some of these instances, the cinematic purpose would seem to be to exhibit the star, in various combinations of nakedness and passion, as the paragon of a sexuality so truthful and fully formed that the men in her movies, with their twisted moralities, must be either converted or undone. At least since Theda Bara, the Love Goddess has been a standard commercial venture in the movies—a venture which must be satisfactory to the banks which invest in these movies.

But the relations I have mentioned would seem to persist beyond the requirements of finance, and persist even when our directors and

This chapter originally appeared in *Harper's Magazine*, June 1969.

stars have arrived at a security which would allow them other cinematic possibilities. Moreover, the notoriety all these relationships have achieved—with the help of the press, television, and radio—soon makes these arrangements as compelling for the average moviegoer as the movies in which these stars appear. Thus, to watch Mercouri enacting the amorous necessities of her life with her screen lover is to be reminded that Dassin sits behind the camera governing her overtures and responses. If Gena Rowlands, cast as a prostitute in *Faces,* fondles her reclining co-star with what appears to be uncalled-for restraint, we are forced to wonder whether Cassavetes is not falsifying her characterization in order to protect his own jealous interests. Or, to take another extreme, when Vadim sets up his camera at the foot of the bed so he can record minutely the fondlings his particular star of the moment will undergo with her screen lover, we must wonder whether this explicitness is dictated by the movie or by the nature of his tie to his star. In other words, so long as each of these movies about sexuality contains another implicit plot between star and director, our attention will wander back and forth from the movie to the actual relationship between director and star. And naturally we will speculate about the extent their present life together determines each new movie and, equally, the extent each new movie influences their life off screen.

But these are real people whose lives are hardly represented by gossip columns and movie magazines. And even if I wished to pursue this impertinent course, I have no private bank of gossip about these notorious figures of the film world. So I leave these actual creatures, and turn instead to creatures of my own imagining—creatures who seem to capture something of the sexual predicament of our time.

The scene, as I imagine it, takes place in a custom-built Mercedes-Benz trailer, parked in the meadow of a small farm on the outskirts of Madrid, where the entire crew has assembled to shoot two important scenes from *Don Juan Strikes Out.* Briefly, the movie tells of Don Juan's painful liaison with the local farm girl (our star)—the creature whose shrewdness and vigor of flesh call his whole sensual career into question, finally reducing him to those ordinary cries of jealousy and possessiveness he has all these years managed to avoid. Josee Civetta has been sitting in her trailer dressing room while her makeup man places smudges on her forehead, left cheek, left shoulder, and just over her right breast. These smudges will be incurred in the first scene when she is shot spading hay to the horses in the barn. After the last spadeful of hay, a cut will be made to the small stream running through the farm. Here Josee will remove her outer garments as she is about to bathe, when Don Juan comes upon her. Now her husband and director, Sergio Rocco, enters. "Josee, Baby, stand up and show me how you'll look when you first take your dress off." Letting her dressing gown fall to the floor, she does a mock bump and grind in her husband's direction. When she senses he will endure this charade with his familiar patience, she bends down to retrieve her dressing gown, her backsides pointing at him, and on rising slowly dusts and folds the gown before placing it on top of her dressing table.

"Josee, later on you can act. But right now, I want to see how you'll look, so please turn around." Instead of turning full-circle in one motion, Josee defiantly makes abrupt small partial turns, her hands on her hips, and at the end of each turn she stands flat-footed, her legs spread apart, and one hip thrust laterally. Sergio makes no comment until she is at last planted with her back to him. "It's wrong! The panties are wrong! Look—by now everyone in the world knows what your behind looks like. Right? An average guy sitting in a movie house and seeing you in your tenth film, he *needs* to be reminded of your behind. And the best way to do this is to have panties that are too tight."

"Okay, okay, have it your way, Sergio! If the guys in the movie house are just like you—which I doubt—if all of you get a charge out of seeing me in tight panties, well I guess then eventually I'll get a charge out of it too. At least that's the way it's been."

If Sergio's guidance were confined merely to techniques for revealing Josee's body to the world, he would hardly differ from the burlesque coach, instructing his protégée in her little song and dance, her bumps and grinds. Such a coach might persuade his stripper to be comic, patronizing, sincere, kittenish, wistful, acrobatic, depending both on her abilities and his assessment of how they might best be exploited. And once her routine was established, they might—together or separately—look on the matter as a form of show business, whether pleasurable or tedious, which allowed them both a livelihood. Most burlesque performers, I am told, have little sympathy for their audience, which they regard as a tawdry assortment of marginal and lonely souls who come to be teased into a solitary excitement which must later be dissipated, if not in the theater itself, then in public and private toilets, alleys, rooming houses, and convention hotels. Even if partners are sometimes appropriated for relief I doubt that the burlesque queen herself is deceived about the solitary nature of this dissipation. Despite—or because of—their grim evaluation of their audiences, some burlesque performers take pleasure in their powers of erotic manipulation from afar, and I have no doubt their own pleasures improve their effectiveness as strippers—without necessarily making them more objective about the solitary quality of their own excitements, which they share with their audience.

As for Sergio and Josee, their artistic ambitions are too formidable to be contained in such a quaint form as burlesque, whose limitations resist all sentimental attempts to puff it up into folk art. Without doubt, their goal is to capture and project the reality of love and sex in our times. Unfortunately, their artistic endeavors are both broadened and blurred by the withering of censorship in the movies over the last few years. These days too much craft must be given over to the struggle to discover new ways of illuminating the landscape of sexuality. And not unlike ordinary erotic life, the movie itself may be neglected in the consuming and frustrating effort to improve the sexual cliché which was yesterday's novelty. The problem is that any visual and objective view of sex is necessarily limited by our anatomical range of behavior. And, obsessed by this view, the modern realistic camera is therefore driven to look more and more at less and less, pursuing with mounting magnification those scant details which cannot and will not yield the essence the moviemakers seek.

Not so long ago, when censorship still obtained, the subject was easily represented by a simple cinematic convention which taxed no one's ingenuity, though repetition eventually rendered it ludicrous. In the final "clinch" the hero clasped the heroine in his arms, and as he pressed his face to hers, our view became that of a rear camera pointed at the back and side of the hero's head—so that when their faces met, their mouths were concealed from the camera's eye. Though we were expected to accept the illusion that our stars were kissing each other, we had the option of assuming—if these two seemed mismated—that their lips never met, or if they did meet, their kiss was no more than the desultory peck of two young people arbitrarily paired by the democratic rules of the game of post office rather than by their own inclinations. (If we were to see two modern movie lovers kiss with mouths closed rather than open, we should have to assume they disliked each other.) At this distance, it now seems to me there were distinct moral and aesthetic advantages to the convention—which should have been spared some of our ridicule, considering the more literal fleshly conventions which have replaced it. For one thing, the final "clinch" affirmed the old-fashioned virtues of privacy and modesty, asserting that the real physical facts within this ideogram of an embrace were none of our business as audience and, moreover, none of the legitimate business of art itself, including all the technicians who make movie art possible. By no means, it should be emphasized, did this refusal to be explicit about what should be implicit interfere with our freedom to imagine this amorous union.

Some of the audience, I have no doubt, turned their imagination to the specifically lustful potentialities of this relationship, while others took a larger view of the ups and downs of the subsequent course of the life of the pair. But in either case, it is worth stressing the paradoxical point that our present freedom from censorship has deprived us of our earlier freedom to have our own imaginative way with a movie. Whatever its artistic limitations, the "clinch" at least was an illusion so safely responsive to even minimal dramatic skill that it could easily be put aside once the day's shooting was over—

which must have been a relief both to audience and actors. Plainly said, there was nothing about the illusion itself, however it was exploited, which demanded it be *lived* as well as acted. Thus, in addition to all else it might have suggested, the illusion contained the illusion of being an illusion. And without that radical ingredient the audience might well leave the theater with the unpleasant suspicion that these two actors were continuing to embrace long after the camera crews had gone home.

Sergio and Josee, as it has already been suggested, loyally support the modern creed that the craft of moviemaking must include in its repertoire not yet all but still a good deal of sexual play. Therefore, in his profession as director and hers as performer, they will strive for an erotic authenticity which emulates—in appearance, at least—their own marital intimacies. In effect this means they believe—or profess to believe—that the visible mannerisms of sex can be separated from the entirety of affective life, and then willed into actuality whenever the dramatic occasion so requires.

Now, Josee's ability to enact her role with almost any leading man must be as gratifying to the director in Sergio as to the actress in Josee. At the same time, her ability may reassure the husband in him (and the wife in her) that her amorous conduct before the camera is merely a dramatic accomplishment, involving no actual entanglement with a real man. Yet, if he is as like the rest of us as he insists, his faith will waver from time to time, making him wonder to what extent her so-called ability is an appetite in disguise—an appetite addressed indiscriminately to every man or, worse yet, to no man at all. In such a state, the knowledge that he bears some responsibility for this enterprise can only increase his distress. After all, he is the one who procures and then directs these actors in their love scenes with his wife. So there is a sense in which, if his pain is sharp, he could regard himself as a respectable pimp. Hopefully, this self-chiding will subside as he regains his belief in his split existence—in other words, as he remembers it is *only* a movie. On the other hand, should Josee be sensitive to his jealous lapses, she will be careful not to repeat her movie gestures in her nights with Sergio. She may even be tempted to invent gestures which are reserved only for her husband. But even if she were up to the artistry necessary to dissemble the deliberate nature of her invention, thus preventing him from confirming his worst suspicions, her predicament would still be disagreeable, inasmuch as she could no longer be sure that her marriage was *not* just a movie.

While her conscience may enable her to resist such domestic artifice, what is to prevent her from appropriating the surfaces of her marital intimacies for the sake of her cinematic lovemaking? After all, according to her creed, it is possible to abstract for the sake of her art the external mannerisms of her erotic life, without violating those affections which ideally will rejoin these mannerisms when she leaves the set. On the other hand, should her lovemaking with her leading man provoke an excitement more overpowering and enduring than the mechanical stirrings she would ordinarily anticipate, she will remain loyal to her creed, preferring now to question the validity of her marriage. Thus, rather than regard herself a victim of those erotic gestures that were intended to facilitate the movie illusion, she may conclude, invoking the usual romantic sentiments, that her new attachment came about in spite of and not because of dramatic requirement.

Real consummation for a movie, of course, does not occur until it is at last submitted to the paying audiences of the world for their verdict. If out of boredom the men in the theaters close their eyes to the naked Josee to nap with dreams of their own making, or turn away from the screen to whisper about the day they meant to leave behind, or wander to the refreshment stand to giggle over the unintended absurdities of this movie, will Sergio's and Josee's excitement over each other survive this test? Or will their excitement now give way to a restlessness and indifference, not unlike that of the audience? In other words, their attachment to each other must draw some sanction and vitality from the audience response to their creation. It is as absurd to imagine Sergio and Josee without an audience as to imagine them forcibly settled in a distant suburb where they are condemned to find their entire erotic sustenance only in each other.

Why should it be otherwise? Why should we ask more of these two famous people than of ourselves? True, the scope of their lives together is gigantic, their desires depending on the confirmation of millions of moviegoers. But I think if we scale down the magnification, we can see more similarity than difference between their lives and our own. When Sergio argues that tight panties will best set off Josee's behind to her public, he resembles any husband approving or disapproving the dress his wife has chosen for the evening's party. In costume and deportment she must, like Josee, prove herself sexually attractive, without transgressing the bounds of taste and, equally important, without mistaking the illusion she creates for the reality of her life with her mate.

The line she pursues is as thin as Josee's: her performance must be sufficiently convincing to charm her companions and at the same time she must project enough make-believe not to deceive her husband or herself—not to mention the other guests, who have their own loyalties to contend with. She must never forget that a man of course wants his wife to be admired, but to the extent that she presents herself and is accepted as an available sexual object their relation will suffer. All this of course is equally true in reverse—the man's public demeanor and reception (his habitation of "his image") will be inspected by his wife. (Indeed, this objectifying on public occasion extends to each person's sense of himself—and may suggest why "self-image" seems such a dubious concept.) When the party is over the couple will return to their home with as much or as little exhilaration as Sergio and Josee after a preview of their newest movie.

In brief, then, I believe the hazards which beset Sergio and Josee as they try to keep their cinematic and marital lives separate are not essentially different from those which trouble sexuality for the rest of us as we shuttle back and forth between our private and public worlds. At this point, let me mention two opposing views of the problem, both different from my own. In 1922 Freud wrote:

> It is a matter of everyday experience that fidelity, especially that degree of it required in marriage, is only maintained in the face of continual temptation. . . . Social conventions have taken this universal state of things into account very adroitly, by granting a certain amount of latitude to the married woman's thirst to find favor in man's eyes and the married man's thirst to capture and possess, in the expectation that this inevitable tendency to unfaithfulness will thus find a safety-valve and be rendered innocuous. Convention has laid down that neither partner is to hold the other accountable for these little excursions in the direction of unfaithfulness, and it achieves the result on the whole that the desire awakened by the new love-object is gratified by a kind of turning-back to the object already possessed. The jealous person, however, does not believe in any such thing as a halt or turning back once the path has been trod, nor that a social "flirtation" may be a safeguard against actual infidelity.[1]

Not uncharacteristically, Freud is less concerned with the quality of erotic life, in and out of marriage, than with the manner in which society restrains and diverts the sexual drive in the service of preserving its institutions. "What the world calls its code of morals," he wrote, "demands more sacrifices than it is worth." Because fidelity in marriage "is only maintained in the face of *continual* temptation" (italics mine), small excursions in infidelity, in which neither partner holds the other accountable, can have the hygienic function of preserving the monogamous relationship of marriage, since whatever excitement is aroused in these social forays can be turned back to the marital partner. Freud's view is a form of mithridatism: small doses of infidelity will defend against larger infidelity. In a society as absorbed with erotic images as ours, it would be difficult to know whether the small infidelity was a protection against or an indulgence of our sexual proclivities—whether the institution of monogamy is strengthened or weakened by the erotic quality of our social life.

Tolstoy, on the other hand, found nothing to applaud about the "little excursions" Freud found so salutary. In fact, he found the spectacle so loathsome he renounced sexuality altogether.

1. Sigmund Freud, "Certain Neurotic Mechanisms in Jealousy, Paranoia and Homosexuality," *Collected Papers*, 5 vols. (New York: Basic Books, 1959), 2: 233.

> And we men don't know—we don't know because we don't want to know—but women know perfectly well that the loftiest and most poetic love depends not on moral qualities but on physical closeness and on the way of doing up one's hair, one's complexion, the cut of a gown. Ask an experienced coquette which she would prefer to risk: being detected in falsehood, cruelty, even immorality, in the presence of the one she is trying to entice, or to appear before him in a badly made or unbecoming gown—and she will always choose the first. She knows that man lies when he talks about lofty feelings—all he wants is the body—and so he pardons anything but an ugly, unbecoming, unfashionable costume. The coquette knows this consciously; every innocent girl knows this unconsciously, just as animals know it.
>
> Hence these abominable jerseys, these bustles, these naked shoulders, arms, and almost bosoms. Women, especially those that have been through the school of marriage, know very well that talk on the highest topic is just talk; that what man wants is the body and everything which displays it in a deceptively captivating light. And they act accordingly. If we should once forget this indecency, which has become second nature, and look at the life of the upper classes as it really is, in all its shamelessness, it would appear like one luxurious brothel. . . .[2]

Were he alive today, Tolstoy would regard the new sexual freedom as merely further corroboration for his conviction that life between the sexes, having become "one luxurious brothel," was no longer morally feasible. And, even more so, he would be positive that abstinence was the only way to escape this brothel. But today we are less interested in his solution, which even in the monastic orders is undergoing some challenge, and more impressed by his statement of our dilemma: ". . . What man wants is the body and everything which displays it in a *deceptively captivating light.*" (Italics mine.) As a general, even minimal comment on erotic life, Tolstoy's notion that man desires the body seems unexceptionable, although our habit with abstractions of this order may make us forget that it is not exactly the body *qua* body that man desires but rather the body with its coverings and uncoverings. Nor is it remarkable that romantic talk finds its heightening in the same play between conceal-

2. Leo Tolstoy, "The Kreutzer Sonata," *The Kreutzer Sonata, the Devil, and Other Tales"* (London: Oxford University Press).

ment and disclosure, mystery and discovery. But this aspect of sexual desire outraged Tolstoy's moral sensibilities: woman's provocative dress, like man's "lofty" talk, was a deception suggesting a more glorious actuality than she possessed or that he could possess. Or perhaps his outrage lay in his painful sense that the peeling away of her decorations merely exposed an inner enigma that, while it may briefly be transcended, must be probed again and again without ever yielding its secret.

Oscar Wilde expressed his disdain for the special nature—the essential femaleness—of women in his quip that woman is a Sphinx without a secret. While I do not share his disdain, I can appreciate the truth there is in his remark. (It is not quite true that she has no secret: her secret is that she has a secret.) Because man's sexuality is external, visible, objective, he cannot encompass a sexuality whose most formidable powers, including child-bearing, must remain hidden to him. However much he prizes the otherness of his partner, he is nevertheless driven to impose a visible, concrete reality, or a metaphor of such a reality, on this privately contained world. And, of course, because she wishes her interiority to be penetrated, she will accommodate herself somewhat to man's objective need, for in this way her own needs are satisfied as well. Depending on the fashion of the moment, man will fasten on such outward criteria of desirability as buttocks, or legs, or breasts, and woman will join him in valuing these fleshly distinctions, since each hopes to please the other.

Pornography is but a further indulgence of his hunger, now extended to the visual details of sexual performance itself. It is worth mentioning that pornography, as we know it, is a genre made by man for man, exploiting the absolute compliance in literal uncovering that only fictitious women can provide. As such it offers little erotic titillation to most women. It is beyond my competence to say what a female pornography would be, except to suggest that its enticements would probably have to include a fundamental romantic context—a plot, out of which erotic situations may be brought to flower—in the imagination or on the page. Such a pornography will be closer to *Dear John* than to *Fanny Hill,* closer to *True Confessions* than to dirty postcards. I do not mean to suggest, let me make clear, that women's penchant for "situational" erotica makes the sort of pornography they prefer any more "refined" than the more literal, no-nonsense forms preferred by men. The sexual arousal, in both cases, is merely an indulgence of an altogether literal, impersonal sexual hunger, and, as such, is as irrelevant to the possibilities of sex as a truly human encounter as is masturbation.

To return to Tolstoy's assertion that to be desirable the body must be displayed in "a deceptively captivating light": In their attempt to explain this human peculiarity, some writers resort to zoology, pointing to the manner in which colorful and exotic features assist a number of lower animals in their mating rituals. However, such animal decoration, it should be remembered, is no artifact created by the Disney special effects department. Moreover, it is our dissatisfaction with our own pale bodies that makes us judge the peacock's plumage or the mandrill's blue and scarlet rump more enticing than the dull gray fur of the rat—or our own poor parts. Conceived in envy, such biological speculation is more a pathetic consequence than an explanation of our particular peculiarity.

Yet, even if our erotic life is essentially unlike animal mating, why should it strike us as peculiar? Why are we unwilling to reconcile ourselves to the human fact that, unlike other living creatures, we cannot do without the erotic deceptions that outraged Tolstoy? After all, as far as we know, sexual illusion has been necessary throughout history. So, if we are envious, what are we envious of? Certainly not the perfunctory rutting of animals. Much as we may object to the excessive and vulgar prescriptions the mass media offer about how to make the body attractive, still we are forced to acknowledge a portion of truth to their instruction. Any man whose ardor has diminished, if not subsided, before a torn and stained nightgown, can testify to his dependence on sexual illusion, while suspecting this ragged costume betrays comparable failure of passion in its wearer. At the same time, in the midst of such discouragement, we wish it could be otherwise; out of nostalgia and/or hope, we long to shed both the excitements and constraints provoked by our coverings, and recapture—or achieve—a bliss in which our bodies in themselves will be sufficient.

At this point, theology may offer more illumination than biology. Before they ate of the tree of knowledge, even a distant suburb could have been an Eden for Adam and Eve, for they still found each other pleasing without adornment or concealment. However, when the Lord ordered them to cover their parts, their sexuality was already an article of knowledge. And in His wisdom He knew that modesty imposed from without would never quite protect them from an immodesty from within: concealment for one could always be disclosure for another. With the first fig leaf, the quality of the covering became critical. There being fig leaves and fig leaves, now a choice had to be made: not only were fig leaves large and small, adequate and inadequate, but some were more pleasingly shaped and colored than others. And how and where these leaves were to be suspended became as important a consideration as their hue and conformation. Seen in this light, fashion reveals itself as a shifting, yet unresolvable, arbitration between the conflicting demands of concealment and disclosure. But the greedier fashion becomes, appropriating for its arbitration clothing, cosmetics, deodorants, coiffures, and even sexual behavior itself, the more painful is our sense of our fallenness and the more obtrusive our nostalgia for Eden—or what we imagine to be our lost innocence.

Not merely, in these moments, does the machinery of sexual illusion seem too cumbersome for us to bear, but it appears now as the adversary of the body-ness of the body, bent on repudiating all its ordinary messiness—its fat, dirt, blemishes, secretions, smells—and making our own physicality itself repulsive to us. With such an unsettling vision as this, the more energetic among us will move from nostalgia to schemes for a New Jerusalem, in which the body will be restored to its natural state, whatever that may be. Repeatedly, throughout Western history, the state has tried by means of sumptuary laws to legislate the degree of personal adornment—to legislate, in other words, the appearances of innocence, if not its actuality. Organized religion, of course, has again and again struggled to oppose our appetite for sexual illusion or artifice. And church and state aside, our recent past contains a variety of utopian efforts, ranging from Tolstoy's and Gandhi's pleas for abstinence to nudist movements to the Mother Hubbards which D. H. Lawrence required the women in his Taos colony to wear. More recently, we have become aware of a trend in the theater, as anti-pornographic as the Mother Hubbard, to present the ordinary naked human body without fashionable inducements of dress or flesh. Even sexology, with its foolish insistence on making of private experience a public scientific behavior, must nevertheless be credited with the same desire to rescue sexuality from prurience. And something similar might be said of group psychotherapeutic experiments in undress that come to us out of the far West.

Still, much as we may sympathize with and even support some of these efforts to curb or contain that portion of sexual life that has to do with sexual illusion, we must acknowledge that, allowing for the uncommon exception, such arbitrary programs are fated to render us twice-fallen rather than once-born. I think it not farfetched, incidentally, in this connection, to regard the very deliberate casualness toward sex on the part of some of the young today—in which people choose partners, change partners, move from bed to bed with visible disdain for the fussiness of fashion, flirtation, courtship—all the procedures of sexual illusion—as yet another utopian attempt to achieve a kind of sexual purity, this one revolving about the illusion that there is no sexual illusion.

However, the drama of Adam and Eve's banishment from Eden can have little validity for us, even as allegory, unless their loss is to some degree experienced by us in our ordinary existence. Innocence may indeed be beyond our adult capacities. Yet those of us who admit faltering before the ragged nightgown or being aroused by a dirty picture must also admit the times when the entire apparatus of fashion turns irrelevant, when the bodily sufficiency we search for is, in affection, granted us, so that after the event we can be grateful that self-conscious sexual artifice for once has been transcended. On the other hand, it is this reconciliation which leaves us painfully nostalgic—not for Eden or some Golden Age in the past—but for the fulfillment, actual or merely potential, which we have known or should have known and could know again. In chapter 8 I have distinguished sex from other human activity in this manner:

> Its particular difference from everything else in this life lies in the possibility which sex offers man for regaining *his own* body through knowing the body of his loved one. And should he fail that *knowing* and *being known,* should he lapse into all those ways of *knowing about* which he has proudly learned to confuse with *knowing*—both bodies will again escape him. Increasingly, as D. H. Lawrence understood, man has become separated from his body, which he yearns to inhabit, such yearning understandably bringing sentimental and scientific prescriptions for the reunion eluding him. Yet it is through the brief reconciliation with his own and his loved one's body that he can now grasp—and endure—the bodily estrangement which has always been his lot, without succumbing to the blandishments that would betray the realities of both sides of this duality.

Prescriptions for reunion are addressed to a form of perception which, for the most part, does not dominate our day-to-day domestic existence. Even here we shall certainly employ many of the materials and devices of sexual illusion and fulfillment urged on us by the public media—all the coverings and uncoverings, both literal and figurative. But the fact is that ordinarily we do not see, hear, smell, taste, and feel our mates in the manner these media proclaim. In our ordinary life, in private, we *experience* one another—and our relation—and this is not essentially a visual process. We are presences rather than appearances to each other; we "read" each other's visible and objective surfaces as a code to the more substantial invisibilities—of meaning, texture, and habit—of our life together. However, that other, public form of perception, so conspicuous and overblown in Sergio's and Josee's cinematic enterprise, also belongs to us in our private and public worlds. And we feel it most sharply when acquaintances enter our domestic world and we leave it to visit theirs. On such public occasions we fall into experiencing our mates as we imagine they will be experienced by others. Stripped of our private relation, which changes everything, I now see my wife as I think others see her, which is to say that I see her as an aesthetic or sexual or social object. Mannerisms of phrase, countenance, voice, gesture, which usually are no more conspicuous than old prints that have long since merged into the anonymity of the dining-room wall, are now, in this new objectivity, brightly lighted and rigorously framed. Telling an old anecdote, I may, out of the corner of my eye, see more tolerance than amusement in my wife's face, as if she were briefly sitting in Sergio's directorial chair, judging my performance in terms that are neither her habit nor my preference. Or, watching her rapt response to her dinner companion's conversation, I will take my turn in Sergio's chair, to wonder if what I see is appropriate or inappropriate to the improvisation I am now compelled to direct. The dress that I thought decent enough when we left for the party now seems too little or too much for this occasion, but I can no longer be sure whether this new evaluation belongs to the dress or my altered perception—or both: whether, in any case, my new vision is the truth domesticity has obscured or simply an insanity I could have spared myself, had I avoided this party altogether.

For the sake of illustration I have arbitrarily made these private and public worlds more discrete than they can ever be. In actuality both worlds interpenetrate, shaping the reality and potentiality of each. In the midst of any gathering our domestic view may unexpectedly and fleetingly return. On the other hand, there will be discordant times in our solitary life together when we see each other publicly, the members of the party invading and challenging every room we would make our own. And with the mounting clamor of sexological exhortation, the bedroom at these times not only offers no sanctuary but seems more crowded with recipes for bodily satisfaction and/or hygiene than the kitchen or bathroom.

To some degree we must live always with a foot in each realm, hoping that something of our private experience will carry over into the public arena, softening some of its harsh objectivity; and hoping as well that that amount of public imagery that *does* pass into our private world (and it does, for we *are* also appearances to each other, and sexual illusion has been, since Adam and Eve, as necessary as it is dangerous) will be peopled by our private selves, subjected by us, in our relation.

If it is hazardous to legislate an Eden through exiling ourselves from the world in which we live, it is equally hazardous on the worldly side to seek a sexual utopia through succumbing to the prescriptions which bombard us from every direction every day of our lives. In both ventures we attempt deliberately to will what cannot be self-consciously willed. It has long been my conviction that ours is an age of the disordered will, our conceit being that there is no human possibility which lies beyond our conscious will. To mention but a few of our more bizarre willful undertakings: we will to sleep, to read fast, to be creative, to have simultaneous orgasm, and to enjoy our old age. As a result of this particular modern disability, we are reluctant to resign ourselves to our natural and inevitable fate of living within the ebb and flow of sexual illusion in both private and public worlds, while at the same time distrusting the efficacy of any given device to bring us the salvation we seek.

10

He Said, She Said

IN ITS EFFORTS to redress sexual, social, political, economic, artistic, and religious inequalities, the new feminism has thrown into question all those institutions under whose auspices men and women through the centuries have sought to combine their lots or join their fates. Marriage, the family, child-bearing and child-rearing, even the man-woman thing itself, are being subjected to such harsh scrutiny and challenge that it is now difficult for some people to take for granted anything about life between the sexes. At the heart of the dissension, I believe, is a failure of dialogue between man and woman—a failure that to some degree, with notable exceptions, has always existed, and now, with our present self-consciousness, is being experienced with greater anguish. I shall not use the term "dialogue" again—for the reason that the word has become so debased in the last few years that it is used to identify almost any public or

This chapter originally appeared in *Commentary*, March 1972.

private babble. Instead I shall talk about talk—real talk—between a particular man and a particular woman. Be it contentious or amicable, playful or serious, such man/woman talk requires a forthrightness on each side that represents the experience of each, and at the same time is addressed to the experience of the other without duplicity or evasion. Its medium is language, a problematical medium that may obscure as much as it may reveal; yet no other medium will serve.

Man/woman talk has been neglected, even disparaged, in philosophy and psychology, largely because it was deemed inferior to the friendly talk between two people of the same sex—usually male, in the writings of the past, more recently female in the urgings of the new feminism. Because of the commonality of their past experience and the relative absence of erotic strivings, two friends, it was held, could achieve a purer, more honest, more illuminating back and forth. The implication of such notions was that friendship was impossible between men and women, or, if this seemed too bleak, it could be said that men and women had *something* together, by no means inferior to friendship, but still something different—a something which replaced the necessity of talk with a shared domestic and sexual world. The logic of this replacement stemmed from the premise that all real talk between a man and a woman, no matter how carefully disguised, was sexually flirtatious, and if an ongoing sexual life together were agreed upon, talk was no longer necessary except for the exchange of factual information about their shared world. Should the hunger for man/woman talk now arise, men and women both must seek their flirtatious satisfactions outside their life together, and for talk turn to friends of the same sex.

What is flirtatious talk? According to the Oxford English Dictionary definition, and according to our modern understanding, flirtatious talk is a contradiction in terms, if by *talk* we mean something forthright between equals. The OED speaks of "playing at courtship," still a relatively bland description compared to our modern pejorative view, wherein flirtation is a form of double-talk, all seeming subject matter being bent to the possibility or actuality of sexual union through seduction, real or imagined. "Courtship" is by now an old-fashioned, if not obsolete, form of life between a man and a woman; at best it represented a rather stylized manner in which two people could come to know each other before sex and/or marriage. A young man and a young woman today are more apt to begin with sex, and for the kind of knowing which follows between them we have no ready word. Clearly, "courtship" is not it.

The problem with the term "flirtation," as I see it, is that either it must be restricted to describe seductive double-talk, in which sex itself is the overriding object, or else it must be enlarged to include talk where sexuality is present in the sense of acknowledged attraction between a man and a woman, without the intervention of actual sex as motive or compulsion. Unfortunately, even "sexuality" is apt to be reductive in the latter description, in that it suggests merely an instinctual magnetism. Certainly it would be foolish to disown this portion of the attraction, yet equally important, perhaps more important, in real man/woman talk, is the exciting possibility of receiving and offering a range of perception and sensibility whose otherness can be uniquely and surprisingly illuminating. Because playfulness and frivolity are thought to belong to flirtation in the reductive sense, I want to stress that man/woman talk of the order I am attempting to describe, and regardless of how seldom it may be achieved in these times, is not necessarily a somber, soul-searching affair. So long as equality and honesty prevail, and so long as each person tries to imagine the other's reality without dishonoring his own, the manner or mood of such talk can be various: humorous, serious, philosophical, concrete, abstract, gossipy, and so on. Employing Martin Buber's terminology, and at the same time shifting its focus from friendship between people of the same sex, I would maintain that such talk contains the supreme potentiality of confirming the other, not only as a particular human being, but as a particular man or woman, and, of course, of being confirmed in the same way.

There are basically three different male-female contexts or modes within which this real talk may take place. In each one the experience of sexual attraction, the quality of it, the acknowledgment of it, will be different. In the first mode, the man and woman talking have a current, on-going sexual commitment to each other. A common or traditional shorthand term for this arrangement is "marriage," although needless to say it does exist without marriage, and, conversely, there is nothing about the marriage ceremony itself which automatically confers these verbal pleasures on its celebrants. In these committed relationships, the issue of sex having already been settled, as it were, the specter of sex will, ironically, be normally less present than in other categories of encounter, since the couple know that, convenience apart, the conversation can at any point be interrupted—or climaxed or celebrated—in bed, and then, or later, resumed.

In the second mode, the man and woman talking are both sexually committed, but not to each other. (I am aware that the whole idea of sexual commitment—always a fragile reality, often an embattled principle—has undergone some strenuous challenges lately; but neither these challenges nor any defensive responses I might offer are to the point in my effort here. I am speaking about a way of life in which commitment, fidelity, temptation, and betrayal are all real possibilities.) In this second mode, then, both conversationalists have sexual loyalties elsewhere, and do not wish or intend to betray them. Still, a lively ingredient of the talk between them will be an awareness of—and appreciation of—the "otherness" of the other: each will respond to, and take pleasure in, the "otherly" attractiveness of the other, which may in fairness be called sexual attraction, so long as it is understood that it does not focus on—or aim at—an explicit sexual conclusion.

In the third mode, the talkers are not quite yet—or only just—involved in a sexual relation; their talk, in addition to its subject matter, has another—usually quite pleasant if not intoxicating—burden to bear, namely, that of exploring the sexual possibilities that may lie before them. Should these two not be committed to others, this adventure may most delightfully combine the pleasures of real talk with the pleasures of real flirtation, without disservice to either.

When the outcome of these explorations would result in the betrayal of a third or fourth person, however, I think that the issue of bad faith constitutes a threat to the honor and forthrightness demanded by real talk.

One of the risks I run in choosing to talk about talk between men and women is that I may be thought to be describing conversation between beings with vocal cords and ears but without bodies, just as someone talking about sex may seem to be describing beings with sexual organs but without voice and hearing. Let me say as quickly as possible that there is no sex without talk, although pornography is a male venture one of whose purposes would seem to be to render the woman speechless, except for certain obligatory cries of gratitude and admiration. And, on the other side, my talkers are blessed with bodies, clothed and unclothed, assisting, questioning, or contradicting what is said. Most of us, I imagine, can recall the times when we talked rather than had the sex we wanted, such talk concealing our true desires, and, in the same spirit, the times when the poverty of real talk provoked us into sexual consolation—or, to put the matter simply, when the lust for talk was obligingly transformed into sexual lust. Even the most unregenerate seducer cherishes the secret hope of real talk with his conquest, although that is precisely what he cannot abide, what he knows would most compromise his entire career as seducer.

My early discussion, which must have seemed utopian, of the privileges of real man/woman talk must now give way to a consideration of the failure—the reasons for the failure.

Allowing for all exceptions to the contrary, I nevertheless have the impression that women generally are more disposed to talk than men, that men for the most part are more guarded and secretive in their talk with women. This disparity is epitomized by a scene enacted daily in all areas and at all levels of our society. It comes in several versions. Two will give the idea. Version A: He comes home. She is making dinner, diapering the baby, and so on. He greets her affectionately, asks her casually, How's it going?, or Well, what's new?—and she tells him. She talks about the children, appreciating, deploring, concern about Bobby's this, delight at Billy's that, she recounts her entertaining—or boring or outrageous—experiences at the supermarket, she does not omit mention of the malfunctioning vacuum cleaner, and, stirring away at the soup, wiping children's faces and spilled desserts, she discusses her response to an item of general public interest she saw on TV. She also recalls the few free moments in which she read an article called "Radical New Approaches to Being a Woman," and more speculation, philosophy, and self-scrutiny flow freely until, the children more or less bedded down, or banished to homework and/or TV, dinner cleared away, and a quiet moment descending over the last cup of coffee, she turns to him, flushed, expectant, as one who has unstintingly contributed her full share of the sharing, and says, Well? How was your day? Does he start off with who called him first thing at the office that morning, and how that call caused him to doubt a decision he'd made the day before, and does he pursue momentarily the problematic nature of the kind of decision making he's required to do and his capacity or incapacity for it, does he respond to her notions about the TV event or engage her reactions to the article she read, being reminded of something *he* read on that most recently well-publicized of subjects and his response to it, does he. . . . But why pursue this? Once in a while he does. More often he does not. Perhaps he says, Oh, nothing much happened, just the usual rat-race. Perhaps he recites some dry, factual résumé of his activities. Perhaps he grasps at some domestic thread she dangled and addresses himself to an issue concerning her or the children, or even the vacuum cleaner. Perhaps he shrugs and is silent. In any case, more often than she cares to think about, she asks with some bitterness why there must be this inequality, why she is open about her life, her thoughts, and he remains closed.

Version B. He comes home. Pretty soon she comes home. The housekeeper is seeing to the children and making dinner. He (or possibly she) fixes a couple of cocktails and they share a quiet interlude before a family (or possibly a solitary adult) dinner. Well, he says, how did it go today?—and she tells him. She talks about her secretary, or co-editor, or senior research assistant, or cameraman, she appreciates, deplores, analyzes, questions, wonders about the nature of her work, of her place and performance in it, tells of other, more private thoughts and concerns that popped in and out of her day. Eventually she pauses . . . and asks . . . and does he . . . ? Well, once in a while he does. More often he does not. He does something else. And more often than she cares to think about, she asks with some bitterness why there must be this inequality, why she is open about her life, her thoughts, and he remains closed.

In whatever setting this scene occurs, his reply to her complaint may be that there isn't much to be said, that nothing interesting happened, that she is more articulate and more observant than he, but beyond or beneath his talk about not talking there has to be some uneasy recognition of his inclination toward reticence. There may be no deliberate concealment: all he may experience may be a familiar blankness following her invitation or demand that he talk. He can stand on his right to have nothing to say, or he can willfully invent a facsimile of talk, but in either case he is left with the aftertaste of an old inferiority in the realm of real talk with a woman.

In order to pursue the nature of this reticence, I shall turn to an old memory of my own. Early in the Depression, when I was in my late teens, my college roommate and I spent a Saturday evening prowling around the Tenderloin district of San Francisco, searching for sexual distraction of some sort. An actual sexual adventure was what we most wished for, but for reasons of timidity and poverty such a culmination seemed most unlikely. As physical fatigue began to set in, my friend mentioned, no doubt in desperation, that he had heard of a display of rubber goods at a drugstore in the heart of the district, where, on the pretense of being potential customers, we would be allowed to examine a rare and extensive collection of erotic or contraceptive rubber devices. Very shortly we were standing in a back room of the drugstore, staring into a large glass case containing each specimen with name and price beneath. My recollection is that we both tried to assume the demeanor of the casual museumgoer as we inspected the display, while hoping the clerk would not badger us into making a purchase. In fact, I remember our attempt at sophisticated detachment more than I remember what was contained in the case. Except for one item called a French Tickler. This was a rubber condom to which was attached a filigree of thin rubber strands that stood out from the surface of the condom like the bristles of a hairbrush.

From my present perspective I wish to make two different, though related, points about that occasion. First, about our plight. There are a number of common expressions that could identify our condition that evening, but all I know of, though splendidly concrete, lack generalizing power. I shall therefore characterize our state by a term I first found in an article by Midge Decter, namely *undifferentiated lust.* By undifferentiated lust I mean the surgings of sexual excitement—usually chronic, often acute—that first begin to possess the young man in his adolescence. In terms of the world about him, this excitement seems to come from everywhere and nowhere, and to be directed at everyone and no one, as it presses for bodily release. Obviously there is pleasure, or at least the possibility of pleasure, in this lust, but just as often it is experienced as an affliction in its obsessive claims on both the body and the imagination. In time the nonspecific, unfocused nature of this lust may give way to differentiation, as actual relations with actual women develop, the attendant discriminations depending critically on real talk in these relations. But such a passage is a shaky one, for undifferentiated lust can never be wholly banished; it may be transcended, or, more often, deliberately withstood. Every man knows he can be subject, if he so chooses, to undifferentiated sexual arousal, and it should be noted that there is a pornography industry dedicated to the arousal of this undifferentiated impulse.

To return to the subject of man's inclination toward reticence. It is when undifferentiated lust begins to capture the adolescent young man that he perceives a radical difference in terms of sexual urgings between himself and a young woman. He comes to know in his own heart that this form of lust is his, not hers. And how can there be frank talk, given this difference? To admit simply that he is driven by a sexual hunger for anyone or everyone would, he believes, deprive him of release with a woman who does not share this extreme hunger. Of course, with the help of the equalitarian fiats bestowed by the sexual revolution, he may convince her or she may convince herself there is no difference: undifferentiated lust is not only the lot, but the right, of both of them. But more often, he will develop the *habit of disavowal,* pretending differentiation when there is none. Needless to say, in this simulation of real talk, he may be as deceived as she about the nature of their tie together. At first, before there can be said to be a habit, the disavowal is relatively uncomplicated. The lust that constitutes an overwhelmingly important portion of the young man's experience must, so he believes, be concealed or dissembled in his dealings with women. But if disavowal persists and remains uncorrected it soon spreads, almost by contagion, to include all manner of experience, both pleasurable and painful, that has little to do with undifferentiated lust. At this point there may be said to be a *habit of disavowal.* It is frequently misconstrued by both man and woman as his special need for privacy, his need to handle whatever is important in his life by himself. If he asserts that talk will only interfere with his concentration on what is pressing, he in effect resorts to his earlier conviction that talk about his lust would deprive him of the satisfaction he desires. Lest I be misunderstood, I am not questioning the legitimate need for privacy that both men and women have, but rather the illegitimate claim to privacy which is not privacy but rather disavowal, and which stands as enemy to real talk.

The second point I want to consider in relation to the episode in the San Francisco drugstore concerns the rubber object in the glass case, the French Tickler. My response to this object at the time was no doubt a mixture of embarrassment and fascination, but this hardly explains why it remains in my memory. It remains, I think, because it was and is constitutive of an inferiority that man feels before woman. What I am saying is that there was something in me that found this object not remarkable but *un*remarkable. I seemed to accept without question its assertion that man in his nakedness is simply not enough to contend with a woman. And the French Tickler in its complicated manufacture metaphorically represented the proliferating web of measures he would adopt to redress his insufficiency and prove he was enough. With this image we are brought to that aspect of the man/woman problem that has received the bulk of attention in the press. Which words are used to designate the issue will depend on the sympathy or outrage of the individual writer. Without exhausting the list, I might mention the male ego (intransigent or wobbly), male chauvinism, machismo, male fragility or vulnerability.

But let me return at this point to the seeming inferiority represented by the French Tickler. However much my democratic prejudices may be offended by this sensation of inequality, I still believe it to be a fact in every man's experience of himself. So I must ask the question, How did it come about? I ask the question, knowing it is baffling and knowing there are many theories, cultural and psychological, that address themselves to it. With what is to follow, I do no more than add my own theory to the lot of explanations, without, however, dissipating my own bafflement. Though the French Tickler seems literally to refer to that later period in man's life when he is sexually active, I prefer to see the object as a constitutive symbol. This is to say that I believe the feeling of inferiority much precedes puberty, going back to a time when the male child first perceives his mother to be a different order of sexual being from himself. Were I to be more literal here I would refer to incestuous strivings and their attendant castration anxieties as my causative theory. Such strivings may or may not occur, but I do not believe them crucial so far as the issue of inferiority is concerned. I am more inclined to think of them as early attempts to alleviate the experience of inequality through some sort of vain and crude wish for sexual or bodily fusion.

With his early apprehension of the difference between himself and his mother, the little boy tries to comprehend a mysterious and awesome complexity having to do with both sexuality and child-bearing that is, by its very nature, hidden from him. Since his own sexuality (and that of all males, including his father) is external, visible, objective, circumscribed, he cannot comprehend a sexuality whose most formidable powers are concealed. What he cannot know, in his way of knowing, impresses and attracts him—and at the same time frightens him. Comparing his explicit sexuality with his mother's, he finds his own body wanting. Envy and fear conspire to tempt him to exalt the female body and devalue his own, although it will not be long before the same conspiracy will tempt him to exalt his own sexuality at the expense of the female body. Yet even if he tries to settle for the latter, he will never wholly obliterate his feeling of inferiority. Actually, over the course of his life, both temptations will nag him, each suggesting an inequality he fears and yet believes he does not deserve. Envy is no stranger to the human condition, be it male or female. But Freud, because of a misunderstanding of the nature of envy, was wrong, I believe, in his famous formulation of envy between the sexes. It is not literally the body or any specific part of the body that either man or woman envies in the other, in the sense of wishing to possess it as part of his or her physical nature. The primary experience of man before woman is awe, which in turn leads him to envy her mysterious inner complexity. And insofar as women envy men, and I think they do, they do not envy man his penis. Barring the occasional morbidly literal-minded exception, what women envy are the prerogatives and privileges of manhood that they believe or suspect are superior to those of womanhood.

Out of the background I have described, man comes to dread that in his life with women he will be found wanting. The irony is that whatever devices his will or history's will may contrive to protect him from exposure, these devices paradoxically serve to enforce his apprehension. In the light of this predicament it is understandable why the male ego remains vulnerable to all manner of womanly challenge. To the degree that a man regards his inferiority as a constitutional or physical fact, rather than a feeling or apprehension, real talk will elude him, for real talk can exist only between equals. Without it he will fall subject to those domineering and apologetic maneuverings, both institutionalized and personal, with which we are so familiar.

To recapitulate, I have stressed two aspects of man's experience that are obstacles to talk with women. When the habit of disavowal associated with undifferentiated lust is joined to the apprehension of inferiority, forthright talk with a woman can be seen as perhaps the most perilous venture known to man. Still, like other ontological necessities, this venture would be refused only by a fool or madman on the ground that it is not his birthright or will not yield to easy prescription.

Though I suggested earlier that women generally are more disposed to talk than men, this disposition is more questionable and more double-edged than is immediately apparent from the example of the man who cannot respond in kind to the woman's talk about her day. To begin to describe woman's disabilities in the realm of talk, let me return to the matter of man's vulnerability stemming from his habit of disavowal and his feeling of inferiority. While it is true that his vulnerability is, so to speak, of his own making, it nevertheless finds its fruition in his life with women who, in a sense I shall presently describe, choose to exploit this condition rather than engage it honestly and imaginatively. To judge from the current indignation over the male ego, with its weaknesses and excesses, we might be inclined to think we were witnessing a revolutionary new discovery about the nature of man. Not so. Consciously or unconsciously, explicitly or implicitly, women have always known in their bones about male vulnerability. In the failure of real talk between man and woman, she is guilty, too, although her complicity is of a different kind. When real talk is failed, guilt is incurred, in that there is an injury to the human order. When guilt is not acknowledged—and such acknowledgment being indeed painful, it often is not—the guilty one is tempted to seek refuge in contempt for the other. Since both parties can be guilty for the failure of talk, it is easy to see how men and women come to have contempt for each other that is otherwise undeserved.

To return to the nature of woman's complicity, take the issue of man's undifferentiated lust. Are his attentions, in their mixture of blandishment and obfuscation, so convincing that she is blind to the particular demon driving him? Hardly. She is, I believe, as aware of her difference in this regard as he is of his. (This is not to say that women are without raw physical lust. I do believe, however, that its differentiation potential is unlike that of men, making women in the grip of lust both think and behave differently from men.) What she experiences that corresponds to some degree to his undifferentiated lust is an undifferentiated desire to be desired by anyone and everyone. Although lust may be one of its consequences, this desire of hers is not to be confused with his undifferentiated lust, nor does she make this confusion. She knows that he is driven in a way she is not, and it is this perception that gives her an edge in the negotiation that may, she hopes, support the achievement of her own aims, whatever they may be. Gradually, or even suddenly, in a manner that has little to do with who she thinks she is or what she thinks she is entitled to, she realizes she is the object of a consuming hunger that may be complied with, opposed, or manipulated, depending upon her own needs and wishes. In other words, she senses, dimly or not, that her sexuality is not only a source of pleasure for herself as well as procreation, but also a negotiable item in her own endeavors in this world—with the provision that its negotiability will depend on the deceit of non-negotiability. Compared to the deviousness necessary to this enterprise, prostitution is a fairly simpleminded, frank business arrangement in which payment is made for services rendered. At any rate, to the extent this power of negotiation predominates in a woman's dealings, she assists in the sexual objectification of herself that is already the perceptual form of his undifferentiated lust.

Despite her recognition that his physical and verbal overtures are at the mercy of his undifferentiated lust, she may, because she is flattered or excited or encouraged in her own designs, pretend there is a differentiation to his lust that there simply is not. When rather than terminate the negotiation she instead protests, "All you want is my body!" she is being disingenuous, for she knows how eagerly he will, with his capacity for disavowal, lend elaborate support to her pretending. On the other hand, if her response is seemingly more emancipated, such as "Well, why not?," she still dissembles her own experience with its difference from the man's in favor of easy agreement. All this negotiating and dissembling on both parts is ruinous to real talk, since, romantic prejudices notwithstanding, sex, like housework, is to some degree subject to negotiation. Talk is not.

As I have already mentioned, man's recurrent fear that he will be found wanting makes him peculiarly vulnerable to challenge. And that fear, as life proceeds, becomes vague and amorphous in his experience, imposing its painful claim not only on sexual performance itself but also on intellectual, emotional, and even spiritual realms. In his compulsion to allay, rather than contend with, this fear, his gestures will be, in a general way, either self-assertive or self-negating or both. The woman who heeds her imaginative sense of the origin of these gestures will be less inclined to take them literally. But should she fail that heeding, should she see no more than the gestures themselves, she thereby grants herself her own license for self-assertion or self-expression—a license extending to all seasons. If she need fear no real talk from the man that might limit her license, her self-confidence can reach such outrageous proportions that she need no longer attend to any response.

There is a potential background for such an unhappy turn of confidence, having to do with her own relation to her inner mystery that eludes man's objective searchings. Her recognition of essential difference, like the man's, begins in childhood, and with puberty she has intimations of how vast that difference is. For her there is a rush of a hugely complicated intermingling of sexual and procreative possibility, of which she will be periodically reminded for most of her adult life. Though her experience of this possibility will widen and deepen with time, as will her discriminations about her experience, still she will not be a knowledgeable master of her own mystery, in that it will persist as an enigma to her, and, needless to say, to man too. Nevertheless, she will come to appreciate the scope of this enigma. And in this light, man's nature may seem simplicity itself when compared to the unfathomable variety of her own nature. Besides its appearance of simplicity, man's nature can seem almost peripheral to her fulfillment. The danger for her lies in the manner in which she deals with her own enigma: unless she respects what must remain enigmatic she will be tempted to assume more than she knows. This is not to say that she will merely give in to the arrogant assumption of superiority, for that conceit spares no one. Her hazard is worse than that—namely, that she will mistakenly assume for herself a completeness, sufficient unto itself.

As I have said, man's vulnerability stems from his fear of being found wanting. Woman may fear she will be unwanted, but not that her inner parts will be wanting. Her parts, indeed, are Nature's marvel. She is, literally, the embodiment of the miracle of life. What is conferred on her is no less than—and also no more than—the distinction of being Nature's vehicle for the eternal renewal of life. That this distinction is also a privilege, and also a burden, and also a mystery—that she is the vehicle of creation, not the Creator—these realities may blur as she yields to her besetting, in some ways overweening, temptation to experience her own physical nature as somehow primary, inviolable, complete. She is of course vulnerable in many ways, but not in the particular ways I have indicated for man. Her prideful temptation is toward a belief in her completeness—a completeness to which man can make no more than an incidental contribution, reduced to a mere footnote to her existence. Her sense of completeness begins with a misreading of the enigma of her physical possibility, but if she indulges—and is indulged in—this delusion, completeness will soon include far more than physical possibility. Let me be childishly explicit about this extreme situation: completeness is complete, meaning that intervention is not only not needed but will no longer be tolerated. At this stage, man's failure to speak his mind, which has already collaborated in her sense of completeness, is now met by her repudiation of the need for further talk.

Man's sense of inferiority and woman's sense of completeness—both may be regarded as the particular vulnerabilities each brings to the occasion of the possibility of real talk between them, each vulnerability implying in its nature the different ways the two people may betray the occasion. For, in truth, man is not inferior to woman, and woman is not complete.

My concentration on the difficulties of man/woman talk should not be interpreted to mean that man/man and woman/woman talk are not without their own dangers. Although the latter form of talk has not been my subject in this essay, let me say briefly that the commonality of experience between man and man and between woman and woman yields, in the realm of talk, both advantages and disadvantages. Because the talkers have their gender in common, and therefore much of the nature of their experience, they begin with a kind of agreement that facilitates a probing of this shared experience, so that there seems to be almost a shorthand for covering issues quickly and yet incisively. On the other hand, such commonality entails the risk, simply because it is never confronted by a wholly other response, that insofar as the speakers confirm one another, what they confirm are simply previously held presumptions and prejudices.

For man and woman there is no such shorthand, nor should there be. Moreover, where there seems to be a previously agreed-upon shorthand, I would suspect it serves evasion more than convenience. Real talk between a man and a woman has a hard-won, even laborious quality when compared to the easy intimacies between friends of the same sex. If I designate the tempo of man/woman talk as adagio, I certainly do not mean that less is said, for an adagio tempo, though its beat is slow, allows for rapidity and subtlety and a varied texture of expression. The reason for this tempo lies in the fact that for man and woman each is other to the other, no matter how much knowledge they may gain about each other over the course of their relation. And being other to the other, there is an element of startle to the back and forth, of being continually and surprisingly caught off balance. I am of course now talking about talk at its best, in which honesty, equality, and imagination of one's own and the other's reality prevail. Real talk of this order, I must insist, is no permanent state of bliss: rather does it come and go, scrutiny of its wonders being the surest way to dispel it. But even without such scrutiny it falls back or withers into meaninglessness, so that the ground must be won and rewon. Early in a relation both sex and talk give powerful help to the restoration of meaning when it has been lost. But as the relation endures and the years pass, the balance between sex and talk shifts. Sex may still offer brief reconciliation, but unless meaning is restored through talk as well, the sexual consolation will become increasingly barren, even yielding to bitterness and despair. Language is now of the esssence, and real talk assumes a heavier obligation. The words that broke through the last impasse and the impasse before that linger in memory and will no longer serve. Verbal habits have become familiar, and expressions that once carried deep personal meaning repeated use has rendered empty. What is needed now is not mere variety or novelty, but a precision of speech that can be inspired only by a more vigorous, more courageous imagination.

Toward the beginning of this essay I suggested that in real talk men and women could confirm and be confirmed not only as particular human beings, but as the particular man or woman each was meant to be. But this is a rather highflown way of putting the matter, so let me conclude in a more modest fashion that is at the same time more appropriate to my calling. Real talk between a man and a woman offers the supreme privilege of keeping the other sane and being kept sane by the other. As we look about us, it is obvious this privilege is not often fulfilled, and I suspect this has always been true. Nor is it the only way of staying sane. But it will remain, I believe, one of our best hopes.

11

On Jealousy

TO SEE ONE'S MATE across a crowded room, doing something else, with someone else, is to be forcibly reminded of the separateness of our lives, however persuasive may be the imagery of connection and joined fates when we are together. If one's own presence or even existence seems merely inessential to the activity we see our mate engaged in, the sense of separation may be easy to bear. If, however, we experience a suspicion that our presence or existence would be inconvenient, even offensive, to the occasion, our reaction is darker, full of dread.

Jealousy is a condition which Webster defines as that state of mind arising from the suspicion, apprehension, or knowledge of the unfaithfulness of a wife, husband, or lover; or the fear or actuality of being supplanted in the affections of another. At its most unambiguous jealousy is a reaction to a real displacement in affection or an

This chapter originally appeared in *Commentary*, October 1973.

unmistakable infidelity committed by one's mate. *A* reaction or *the* reaction Webster doesn't make clear. My own feeling is that jealousy is *a* reaction, one of several possibilities, although certainly the most common, the most expected, among them. I will have something to say about other responses a little later.

For the moment let us consider the more ambiguous situation in which jealousy arises from a suspicion of infidelity or displacement or—to come closer to our most ordinary experience—from an *intimation* of something even more general: let us call it betrayal. One is compelled, say, to witness from afar or to remember or to imagine (hint and rumor operate here) some action or inclination on the part of one's mate that is disturbing enough to cause a strong reaction and a marked change of course in relation to the world. One acknowledges (to oneself) that reaction as a flurry of jealousy, without identifying the behavior of one's mate as constituting actual displacement or infidelity. The matter of unfaithfulness cannot be restricted to literal sexual infidelity. Perhaps an habitually jealous person will make a rapid extrapolation to a clandestine sexual union, actual or imminent, but for most of us, unfaithfulness, or what is regarded as unfaithfulness, need not be writ large for it to be constitutive, on the one hand, of our mate's availability to intimacy with others, and, on the other hand, of our loss of exclusive claim to such intimacy.

It should be noted that prior to the moment of the onset of jealousy the matter of exclusiveness was not active in our consciousness, although in retrospect we might assert it was assumed or taken for granted. This retrospective rumination belongs to the phenomenology of jealousy. "If I have lost what I had, what was it I had?" and "If I am now a different person, how am I different?" And further, "If it is jealousy I am feeling, why can't I say so and have done?" Why indeed? Yet one seldom does. One raises the issue, but furtively, pretending not to. One interrogates, but affects whatever tone one can command—annoyance, indifference, umbrage, solicitude—to deny one's predicament. And one's mate, in response, offers equal dissembling. Lying answers to lying questions. Jealousy is concealed in the question, evasion in the response. Those with long experience in parrying the jealous intrusions of mate (or parent) soon acquire the habit of disowning or even disparaging any affectionate tie. This is to say that both jealousy and the response to jealousy proceed along paths of indirection.

Why is this so? Why must jealousy pretend to be other than it is? The provocation may be slight or massive, but every jealous person knows jealousy to be a brutally degrading experience and resists with all his might revealing the extent of his degradation. (Even a confession of jealousy, when other strategies seem inappropriate, may be used in an attempt to repudiate the state itself.) Obviously pride makes humiliating the admission of all manner of human weakness—lying, conceit, malice, etc.; but such admissions contain the possibility that the confessor will stay larger than his sin. Such comforting contrast between himself and his jealousy is beyond the reach of the jealous person for, subjectively at least, he *is* his malady: to describe his jealousy is to illuminate his reduction as a human being.

In general I believe that jealousy, when it is not used to mean either envy or zeal—these are possible uses of the word, but since each has its own serviceable synonym neither will be considered here—jealousy, that portion of meaning without synonym, is experienced in essentially similar fashion by men and women alike. Essentially, but not entirely. There are, I suspect, innate differences. Certainly there are cultural ones.

In terms of history and tradition women's jealousy has been given very little in respect or credence, in contrast to the considerable weight credited to both the suspicions and rages of men. A jealous man is often considered to be asserting his possessive rights; jealousy in a woman is regarded as nearly equivalent to shrewishness, fishwifery. The jealousy of the man has, as well, been given striking sanction within the community. In the time of Moses (as described in Numbers 5) evidence against a woman suspected of infidelity needed to consist of no more than unfounded (the text is explicit on this point) jealous suspicion on the part of her husband for her to be subjected to a trial by ordeal whose result, one must conclude, had to be of dubious fairness to the innocent. On the issue of the legitimacy of the man's jealousy—or of any consequences to him of the wife's proven innocence—the passage is silent.

Throughout history the sexual infidelity of women has been punished far more harshly than that of men, ranging from social ostracism to banishment to death, and including the occasional American Indian practice of amputating the nose of an unfaithful wife.

Traditional assumptions about jealousy are also interesting. A man is cuckolded; a woman is unfortunate. The wife's infidelity strikes at her husband's honor and pride, it humiliates him. The husband's infidelity, however much it hurts his wife, need not humiliate or dishonor her; it reflects upon him rather than her, whereas hers also reflects upon him.

In short, history would seem to be telling us that a man has much more to lose from his mate's infidelity than a woman has, and that his vulnerability must be well protected by law and custom. Whether there is any truth to this or not, traditional practice has clearly been most unfair to women. However, I doubt if history's legitimation of male jealousy has had either a consoling or an improving influence upon men. If virtue is its own reward, jealousy is its own punishment, though not, frequently, its only one.

But is there, we must now ask, any truth reflected in or represented by the cruel practices and assumptions of history? Do male and female jealousy differ in any important way? My impression is that they do, and I would propose that the difference is this: while men and women alike fear both displacement of a mate's affection and his or her sexual infidelity, a woman is more apt to conceive of the larger picture and fear displacement; a man is more likely to center his attention on the sexual fact. For her the sexual betrayal is emblematic; it refers to the larger replacement. For him the sexual betrayal is constitutive; it represents the larger replacement, at the same time that it stands for itself.

We may better understand the difference of emphasis upon sexual jealousy if we consider briefly the difference between the male and female experience of sex. The act of sex, for the male, is a contained event. Its onset of desire, or need, or even compelling urgency, its crescendo of development and its final climax and rapid dénouement, constitute a drama of rise and fall which is literally transforming. Physiologically and psychologically, visibly and spiritually, he is changed. His disinclination to linger at the scene of his transformation, usually felt and expressed as an abrupt urge to turn his attention elsewhere, to rejoin the world, is not a failure of affection on his part or a wishful repudiation of his larger tie to his mate—although it is sometimes so interpreted by her. One of the reasons whores may please a man is that they too, though for reasons more professional than natural, prefer to minimize post-climactic cuddling of either a consoling or a celebrating nature.

Whores aside, a woman's experience of the act of sex is different. For her the event may be entered into with, or arise out of, desire—though seldom the undistractable urgency men sometimes feel—but desire is not necessary to her participation. The conclusion of sex, whether she is technically fulfilled or not, represents no decisive change in her being. The sexual event takes its place along—and derives much of its significance from—the continuity of the life of affection she and her mate lead together. (If it is essentially a life of *dis*affection, that will change the nature and mood and significance of sex, but not its place within continuity.) Because she is not transformed, and particularly when the experience has been satisfying, her inclination, unlike his, is to prolong the dénouement of passion in order specifically to mark the relation of sex to the larger affection they share. There is some sense, too, in which she understands the significance of his transformation, and wishes to console him with her undiminished affection. This is not the moment, however, for him to mark the connection between sex and love. His moment is more likely to occur with the onset of sexual desire and its focusing on his mate.

In sex, then, the woman consumes without being consumed. Jargon has it that a man "takes" a woman, "has" her. In reality it is she who "has" him. She uses him up—renders him, for the moment at least, incapable of any further sexual activity. In this sense (which of course is illusory) she "possesses" him. But sex does not use her up—it does not change her. It may exhaust her, it may fulfill her, it may do both. But neither condition—total fulfillment only dramatizes this difference—makes it impossible for her (potentially) to continue to function sexually, with or without desire. Theoretically, she is still available: he never succeeds in conclusively possessing her.

Now what does all this mean in relation to sexual jealousy? Sex for the man is a drama of conquest and withdrawal. The territory is never won but to be lost again. Since he can never possess her absolutely he must possess her exclusively. For her to act on her potentially continuous availability would be to defile his manhood, his vulnerable and self-renewing manhood, which he entrusts to her discretion. Not only a man's experience of sex but also the nature of his sexual parts induce him to be more literal about sex than a woman, both whose experience and parts lead her in an opposite direction. In terms of betrayal, the ultimate betrayal for him, therefore the focal one, is sexual. For her, sex is less literal, less isolated. She naturally sets it—as she experiences it—in a larger picture. For her the ultimate betrayal is her displacement from that larger picture, her banishment from the *ground* of her life with her mate, which to a considerable degree may constitute her groundedness in the world. (A career, incidentally—an alternative groundedness in the world which does not include her mate—appears to offer some sort of protection against this fear of displacement. However, it is no simple solution. It makes some things easier, some harder. And it guarantees nothing at all to the actual torments of jealousy.) In view of this more diffuse apprehension of displacement on the woman's part, she tends to find more occasion for jealousy that is not specifically sexual than the man does. She may become jealous of his friends, family—even their children, and even his absorption in work, hobbies, TV, etc. This female sort of jealousy is always surprising to the man; it is, by and large, outside his own experience, and catches him unawares.

I do not, let me make plain, think that a man's sexual infidelity is not painful and devastating to his mate. As I said, history has been brutal and unfair. Women do indeed suffer horribly at both actual and suspected sexual betrayal, and very little respect has been granted their anguish. Worse yet, the popular assumptions about the difference of the *response* of men and women to the infidelity of a mate have never given women proper credit. The difference, of course, well documented and long assumed, is that women tend to forgive sexual infidelities, and men don't. It is true enough. So intransigent indeed are men on this point that uncomplicated forgiveness for sexual betrayal from a man immediately arouses suspicion. From a woman it is often accepted with minimal comment or gratitude. The usual explanations offered for this difference contain elements of truth: women care, but not in the same way men do; women care, but they are dependent, what can they do; women care, but they have a powerful urge to preserve the family, the home; and—women are simply and by nature more forgiving than men. In my view, allowing for the portion of accuracy contained in all of the above, the difference of response of men and women to sexual betrayal is essentially to be found in the particular nature of their sexual experience.

Let us return to an investigation of the jealous state as it is experienced by men and women alike. What sets jealousy apart from other possible responses to a real or imagined infidelity—such as rage or grief—is its quality of obsession. (This is not to say that jealousy is not full of both rage and grief, but that rage and grief, and even resignation, each in its own right, need not be obsessive.) Literally, obsession means being oppressed or besieged, as if by an evil spirit. On the one hand, one wills one's obsession to disappear, thereby ensuring its perpetuation. On the other hand, the obsession *is* the condition of the will—simultaneously assertive and impotent, simultaneously frenzied and paralyzed. The role of the will here is crucial. Whether one is alone or with others, whether one rages or is silent, berates one's mate with questions and accusations or refrains from berating one's mate with questions and accusations, the internal drama remains the same: the will has become fixed in a rigid orbit of injury—it spins and burns, but cannot escape its tiny, terrible sphere.

Obsession being so poignantly lonely a condition, the opportunity to engage one's mate, either beseechingly or angrily, on the subject of one's injury is constantly tempting. At least one's obsession can assume the illusion of dialogue—one can talk it over with its object. The obsessed one craftily guards himself [1] in this enterprise, however, for harsh words and excessive demands may drive his mate away, and that deprivation would be the ultimate horror.

In the grip of jealous passion one's state is reduced to a kind of craven non-being. One strives to appear to be the person he was, but he knows that he has lost his autonomy—his sense of self—and has become a slave whose diminished existence is at the mercy of his mate. His human space has shrunk to the narrow boundaries of the jealous melodrama in which he must perform. The world beyond those boundaries seems utterly alien, unreal, and his participation in it—insofar as it is compelled—will strike him not as reassuring and comforting, but hollow and mocking.

Nor can he bear for the object of his jealousy to step outside the boundaries of this melodrama. He may tell himself that it is his suspicion of possible or further infidelity that requires his mate to be visibly and audibly within reach (phones are crucial, the mails will no longer serve). But the fact is that his tie to his oppressor has become so tortured and so fragile that it must depend on the most literal sensory validation. Once the mate goes through the door, moves outside the allotted space, the jealous one dies; the mate holds, in the shift and attention of his or her very eye, the power to grant or withhold the permission to be. Small wonder that jealousy contains so striking a portion of anger. In his desperate need to prove the unprovable—namely affection, both his own and his

1. The language of sexual neutrality is impossible to sustain gracefully beyond a certain point. I will therefore generally be using the masculine pronoun, but I ask the reader to bear in mind that I am speaking in this section—and, except when otherwise explicitly indicated, throughout this essay—of jealousy as experienced by men and women alike.

mate's—he wills what cannot be willed, demanding an enactment of relation that can only be grotesque in its deceits and disgusts. Although the issue of "love" may be raised again and again as he implores and interrogates and she demonstrates and defends, it must be pointed out that neither one at this moment is morally qualified to use the term at all. His is a despairing dilemma; he is driven to prove an infidelity he cannot tolerate and is unable to prove a fidelity he so obsessively requires. No gesture of hers is reassuring enough, and, insofar as he perceives the inevitably forced and willed nature of her performance (it is very rare that a fit of jealousy, whatever the provocation, is met with an outpouring of love from a guileless heart), every gesture of hers confirms his suspicions. In this way jealousy is self-confirming; it breeds itself. And when evidence is offered, as it often is, that his jealousy is inappropriate, uncalled for—and unquestionably damaging to the relationship—does he subside, satisfied? Does he abandon his jealousy willingly and with relief? Far from it. For one thing, evidence, like for instance, is not proof. More importantly, jealousy is not only passionate but imperious; it treasures its own being, and in a sense forces its host to do so too. In no simple way (such as: OK, I was wrong all along) will this state of torment and anguish give up its claims or its existence.

Not even the idea of the harm he is *causing* will sober someone in a jealous fury. In fact, such a notion will more likely enrage than restrain him. The experience of jealousy always includes so strong a conviction of *being injured* that it is most unusual for the jealous person to be able to consider the injury his jealousy causes to others. For this reason, the real guilt that is jealousy's inevitable consequence is seldom acknowledged by a jealous person; it is obliterated by his overriding absorption in his own injury.

The role of the rival (or suspected rival) has some importance in jealousy. If he or she is unknown or barely known, one's speculations as to his or her nature will cover a large range of qualities, as one futilely searches for just that combination that will reduce the jealous imperative. In point of fact there is no ideal rival, one that makes jealousy an easy condition to bear. If he or she is believed to be an enormously superior, attractive creature, envy and bitter self-doubt are joined to jealousy. On the other hand, if one regards the rival as a trivial, inferior person, one's pain is not much assuaged, for this makes the involvement of one's mate all the more dismaying, shocking. However one conceives the rival, the illusion persists that a different sort of rival would ease the situation. By and large this is not true.

However much or little is known about the rival, the jealous person makes an attempt to see that rival as the seducer, the initiator of whatever has taken or is taking place—from mild flirtation to actual betrayal—between him or her and the mate. This view of the mate as victim offers the possibility of reconciliation, even forgiveness, or, more bleakly, perhaps merely rationalizes one's jealous efforts to possess again what has been lost. Most importantly this interpretation permits the jealous one to dismiss from his mind the maddening image of his mate freely undertaking—even initiating—an unfaithful act.

An unknown rival is distressing enough; when the rival is—or has been—the jealous one's friend, good friend, even best friend (this is not so rare as one would like to believe), the situation turns drastic. In the case of an actual infidelity between the mate and the friend, this double betrayal, the shattering of the worlds of both love and friendship, constitutes a virtually intolerable burden of demoralization and pain. (The messy complexity of motives in these situations of multiple betrayal sometimes seems to suggest that jealousy may have been as much a cause as a consequence of the betrayal.) Again one tries to fix the blame on one or the other—most likely on the friend—in order to salvage something of the remaining relation. However, one is also tempted and crazed by visions of revenge. With so much of the world now lying in pieces, one yearns to make the destruction absolute—if only one could somehow be sure, oneself, of surviving, to witness the desolation.

As the jealous person's obsession grows, he finds himself seized by visual reenactments of his injury, usually fragmentary. They may involve plots of revenge against his rival, and these may be spun out endlessly. Or the fragment may fasten wrathfully on the intrigue and deceits that led to the bedding down. But as he approaches the act itself, he will almost physically interrupt the vision because it seems too dreadful to endure. At this point his very jealousy convinces him, however, that he must master his dread and view the literal sexual possession in its entirety before there can be any turning back—or turning away. We can see the obsessional workings of jealousy in this conviction because it represents such a defeat of imagination, one of whose functions is to guide the movements of one's attention. The imagination *not* to imagine is an important power of intelligence, disabled here by the seeming necessities of obsession. In his repeated interrogations of his mate he may press for sexual details that will do justice to the movie in his head that lies at the center of his jealousy and that he cannot bring himself to witness. What he cannot bear is opposition, whether it be silence or a remark that questions the validity of the interrogation itself. Should she ask, "What difference do the details make?" he will understand her question as evasion, for he knows it is precisely such details that *do* matter and have become the measure of his fate. And yet from time to time there will be the flickering realization that there can be no end to his craving for such details, for they will never yield the certainty he believes he requires. Still, any particulars she offers, out of anger or compliance, will be seized upon and elaborated in his home movie, so that his obsession assaults him with sexual scenes he would avoid if he could.

Though this home movie remains necessarily incomplete, its impulse is essentially cinematic in form (no still shots will do) and pornographic in content, having some resemblance to commercial pornographic films that portray, with a minimum of artifice, all the sexual posturings within reach of human bodies.

I suspect that pornographic movies of the solitary, secret, home variety long preceded the commercial venture. Admittedly lust is the more common author of pornography, but jealousy has not been given sufficient credit. Can a distinction be made between these two states of mind on the basis of the images they inspire? Both may be obsessive, in that their presence causes other human considerations to evaporate. The difference that immediately springs to mind is that the home movie whose author is jealousy has an unhappy ending, in that possession belongs to another, while lust's movie allows its audience the happy illusion of sexual possession. Though the difference is critical, the fact remains that the erotic materials of both movies are similar. I have labored the comparison in order to stress a paradoxical point about one's jealous imaginings: namely, that in the midst of his painful movie sequence, anguished though he be, he may find himself sexually aroused by this objective view of his mate as naked actress. His arousal is, of course, reinforced by the possessiveness of jealousy, under whose simplifying, crudifying provenance such need for possession turns literally physical. Sexual union now offers his main illusion, however brief, that he can possess his mate. These paradoxical surges of desire, in the midst of reduction and alienation, may be misconceived by either partner or both as a transcendent return to being-in-love and an escape from jealousy's claims. Because of this misconception, jealousy has brought about marriages that were ill-advised, and prevented the dissolution of relationships in which meaning had altogether failed.

Let me return again to the similarity between the jealous home movie and the commercial pornographic movie in order to ask what the latter offers the jealous man. Obviously for most men it offers erotic excitement in the guise of vicarious involvement with the sexual minglings of strangers, seeming to serve their lustful inclinations, even though the excitement be later discharged with their mates. But I have noticed that those who return again and again to hard-core pornography seem to be straining for a distance from the subject matter that places them beyond such inclinations, allowing them the critical detachment, say, of the ideal sex therapist or movie critic. Similarly, the jealous man hopes that immersion in the materials of his betrayal will lead to a mastery of its images, permitting him relief from his enslavement. His aim is to trivialize the details through repeated viewings.

So far as jealousy is concerned, sexual emancipation and the decline of censorship have proved to be a mixed blessing. It was inevitable, I think, that there should be a proliferation of experiments with "open marriage," swinging, wife-swapping, etc., all ideologized in the name of freedom from old-fashioned monogamous constraints. From this point of view, jealousy is an inherited encumbrance rather than an unpleasant given in human affairs. The proposed solution would seem to be a "hair of the dog" prescription: if the fear or knowledge of infidelity can bring such a painful state as jealousy, then infidelity must be legitimated and embraced in such a way as to undo the jealous impulse. By way of the same regimen of immersion, trivialization, and—it is hoped—mastery that encourages attendance at home or commercial pornographic movies, swingers, swappers, and partners in open marriage would seem to be aiming at a similar state of desensitization: the achievement of an attitude toward, and practice of, sex that would combine total freedom with total invulnerability. It seems unlikely to me that such an ancient fox as jealousy will be so simple-mindedly outwitted. I suspect that the new permissiveness offers him a vastly enlarged arena for his operations. If the new generation is serious about its ambitions in relation to sex and serenity of mind, it may be forced to reinvent fidelity.

There is another affliction of passion which may be seen as a companion obsession to jealousy; that is the state called being-in-love. Unlike jealousy, about which, to my mind, there is really nothing redeeming to be said, being-in-love does have pleasures, even virtues, which can survive its transformation into some more reasonable relation. But the state of being-in-love itself is strikingly similar to jealousy. The imperative of total possession rules them both. In being-in-love each appropriates the other's history as painlessly as possible ("I want to know everything about you, but be careful with the details"), at the same time that they rush to develop their own history and mutuality together, metaphorically fortified by *their* restaurant, song, drink, movie, first fight, and so on. Not only do they merge their lives, loyalties, passions, but their beliefs, attitudes, and opinions must match as well. Any hint of imperfection in this fusion ("But you said you *did* think Woody Allen was America's most important comedian") causes crisis. The smallest real difference of opinion (compromise and accommodation are constant in this enterprise, so that dishonesty is never more than a sentence or two away) stands for the impossibility and unreality of the ideal of total mutual possession, and thus provokes jealousy, even in the absence of any rival whatsoever.

There is a blasphemous character to this endeavor, in which each singles the other out as an object of worship. To do this, and to be "worthy" of it, each implicitly yields—or tries to yield—up his separate existence to the exalted unity. He abandons—or tries to abandon—or tries to appear to abandon—his independence of spirit as though it were a false idol. Of course it doesn't work. No matter how willing, one can never totally possess or be totally possessed by another. But before disillusionment sets in, and while the inevitable interruptions of jealousy are serving, paradoxically, both to cripple and to keep feverishly alive, being-in-love is often experienced as a miraculous rebirth, a time of exhilaration, inspiration, and ready transcendence, not to mention overstatement. Like jealousy, and all obsessions, it is addictive, requiring larger and larger doses of itself to satisfy the terms of its illusions.

Unlike jealousy, being-in-love can have a happy ending—happy continuing might be more accurate. The only happy ending to jealousy is, for whatever reason, its disappearance, experienced usually as something closer to relief, leaving, as it must, so much damage and unhappiness in its wake.

But it is possible for two people and their relation to survive being-in-love. With enough appetite for each other's company and enough hope in the possibilities for commonality that this life affords, they may go on to find a way of being together that includes being apart, a way that combines passionate affection with the reality of distance. A way that is also uncertain, vulnerable, and ever open to the contaminations of jealousy. There is no happy ending. But there is happy getting on with it.

What can be said about the ground out of which jealousy springs? In his essay on the subject, Freud thought jealousy to be "one of those affective states, like grief, that may be described as normal." Moreover, he said, "if anyone appears to be without it, the inference is justified that it has undergone severe repression and consequently plays all the greater part in his unconscious mental life." Of "normal jealousy," having to do with the pain of the thought of losing the love object, he at first noted there was little to be said from the analtyic point of view. But a few sentences later he located its origins in the Oedipus complex of "the first sexual period." In other words, adult jealousy, of the "normal or competitive" variety, was due to the childish jealousy of one's early sexual stirrings. There is no question that the latter precedes the former. But whether one is the cause of the other or is merely an early manifestation of the normal human inclination to jealousy is harder to say. What I have labeled as "sexual jealousy," Freud calls "projected" jealousy, being "derived in both men and women from their own actual unfaithfulness in real life or from impulses toward it which have succumbed to repression." Because fidelity, "especially that degree required in marriage, is only maintained in the face of continual temptation," asserts Freud, anyone who denies such temptations will look for "absolution of conscience" by making his partner responsible. Thus, "the person can justify himself . . . that the other is probably not much better than he is himself."

Freud must be admired for discerning that sexual or projected jealousy represents an illegitimate way of absolving oneself of bad faith, whether because of actual sexual infidelity or merely impulses toward infidelity that have been disowned or repressed. My criticism of Freud's view of jealousy has nothing to do with his clinical observation, which, in my experience, has unmistakable though partial truth; rather it is that his theory is too circumscribed, thus failing to account for the ground out of which jealousy erupts, often surprisingly, with little or no provocation. To consider this issue, I must now discuss the relation between jealousy and promiscuity.

I use promiscuity here in its original meaning, namely an "indiscriminate mingling"—primarily in one's dealings with others, of course, but also in relation to ideas, emotions, morals, etc. Thus, sexual infidelity would be but an instance of promiscuity. Though my emphasis here will be the experience of a developing promiscuity, flagrant examples of the full-blown variety in adult life are easily come by, examples in which the issue of promiscuity is unmistakable to the outsider. Particularly in public life do we see people whose necessity to join with their audience leads them to forget private doubts and settle on easy and optimistic pieties (including those labeled "The Tragic View of Life") which they buttress with indiscriminate bits and pieces of corroboration from anywhere and everywhere. But in their will to win quick admiration they often misjudge their hearers, or at least those among them whose convictions oppose such intellectual vulgarity. To the latter it may seem that promiscuity, having become a way of life, has resulted in a coarsening of previous discriminative powers, suggesting not that the promiscuous one has forgotten such possibilities, but rather that he is no longer capable of them. Using a sexual metaphor, we say he whores, though we may have trouble deciding whether he whores out of temporary necessity or out of acquired, hardened disposition. If we favor consistency, we may infer sexual promiscuity as well, identifying him as a seducer. This is frequently true, but not necessarily, for sexual fidelity or at least its appearances may be preserved either out of fear or some lingering sense of its value in the midst of a prevailing promiscuity.

Because we focus on the seductive overtures of these public figures we may fail to note the jealousy that inevitably accompanies their efforts. Should their audience become restless, should they yawn or doodle or whisper to each other, it is jealousy that prods these figures to ever more strenuous exertions to recapture their audience's devotion. It is as though, figuratively speaking, they were willing to undress, if nakedness would restore the attention they hunger for. But, as I have mentioned above, we will be struck more by the increasing vulgarity of their message than by the jealousy that drives them. Of course, winning one portion of the audience will antagonize another portion, bringing new jealousy in its wake. As a result they are driven to scatter their overtures, as though they would be everything to everyone—which in itself is a serviceable definition of promiscuity.

Do not be misled by my example, chosen only for its cartoon-like clarity. By no means do I mean it to acquit you and me of such ignoble strivings. In varying degree we have all, from an early age, had to confront promiscuity, both in inclination and actuality, our own and that of others.

As the child grows gradually aware of the absolute separateness of his being from all other beings in the world, he discovers that this condition offers both pleasure and terror. On the one hand he cherishes his separate, individual, regal self, and on the other he yearns for the loneliness of his autonomy to be relieved by relation with others. The manner in which he seeks and finds such relief, and the manner in which those about him not only answer his overtures but also turn to him for their own consolation, will have considerable bearing on his interpretation of his (and their) condition—and his handling of it.

To the extent that he must—or believes that he must—toy with his own presentation of himself to others to earn the attention and approval he craves—and to the extent that he senses that those others are also busy with their own adjustments and accommodations, he will experience a queer, unnamable apprehension in regard to his worldly enterprise. This apprehension will, of course, proceed from, and present itself as, sensations of inadequacy, unacceptability, and so on, requiring an habitual dissembling on his part to render himself lovable. This uneasy state is both painful and corrupting, the pain and the corruption, it is commonly believed, being consequences of his low self-esteem and fear of others' indifference or rejection, which in turn causes him to project himself falsely. It is more likely, I think, that once this habit begins to harden the crucial source of his pain *is* his corruption. In his constant inability, or unwillingness, to tell the truth about who he is, he knows himself in his heart to be faking. If he suspects that those about him harbor a similar discrepancy between what they think and mean and what they say and do, this will offer not so much consolation as confirmation of his developing cynicism in regard to the life of affection, indeed in regard to life in general. As everything that can be is bought and sold, and the rest hidden, he may alternate between frantic activity in the marketplace and a savage repudiation of relational bargains altogether, this repudiation requiring of course its own sort of willing and dissembling. And as he performs some version of himself he hopes will win him the regard, the congratulation that is so essential to his very existence, he will attempt to persuade his audience of the absolute authenticity of his behavior—that is, much of his effort will be directed at denying the split that has prompted this impersonation. But the person to whom these efforts are principally addressed is himself.

Not merely is he ashamed of having and harboring a secret, unlovely, illegitimate self. The spiritual burden of not appearing as the person he "is," or not "being" the person he appears to be—the extended and deliberate confusion of seeming and being—is by and large intolerable if held in direct view. If the integrity he craves is to be denied him, at least he will have its illusion. If he cannot (he believes) publicize his private self, adjust his public gestures to conform with his private thoughts and feelings, then he will command his private self to conform to the public one; he will beguile his judgment into believing that what he says and does is what he thinks and means. What this endeavor will do to his relation to truth may easily be imagined. Truth will be ever on his mind and never in his speech. He can neither fulfill it nor abandon it, but must always be striving for some irreproachable imitation.

Telling the truth is, to be sure, no simple thing. Sometimes it is uncalled for; often it is hard. But *telling* it is by no means always the most difficult aspect of truth. That may be *knowing* it. Ordinary people—you and I—not in the grip of an inner separation such as I have been describing often encounter uncertainty and confusion in their efforts to reveal by word and gesture what they do actually think and feel. They, too, cherish their integrity, and tend to believe that what they say, by virtue of their saying it, does indeed accurately represent them. Often it is only later, when the moment has passed, that one realizes, gradually and grudgingly, that, for one reason or another, caught up in the occasion, one falsified. One spoke when silence would have been truer; one was silent when he should have spoken. One spoke, and aimed at the right meaning, but used words of the wrong color. And so on. Most of us do not habitually betray ourselves—or others—with sweeping deceits. We just crowd a little here and there, we make ourselves a bit more comfortable than our good sense or loyalties should permit, we take refuge in discretion—or we overrule an appropriate discretion in favor of some fleeting self-indulgence justified as "straight-talk" or, indeed, "truthfulness." One way and another we compromise in tiny steps until, we come to realize—perhaps with a shock—we are standing on alien ground. To make such discoveries, and to retrace our steps, it is essential not to be willfully caught up in sustaining an illusion of truth-telling. It is hard enough without it.

As for the child already steeped in separation and deception—or the adult who was once that child—what will be the condition of his belief in his ability not merely to tell (or not to tell) but to know the truth? It will have been more or less forfeited. The aim of his will is the invention of a successful illusion. The actual ground he is standing on, having disappeared from his words, will also have passed from his attention. There are some things it is impossible both to do and at the same time to impersonate oneself doing. Speaking truthfully is one of them.

Whatever imagined unloveliness originally drove him into habitual deception in his relations with others becomes, in his own eyes, explicit and institutionalized, so to speak, by the habitual deception itself. How much more now, in the face of his recurring sensations of self-disgust, he must seek the reassuring approval of others. His own low self-regard is now diabolically joined to a craven dependence on the inflated regard of his fellows. It is as though he abandons his responsibility to assess his own standing in the world, capering madly before all those omnipotent others who have become his collaborators, his judges, and the keepers of his fate. His very reliance upon "regard" itself, to justify his existence, indicates the reduction of his being: he has lost that ground upon which he might stand to reveal—with speech or silence, action or withdrawal—who and what he is, according to his own counsel. With that loss of ground comes a pervasive suspicion of the legitimacy of his entire career in the world, indeed of his life. He has lost moral authority with himself, a condition he will encounter again and again, along with his sense of illegitimacy and his addiction to his "image" and his impersonation of "truth-telling"—in the inevitable jealousies that lie in store for a life lived on these terms.

Puberty, adolescence, and the beginnings of adult sexuality bring a new dimension to the problem of jealousy. In the midst of an ongoing maturation of physical and intellectual powers that enhance the capacity for separateness, self-sufficiency, and particularly the discriminations requiring distance for their fruition, the burst of sexuality provides new urgencies for union that seriously challenge the developing selfhood. The period is promiscuous in the original meaning of the term, it being a time when young people band together or hang around with each other on almost any pretext. Moreover, as I wrote in chapter 10, the undifferentiated lust that overwhelms the young man's consciousness is promiscuous in the sexual sense, in that it presses for discharge anywhere and everywhere, even in solitude with imaginary lovers. And the combination of lust and undifferentiated desire-to-be-desired that overcomes the young woman is also promiscuous in its own way. Each sexuality invites its own dissembling for its fulfillment, whether in the form of actual deceits or romantic and idealistic fictions. The well-known turbulence of the period is to be found in the alternation between infatuation and disillusionment, bad faith being the common experience at either pole.

I have been describing the nature and development of what I call the *ground of jealousy;* that is, those hardened assumptions about oneself and the materials of one's life (not constituting but underlying and determining thoughts and attitudes and actions) which together produce a habit of promiscuity—a habit characterized by deceit, cynicism, and bad faith. Out of this ground, with its racking insufficiency of self and harsh dependence on the excessive regard of others—no degree of excess ever being truly adequate—springs again and again the inescapable jealousy that follows the failure of one person after another to fulfill the impossible demand: make me whole.

This is the ground of habitual jealousy, and, obviously, I have pictured it at its most extreme. One may be rooted here for life; one may get free only to be drawn back from time to time; one may be no native, and yet pass this way in periods of duress. Some few have perhaps never sniffed this air at all. But impulses toward promiscuity (and I am still using the word in its largest sense) are probably not so utterly alien to most of us that we have not strayed close to this ground at one time or another, and borne the painful consequences.

Freud's notion of *projection* postulates an explicit, virtually mechanical displacement of an act or impulse from one person onto another. In my view such projection is but one representation—among many—of the connection between promiscuity and jealousy. One whose life is governed by a prevailing promiscuousness need not harbor the slightest inclination toward sexual infidelity to his mate to be seized with a tormenting jealousy in regard to her sexual conduct (which may be entirely above reproach). The self-doubt and self-disgust that are both antecedent and consequent to his promiscuity counsel him that of all creatures he is most unfortunate; all others have those precious spiritual commodities —integrity, independence, self-reliance, peace—he alone lacks. And at the same time the cynicism which also has a cause-and-effect relation to his promiscuity promises him that all hearts are ruled as his is: of that of which he is capable, all are capable. Cynicism, like its offspring, sentimentality, is a great leveler.

Needless to say, an occasional encounter with jealousy (provoked or not) is no clear indication of rotten moral fiber. (There are people with utterly destroyed moral fibers who are never jealous—but that is a curious condition outside the scope of this essay). It is habitual jealousy that suggests the issue of promiscuity.

There is another perhaps peculiar aspect to habitual jealousy. An habitually jealous person is someone who lives with constant dishonesty. This dishonesty leads him into unlikely relationships. Lacking the courage or clarity to identify their essential meaninglessness and wrongness for his life, he may resort to something easy and known: that is, he may deliberately expose himself to jealousy, as a way of animating a dead thing, and postponing his inevitable repudiation of this relation. This is to say that habitual jealousy may often mask not only dishonesty, but also an essential failure of moral courage.

I have been speaking here as though it made little difference to the genesis and experience of jealousy whether it was provoked or not—whether it would be understood by an outsider to have "sufficient cause." This is both true and not true. Obviously, someone constantly plagued by jealous suspicions in the absence of provocation would seem to be exhibiting that sort of habitual jealousy that I have associated with a promiscuous nature. (Incidentally, I do not think the promiscuity I have been discussing, whatever its range or degree in a given individual, is freely chosen—or freely abandoned. It is a deeply ingrained aspect of character whose origins probably reach far back into early life. One can, I think, in some cases, repudiate it and move beyond it, but that constitutes a significant transformation of character, and will very infrequently be achieved by a tidying up of, say, one's party behavior.)

But what of provoked jealousy, jealousy as a response to a real infidelity or threat of infidelity on the part of one's mate? As I mentioned earlier, jealousy is not the only possible response to such a situation. One may react with grief or rage or even forgiveness without having entertained jealousy at all. Jealousy, as I have described it, is an obsession; it is a state of virtual paralysis in which the will races around a single point. There may be—there usually is—a great deal of activity, but no essential action. In a state of jealousy one exhibits a curious inability to act on his options. Such real action as I have mentioned could take several forms: it might be a considered resolve to terminate the relationship. It might be a heartfelt resolve *not* to terminate the relationship, even though the provocation may have been actual and massive. In this case an essential action would require not only the desire but the capacity to forgive. Another form of essential action might be the illumination of one's own ground—one's own standing in the lists of good faith and fidelity.

Such actions may constitute alternatives to the state of jealousy; but they may also serve to rescue a jealous person from his static affliction. It is interesting that often, when some essential action is undertaken, jealousy tends to diminish, even to disappear. It is no sure thing, however. Maddening though it may be, the truth is that there is no reliable cure for jealousy at all. There is no dependable, deliberate move one can make that will assuredly liberate him from his jealous enslavement.

Since the will *is* distractable, flurries of jealousy may come and go, giving way to this or that distraction, or to reassurance, or to decision—all without disturbing the ground of which I have spoken.

I have said there is no cure. And yet jealousy—habitual jealousy—does sometimes disappear. There is no cure, but people are cured. The ground can be illuminated, and its prisoners can be set free. It is rare, but it is not miraculous.

III

12

Lying on the Couch

IT IS VIRTUALLY IMPOSSIBLE to find references in the psychoanalytic literature to liars or lying, even in the form of studies of the impostor or confidence man. If we are surprised by the psychoanalytic neglect of such a commonplace activity in our ordinary lives as lying, we should remind ourselves that psychoanalysis has, like other professions, had its share of practitioners of the lie. In fact, one of the early stalwarts of psychoanalysis, Wilhelm Stekel, at the time an editor of the *Psychoanalytische Zentralblatt,* was expelled by Freud from the inner circle for precisely this reason. I quote briefly from a letter of Freud to Dr. Stekel, dated January 13, 1924:

> Dear Dr. Stekel:
>
> I acknowledge receipt of your letter of December 31, 1923, and thank you for your good wishes regarding the improvement of my health. But I cannot refrain from contradicting you on a few important points.

This chapter originally appeared in *Salmagundi*, Spring 1975.

> You are mistaken if you think that I hate or have hated you. The facts are that after an initial sympathy . . . I had reason for many years to be annoyed with you while at the same time having to defend you against the aversion of everyone around me, and that I broke with you after *you had deceived me on a certain occasion in the most heinous manner*. . . . I lost confidence in you at that time and since then you have not provided me with any experience that would help me to regain it.
>
> I also contradict your often repeated assertion that you were rejected by me on account of scientific differences. This sounds quite good in public, but it doesn't correspond to the truth. It was exclusively your personal qualities—usually described as character and behavior—which made collaboration with you impossible for my friends and myself. Since you most certainly will not change—you don't need to, for nature has endowed you with an unusual degree of self-complacency—our relationship stands no chance of becoming any different from what it has been during the past twelve years.
>
> With good wishes, yours faithfully, Freud.[1]

Without knowing the content of Stekel's alleged deceit, I am rather heartened by Freud's response. He does not turn to psychoanalytic theory to accuse Stekel of trying to murder the father of the movement, as he had with other apostates. Instead he says, in effect, "Wilhelm, you have a rotten character, which, given your self-complacency, is not going to change. So let's call it quits."

We would be mistaken to assume from Freud's outrage that he regarded the human being as essentially truthful. Stekel's deliberate deception caught him off-guard, I imagine, but I am sure that his customary pessimism about the human condition remained unshaken. It was only a few years before that he had written the Reverend Oskar Pfister, "I don't cudgel my brains much about good and evil, but I have not found much 'good' in the average human being. Most of them are in my experience riff-raff, whether they proclaim this or that ethical doctrine or none at all."[2]

While psychoanalysis paid little or no attention to the conven-

1. *The Letters of Sigmund Freud,* ed. Ernst L. Freud (New York: Basic Books, 1960), pp. 347–348. Italics added.

2. *The Life and Works of Sigmund Freud,* ed. Ernest Jones (New York: Basic Books, 1955), 2:457.

tional notion of the deliberate lie, it compounded man's capacity for deceit by adding to his concept of himself what we might call the unconscious lie—the lie that is hidden from our conscious awareness. The early literature on hysteria and repression suggested that the neurotic disorder itself was the result of a disagreeable bit of personal history that had been unconsciously disowned. Treatment required that the truth behind this neurotic deceit be retrieved and exposed to consciousness and responsibility. Since the beginnings of psychoanalysis, there have been several techniques for penetrating the unconscious and retrieving the truth behind the neurotic deceit. At first hypnosis was the method of choice. But then it became apparent that not everyone was subject to hypnosis. Worse yet, whatever the hypnotic state might be—to whatever degree it seemed to resemble the unconscious itself—it soon became clear that this state was not lie-proof: in fact, hypnosis seemed to offer an histrionic setting for lying which enhanced the capacity for deception. Drugs still find favor as lie detectors. Ancient sexual encounters and acts of cowardice or brutality on the battlefield have been vividly reenacted with the stimulation of various drugs, but again, as with hypnosis, dramatic verisimilitude proved to be no guarantee of truth. After hypnosis, the technique of preference in psychoanalysis became free association—and, of course, the interpretation of dreams through free association.

I should now like to offer an example of the hazards of free association from my early days in psychoanalysis when I was first a candidate in training with a psychoanalytic institute. I am compelled to warn you that my initial conception of free association was rather cinematic in character. As nearly as I can recall, I believed this esoteric art was primarily visual—a sort of movie which would be projected on the screen of my inner eyelids after I had closed my eyes. Naturally I considered myself honor-bound to describe to my analyst, without deletion or censorship, the course of this movie, that description being what I considered free association.

On the day I have in mind I had lain down on the couch, closed my eyes, and was waiting for the movie to begin. I saw no more than an image or two when I heard what could only have been a fairly young child practicing the violin in a room nearby. I could close my eyes but not my ears, and my movie stopped altogether as I listened to the kind of screeching that can be obtained only by a novice with a tin ear playing forcefully and out of tune. It struck me as a hopeless situation: the two of us could not pursue our art forms at the same time. Summoning up my courage (after all, I was paying for my time), I asked my analyst if it would be possible for the young man (her son, perhaps?) to do his practicing at a time that didn't coincide with my analytic hour, because I found it impossible to free associate (I did not reveal the idiosyncratic nature of my free association, which I felt was my own business) as long as the young man fiddled. Out of politeness I spared her any critique of his music-making, implying that even Heifetz would have got in my way. "Of course," she said, and moved quickly to the practice room to silence the young violinist.

When she had returned to her easy chair behind the couch, she said, "I didn't realize you were interested in music." Caught completely off guard, I blurted out, "Well, of course, but I wouldn't tell *you* about that!" For a moment I was somewhat amused by my snotty remark, which suggested that while I was willing to recount all manner of sexual indiscretion or infantilism, there remained a few other matters that were too private for psychoanalytic dalliance. However, my amusement was short-lived; in no time I became ashamed of my pretentious nonsense.

As I awaited my movie, violinist now silenced, my eyes shut, not surprisingly my mind turned to early musical experiences of my own, in particular to a painful time when I engaged in a state violin contest, all of us young fiddlers being assigned Sibelius's "Valse Triste," a lugubrious little tune consisting of long sustained mournful tones. Stage fright overcame me, a tremor overtook my bow arm, Valse Triste became Valse Stacatto. My opponent, known throughout the community as my inferior—I was, in fact, considered a shoo-in for first place—my opponent was an easy winner, if for no other reason than his steady bow arm. When I returned home that night my father asked me how the contest had gone. "I lost," I said mournfully. The movie began to go very slowly in this portion of my associations. Looking at my father's face I saw no trace of commiseration on his features. To the contrary, he looked furious, as though my defeat were a cruel reward for all those months of listening to me rehearse my dreadful piece. As I tried, in my analytic hour, to describe the effect of his anger piled cruelly on top of my humiliation over my musical collapse, my eyes filled with tears, my voice choked, and, to my astonishment, I found myself weeping noisily. Ordinarily I do not weep, so my tears seemed fraught with significance. It was as though without warning I had been plunged into a sizeable pocket of grief that I never knew existed. I seemed to have stumbled on a momentous event explaining a parting of the ways between my father and me. As if that were not meaning enough, I thought I now understood, or so I explained to my analyst, why I had chosen not to pursue a musical career. That renunciation, to judge from my tears, represented a far greater loss than I had ever been willing to acknowledge. Afterwards, as I mulled over this tumultuous hour, I thought to myself: What a marvelous thing is this psychoanalysis, that it should provide me with such revelations. I felt illuminated—though saddened—by my new insights and also, I confess, quite exhilirated to be a part of this remarkable profession, whose extraordinary theories I had just verified in my own analytic experience.

My revelatory binge proved to have little staying power, however, giving way shortly to a sobriety in which I was compelled to make certain important revisions. First, there never was a dramatic parting of the ways between my father and me. Our life together was hectic, full of struggle and reconciliation, both rewarding and disagreeable, depending on forces I shall describe in my next novel. Second, my musical talent was modest and I knew it. There was never a serious inclination—leaving my fantasies aside—to make music my profession. When the time came to pack away my violin and get on with my medical studies, I did so with relief, not grief.

If we recall Freud's pessimism about human character in general we may be able better to understand the curious circuitry that connects psychoanalysis to truth and truth-telling to psychoanalysis. The aim of the enterprise is, of course, truth, and an essential rule of the contract is truth-telling. On the other hand, the party who will be doing most of the telling is also deemed inadequate to the task on prima facie grounds: most people lie and deceive themselves a lot anyhow, and even an unusually truthful person wouldn't be able to speak the real truth about himself, since by definition it is hidden from his conscious mind and may be discerned only by, first, outwitting consciousness using the various devices I have mentioned (hypnosis, drugs, free-association, and so on) and, second, subjecting the material thus produced to the analyst for decoding.

While the analyst remains the principal decoder (being the one trained in the basic Freudian lexicon of human nature and therefore the one who owns the decoding manual), the patient is usually encouraged to participate as fully as possible on these archaeological expeditions; true, he is only an amateur, but on the other hand it is *his* dream, *his* free association that is the shard of pot, the splinter of bone. And not only *his* dream, *his* free association, but also *his* therapeutic moment, *his* scene, *his* production at—and of—the moment—and momentousness—of discovery. The revelation of his revelation.

At this point the paradoxical relations between psychoanalysis and truth become even more complex. It is given to human experience not only to contemplate its own nature and existence, but to historicize itself. Of epochs and eras and periods we hear much from chroniclers of public life. But rare is the individual who does not seek, in one way and another, to trace his own trajectory in time and context, to question his own life for shape and direction. Here I am today, sixty-two years beyond my beginning, the embodiment —refugee, survivor, and witness—of the forces that have moved across and within my life. As I survey this pastness that belongs to me alone, this unique tangle of public-private, shared-solitary, accidental-intentional, known-unknown that is my life-so-far, and is in some way accountable for my arrival in this present, and for whatever present-ness is yet to come for me—what I long to find is some particularity, some singularity that makes it not only in fact, but in truth, mine. I search for some continuity that is more than mechanical, for something thematic in the moving parts; I search, above all, for a *point,* a meaning; and the truth is that if there is a meaning *I am* the meaning. (Some lives could, perhaps, be considered useful for making general points, cautionary or exemplary, but not, I trust, yours or mine.) I say "if there is a meaning" not because some lives have meaning and some don't, but because some lives *find* meaning, and some don't. And where is meaning found? It is found in the search for truth—about what one has been and done, about what one is and is doing. And so, it turns out, Freud and I have no disagreement here. The point is to look for truth, and truth is the point. But the crucial question now is: what sort of truth? And what sort will, of course, determine to some extent the means to be employed in finding it—if, indeed, the means have not already determined what sort.

The truth I have in mind to look for is not the sort that, once you find it, you can have it wrapped to go. And once you get it home it fits right in and never wears out. My view of the truth is, first, there is such a thing, and, second, I can approach it only if I keep in mind the impossibility of my ultimately grasping it. As Martin Buber (who, you will notice, was comfortable with terms that do not come easily to us in our calling) wrote: "The truth belongs to God alone. But there is a human truth, namely to be devoted to the truth."

The truth that interests me is problematical, partial, modest—and still breathing. It is not normally dramatic or revelatory, and its attainment depends far more on thinking hard than feeling freely. To put it another way: I think that speaking truthfully is a more fitting ambition than speaking the truth.

It is a different kind of truth that is sought and produced by the devices of psychoanalysis. It is a revelatory truth; it is usually attended by—indeed identified by—considerable emotion, which is often understood to have been repressed or denied and is only now breaking through to the surface—a formulation I find somewhat dubious, quite incompatible with much of anything else we know about emotion, which is hard to conceive of as something not-present. In any case, the truths yielded up by these means are remarkable for their clarity, their completeness, their shapeliness, so to speak. Revelation tends to have a certain loveliness of form that is quite unrelated to—and in fact may be quite in defiance of—what is revealed. "I see it now: I am a monster of self-absorption," may not seem especially self-congratulatory, but it is the sort of pronouncement that yields genuine satisfactions to its pronouncer, and these satisfactions are essentially esthetic in character.

There is, in my view (Keats to the contrary notwithstanding), no natural or inevitable affinity between truth and beauty; or, to put it another way, one would do well to cultivate an alert suspicion of any such claimed connection. I do not mean to say, of course, that this probable incompatibility of art and life pertains to art—only to life. In the pursuit of meaning in one's own life there is inevitably a temptation to estheticize not only one's experiences but one's conclusions as well, in both cases not so much, or so specifically, beautifying what was ugly (in fact, just as often uglifying what was difficult or confused or uncertain) as giving more deliberate and dramatic form to occasions and relations than they merited, or could, without falsification, accept. Everyone has, I imagine, experienced this temptation, and the difficulties it produces, in trying to present himself (to "tell it all") to a highly prized new friend. He swoops and sweeps across the past—and into the present—shaping, structuring, summarizing, condensing—lying, lying. That is not how it was; that is not who he is; not at all.

I had once, in supervision, a young psychoanalytic candidate who was enthralled—as I had been, briefly, those many years ago—by the possibilities of psychoanalytic revelation. His specialty was dream analysis, and he was marvelous—inventive, enthusiastic, colorful—his interpretations were radiant with ingenious plausibility. The only problem was—and this dismayed him—his patient refused to get better. "I'm giving him all this great stuff, every time, and it never makes any difference at all," he complained again and again. Possibly, of course, the patient was merely a pathologically stubborn fellow, or—possibly he just wasn't as subject to revelatory rapture as his therapist. The "Aha!" phenomenon is more compelling for some than for others. And of course for an analysis—or a friendship—or a marriage—to proceed compatibly according to the principles of revelation it does require *two* "Aha!" hounds as its participants.

Revelation is addictive because the pursuit of the esthetic—at the expense of the accurate—is essentially coarsening. Ordinary, fragmentary truth, on a more modest scale, appears by contrast trivial and inadequate—appears, in short, untrue, since it so conspicuously lacks the splendor and intensity of feeling by which one has come to recognize the validity of revelation. In this way one's assumptions about truth fasten on the revelatory, and this habit of discovery quickly becomes addictive.

It is clear by now, I suspect, that I have come to consider the revelatory mode to be a form of lying. It yields something that calls itself the truth but is untrue, is an essential falsification of its subject. But can it be called lying? I think of myself on the couch on that day I have described. I had accepted wholeheartedly the ideology that taught me that such things were possible. My tears, being so unaccustomed, seemed then, as I said, fraught with significance. (It seems to me now that since my tears were so unaccustomed they should have seemed fraught with false significance.) However, everything about my experience on the couch, and the conclusions I drew from my emotions, seemed utterly genuine, without guile, in good faith. Does the fact that a short time later I decided the evidence all pointed a different way mean anything more than that I had originally been mistaken? It could be quibbled over, but I would rather not. The same evidence that persuaded me of the genuineness of my revelation at the time—my tears, my thrilling, painful emotions, the general commotion—I later saw to contain the very clues that might have restored my sanity during the occasion itself, had I grasped them. That performance was not merely uncharacteristic of me, it was alien and unnatural, it was inherently false, and I should have known it. Enthralled already by the ideology that permitted—indeed provoked—these novelties of self-expression, and too naive—or too cowardly—to heed my tiny intimations of doubt about the authenticity of my behavior, I played out the drama of my willed self-deception to the hilt. Self-deception, but deliberate. Also known as lying.

It is interesting to note that just as psychoanalysis, in its origins, was rigidly mechanistic and utterly committed to revelation, so, too, the pop therapeutic spinoffs that surround us today—group encounter in various forms, self-actualization, primal scream, and so on—all share this dependence on the revelatory mode. That is, the paths to salvation take different turns, but salvation itself remains a real and realistic goal. It is represented in psychoanalytic doctrine, of course, as the state of being "completely analyzed." It is some time since I myself gave up my allegiance to that possibility; now I am truly gratified if a patient gets somewhat better.

In these remarks about revelation, let me stress that I do not wish to challenge the possibility of genuine revelation. What I do mean to convey is my distrust of any psychological—or, for that matter, religious or artistic—doctrine in which revelation is obligatory and ideological. What such a doctrine requires is the repeated fancying-up of some item of experience—memory, dream, feeling, what have you—to give it an epistemological razzle-dazzle it couldn't manage on its own; and in the process essentially falsifying it. I spoke earlier of the "paradoxical relations between psychoanalysis and truth." The paradox is this: the entire enterprise of psychoanalysis is predicated on a person's capacity for truth-telling. And yet the very devices and strategies traditionally employed for facilitating his search for truth (designed, as I mentioned, to outwit his *in*capacity for truth-telling), not to mention the tools for deciphering and celebrating the truth, once it is found, all seem to encourage the patient's capacity to embellish, to dramatize—in short, to lie.

When an anthropology or psychology gives insufficient weight to the possibility and reality of lying, the chance is increased for the double lie—one not only lies, but lies about lying, claiming to be speaking the truth—particularly if truth-finding has become an important part of the ideology. The more a given psychology (or any creed) approaches a form of gnosticism, the more vulnerable it is to —indeed the more imperiously it requires—the lie that passes as truth. In gnosticism, I quote from Hans Jonas' book, *The Gnostic Religion:* "knowledge as a mental act is vastly different from the rational cognition of philosophy. On the one hand it is closely bound up with revelatory experience, so that *reception* of the truth either through sacred and secret lore or through inner illumination replaces rational argument and theory (though this extra-rational basis may then provide scope for independent speculation), on the other hand, being concerned with the secrets of salvation, 'knowledge' is not just theoretical information about certain things, but is itself, as a modification of the human condition, charged with performing a function in the bringing about of salvation." [3] That day on my analyst's couch when I had those (false, as it turned out) revelations about music and my father, it was psychoanalytic doctrine, psychoanalytic training, and psychoanalytic technique that led me to a gnostic certainty about my discoveries, a certainty depending far more on faith than fact or reason. Gnostic certainty is, not surprisingly, characterized by contempt for the world, which is regarded as irretrievably evil. It is not difficult to see how agreeably Freud's grim view of man fits into this picture and how inevitably psychoanalysis took on, from the beginning, a gnostic cast. One of the curiosities of gnostic certainty is that it renders the believer so gullible. There are psychoanalysts who will believe absolutely anything a patient tells them about himself provided it is sufficient testimony to his morbid or pathological condition. Having said this, let me also point out that there are all sorts of psychoanalysts in our profession who go about their business without falling into the gnostic temptations that our traditional doctrine provides.

Let me leave the field of dubious revelation and move now to a more ingratiating form of lying. I shall cite an example from the supervisory part of my psychoanalytic training. After finishing my psychiatric residency at St. Elizabeths Hospital in Washington,

3. *The Gnostic Religion* (Boston: Beacon Press, 1958), pp. 34–35.

D.C., I found a position on the staff of Chestnut Lodge Sanitarium in Rockville, Maryland. Under the influence of Frieda Fromm-Reichmann and Harry Stack Sullivan, the young therapists were caught up in the intoxicating possibility of treating schizophrenia with a form of psychoanalytic psychotherapy. I was assigned to treat a thirteen-year-old schizophrenic boy who had been mute for several years. Frieda Fromm-Reichmann was to give me one hour of supervision a week. Under ordinary circumstances I would have felt myself enormously privileged to undergo this apprenticeship with such an estimable psychoanalyst. By ordinary circumstances I mean having a patient who would afford me something to talk about with my supervisor. Five days a week, an hour each day, I sat with the boy. Sometimes I was as mute as he, seeming to emulate the silent psychoanalyst of tradition. At other times I tried to make conversation in one way or another, always unsuccessfully. But whether I free associated or read aloud to him or sulked, our impasse remained absolutely intact. Meanwhile, I would meet once a week with Frieda, talking mostly of the ways in which I had tried to get something going. Frieda's suggestions were not uninteresting. She came up with ways different from my own, correctly charged me with impatience with this boy's silence, and urged me to try to examine my inflated therapeutic ambitions in my own analysis and to try to be more imaginative about the inner life of this young adolescent. All this seemed fair enough. None of Frieda's interpretations of my therapeutic endeavors would qualify as a cheap shot. Still, week after week, regardless of what she suggested and I did or did not do, the boy's silence remained unbroken. I began to dread each hour with my patient and dreaded, even more, each supervisory hour when Frieda and I would try once again to make something of nothing. After a few weeks I was ready to throw in the towel, suggesting that my patient and I were mismatched, that surely he would do better with another therapist. Frieda seemed to regard my wish to be relieved of my assignment as *quitting,* and she turned what I can only call stubborn. I should emphasize that the mythology at this sanitarium included the vainglorious conceit that there was no one so disordered that he could not effectively be reached through psychoanalytic psychotherapy. Stories circulated around the staff dining hall about patients who awakened suddenly from years of catatonic stupor to pass the time of day with the therapist who had devotedly, or perhaps doggedly, appeared each day for the obligatory hour. This was a different sort of gnosticism, more like the martyrs of the East who, year after year, sought God from the isolation of their caves in the desert.

In the foregoing passage I have sought to give something of the background to that particular supervisory hour when Frieda asked me once again to describe what had happened in the previous week, and I said, "To tell you the truth, Frieda, nothing comes to mind. My mind is a blank." My lie was beginning: I was resorting to a stale psychologism in order to avoid saying, once again, "Nothing happened. Five more empty hours." Looking at her expectant face and knowing my own emptiness, I don't know whether I felt sorrier for her or for myself. Both of us were famished in our craving for some sort of therapeutic meaning. "It's peculiar you don't remember anything," she said. "Perhaps your amnesia has something to do with our relation." "Perhaps," I said hopefully. I knew where we were headed: a familiar psychoanalytic shore lay ahead, at that moment seeming to me better than anything I had to offer. I heard Frieda continue, "After all, I am an older woman, no doubt about the same age as your mother." Two more dissimilar human beings I could not imagine; any comparison would be truly absurd. And yet, I found myself thinking, Why not? If it pleases her I can learn to like it, too. "You may have something there, Frieda," I answered. "I do remember times when I had nothing to say to my mother, when I resisted all her entreaties." She nodded thoughtfully and suppressed a sigh of gratitude. I hastened on. "Perhaps it is possible I've fallen into an old pattern . . . ," and so on. We spent a fairly pleasant hour in this manner, handing each other helpfully and courteously across this stretch of time we had to spend together, which, but for this invention, loomed vast and meaningless.

As to whether it was lying, I cannot convict Frieda. She was a true believer. But as for me, I didn't even have revelation for an excuse. Certainly there were times during the hour when I entertained—or tried to entertain—the possibility that all this might contain some sort of truth. But on the whole I have to say that mine was an expedient and deliberate deceit, undertaken to relieve us both, and indulged in with the certainty that it would be received not only graciously but uncritically. In other words, I was bound to get away with it.

Although I am the villain in this story, I have to say that I don't think there is anything about my experience in this instance that is unique, either in psychoanalytic training or practice. Psychoanalysis is backbreaking work, constantly threatened by loss of meaning. Since almost any content, no matter how debased or even untrue, is more bearable than meaninglessness itself, it is both our fortune and our misfortune to have a doctrine that makes itself available to our hunger for content at any cost.

It is not merely in therapy, of course, that meaning fails. Friend and friend, lover and beloved, parent and child, husband and wife, teacher and student—all important relations in this life are subject to meaninglessness from time to time, and vulnerable to invasion by one deceit or another in order to revive meaning that has been lost.

The construction of fictions—of various degrees of falsity—to ease our path occasionally, to repair a faltering relation, is one of the functions of imagination, and we would do well to be in no hurry to despise imagination, upon which we are also dependent, after all, for the construction of nonfictions, which we can hardly do without. That is, imagination is the ally of both lying and truth-telling. It is double edged; it has its uses and abuses, its privileges and penalties. On the one hand it is one of our most powerful tools for knowing reality, and on the other it reverts to its original, idolatrous, form of image-making, which is inevitably destructive of truth.

Let me suggest here that lying may be divided crudely but serviceably into two categories. One category contains those gestures of kindness, convenience, cowardice, courtesy, and so on that are less than candid—sometimes a great deal less—and sometimes appropriate and even admirable, and sometimes inappropriate and deplorable, but which, in their category, share one thing: they somehow leave open-ended their relation to utter truth; that is, they do not identify themselves as deceit, but neither do they pose as truth. In this essay I have concerned myself with lying belonging to the second category.

There is a proverb that goes: "Man is a creature who was given a tongue to speak and words to conceal his thoughts." When I was reminded of that saying, but couldn't recollect it properly, I reconstructed it as: "Man is a creature who was given words with which to think and a tongue to conceal his thoughts." Neither formulation really quite gets to the heart of the matter, which is that man is a creature who can speak truthfully, and who lies. That's not very catchy, but it's closer. We all lie—to ourselves, to others, to the world itself. It is in our nature to lie, but I think I must add that it is also in our nature not to lie.

Lying, however natural to us, is also, in another sense, a treachery against ourselves. A lie is a desecration of the given. And the given is exactly that—that which is given to us to receive by calling it by name. When I suffered my revelation about my father I lost him. He literally disappeared from my imagination and was replaced by a sort of cartoon figure I could barely recognize. I had lost him, and I had to work to get him back. I remember that occasion, too, for when, after considerable struggle, I changed my mind about my revelations, when I repudiated the simplicity of my therapeutic inspirations in favor of the much more complex and difficult realities of my relation with my father, I experienced this change of mind—and heart—with a sense of deep relief—I suppose it could be called joy. I would not have so named it at the time; it didn't seize my consciousness with cries of "I am Joy! An important emotion! Observe how I fill you with feeling!" On the contrary, what I felt then was a profound rightness about my decision, I felt that something significant and truthful had been restored to me; I had retrieved one of my givens.

I seem to have had many harsh things to say in this essay about feeling, and I would like to clarify my position somewhat. There has been a rumor around for a couple of hundred years, probably more, that you only know it's a feeling if it bites you on the nose. Or, to put it differently, there is a decibel scale of emotion (often curiously congruent with the more familiar decibel scale of sound), on which intensity, significance, and validity are all directly proportional, and increase as they climb the scale. Of course I have emotions of this nature, as we all do, but it is usually my inclination to endure rather than to cherish them. There is another sort of feeling that I do cherish—but only in retrospect, or in theory—for it does not single itself out as feeling during the experience to which it belongs. It stays bound to its subject, its content, as it did in my reconciliation—in my own mind—with the reality of my father. I suppose this might be called the feeling of truth-telling.

13

Family Reunion

SOCIAL CRITICS often decry the absence of ritual in our culture, noting that our hunger for ritual leads us to devise all manner of pomp and circumstance, some of it as foolish as a conclave of Shriners in funny hats, some of it as ominous as a troop of Ku Klux Klanners in hoods. In their headlong rush down this inviting ideological path, however, critics may miss altogether the multitude of pompless rituals that engage us in our ordinary lives. Not merely birthdays and holidays, but such simple festivities (or ordeals) as the evening dinner and the favorite TV program may qualify in this category.

By far the most powerful ritual to celebrate the institution of the family is the family reunion, a gathering of interconnected family units, spanning several generations, related by blood or marriage. The occasion may be a wedding, a birth, a death, an anniversary. Or the reunion may arise out of no impulse other than a mutually felt

This chapter originally appeared in *Commentary*, January 1974.

obligation that the clan should gather again. Indeed, many families have regular, scheduled gatherings, the gathering together itself providing both the occasion and the regularity.

Some years ago I attended a reunion on the occasion of my parents' fiftieth wedding anniversary. In my memory the event has unfortunately merged with an 8-mm movie, which I tend to confuse with my actual recollection. Still, in both the movie and my memory a cousin cradles my infant son and sings "Bill Bailey" to him. In the movie he merely mouths the song, but in my mind his voice is true and confident, not very different from what it was when he was a Dartmouth undergraduate home for the holidays with all the newest songs in his repertoire, and I was only a callow thirteen, dazzled by his sophistication and assurance. I remind myself that he has had two coronaries, three marriages. And I see his father's face hidden in his face. His father, my favorite uncle, my father's oldest brother. If I try hard I can even find my father's face somewhere in his features as I am sure he can find my own father in my features. This is but a small instance. Actually there is a profusion of small and large family resemblances to be seen in this gathering. There is something unnerving about all this resemblance, as though we all wore masks. Or as though we were science-fiction creatures all of whom developed from the same intergalactic spore.

In watching my cousin, then a man of about fifty-five, singing to my baby, reminding me of the person he had been, or seemed to both of us to have been, so many years earlier, it crossed my mind to wonder at what he was doing. Had it become his habit, at his age, to dandle infants on his knee and croon hits from the 20's to them? Would he, when he left this party, search out someone else's newborn, in order to repeat the performance? Not likely. The performance, and surely that is exactly what it was, was for me, for him. He was performing a version of himself we both remembered and could endorse as genuine, if not to this time and place, then to some other, then to history. He was identifying himself in the group portrait.

I also appear briefly in this movie (my wife and I took turns behind the camera). I appear in a manner that perhaps tends to justify its existence, for what I behold on the screen is not what I would likely have remembered. I am first glimpsed standing in the corner of the patio chatting with a young man, my nephew. My head is slightly inclined toward him as he speaks; I am looking noticeably thoughtful and attentive. Later, the party and the camera move into the house, and I may be seen sitting near my mother as she opens and exclaims and weeps over her anniversary gifts. Despite the extremely dim light of this indoor scene, it is clear that I am still looking noticeably thoughtful and attentive.

Prodded by this pictorial record, I have to acknowledge that a portion of my consciousness on that occasion was occupied with how I appeared, not merely to my nephew, or my mother, or the camera, but to the entire company. I was not dissembling—exactly. I was then and am now a thoughtful and attentive person, as befits my age, profession, and character. On the other hand, I wasn't breezing through the afternoon, looking bored if bored, wandering away if distracted—letting the chips fall as they might.

My wife, too, turns up now and again in this movie, and she offers an entirely different dish, but clearly part of the same banquet. She is seen having a very good time, time after time, talking and laughing animatedly with a number of people, not singing, not looking especially thoughtful, but doing her own little number in her own way. "It's the jolly me," she says. "It didn't feel too bad at the time, but please don't make me look at it again." This movie, by mutual consent, is not shown often at our house.

Yet let me point out, while neither of us relishes witnessing ourselves performing these—or any—versions of ourselves, neither of us felt that he or she—or the other—falsified himself in any important way. What we were attempting—what everyone there was attempting—was to provide a sort of snapshot identity by which the company might refer to us, evaluate us, if they would (and they would, they would); a stereotype, to be sure, yet one that did not, we hoped, deliberately misrepresent our more private conditions.

This matter of stereotypes is worth dwelling on for a moment. We present ourselves and see one another as stereotypes at a family reunion not in order—or not merely—to deceive, but in order both to create and to survive the event.

As for the creation of the event: the purpose of a family reunion, after all, is not to take everyone's spiritual temperature, but to confirm this family, as a family (and through this family all families, Family itself). Naturally, the subject of the occasion is *the family,* and the most significant expression of this subject is the updating, the revising, of the Family Chronicle, for which purpose each individual must be ticked off in time and place and worldly enterprise; his accomplishments must be reviewed and measured against his earlier promise. All this may have relatively little to do with his private, subjective concerns, but the Family Chronicle does not record its members' progress—or lack of it—toward the moral life, and perhaps we should be grateful for that. It does not ask, "Are you a good person?" but "How are you getting on in the world?"; and since that is a question the world often asks us in its own many ways, it need not be considered impudent or unfair. On this great secular Day of Judgment the family seeks to chart its own worldly progress, which is the only progress it can measure or understand. The family is an entity, but it is not a person; it has no collective subjective dimension; its concern, in addition to its history, is with its survival, its prosperity—these being its rough equivalent of moral goals.

So, evaluations are in order, and evaluations are made, usually quite shrewdly, if not harshly. The stereotyping of the individual members is merely a convenience, and usually it is not rigid, but quite responsive to change. Ratings rise and fall as fortunes are made or lost, promising marriages sour and children fall from the fold, or new marriages bring new expectations and new children.

As for surviving the event, the dealing in stereotypes can be a welcome protection against what could amount to a massive personal assault. Can you imagine a houseful or yardful or banquet-hall full of family members all intent on having profound, private exchanges with one another? It could produce mass slaughter. One of the cardinal rules of conduct for the family reunion is: Don't get personal. Nothing must really happen.

Further, the "catching-up" sort of exchange that goes on provides an objectification of one's life that is by and large outside experience—or, at any rate, outside one's customary self-awareness. It may offer a convenient, even a comforting frame for one's own private story.

One's private story *is* separate from the Family Chronicle—surely, at least, they are not identical. The Chronicle, that compilation of events—births, deaths, marriages, divorces, graduations, retirements, promotions, demotions, not to mention moves, accidents, diseases, crises, surprises, tricks and winks of fate—this record constitutes the family story. Few families are without their amateur archivists—those devoted chroniclers whose energetic gift for comprehensive "catching-up" is matched only by their extraordinary powers of absorption and recall. This is probably one of the crudest forms of history ever written—indeed, it is usually never written; it is an oral record, often buttressed with photographs, letters, passports, clippings, and other magical documents; it is also one of the most compelling forms of history we will ever know, for two reasons: 1) It is our first existential experience of history itself; and 2) it is not our own story, but the story to which our lives belong. It is our first experience of history as *story*—how many of us, as children, did not beg our parents, "Tell me a story about when you were little," and how many have not heard our own children repeat the plea? When this tradition of storytelling is once begun, books have a hard time competing—until the children are ready for real books; and even then, they read their books, and still ask an immoderate and unanswerable number of questions about how it was when we were they. Children are passionate historians and "storians." So are we.

Our two accounts—our own story and our role in the family story—will maintain a lively dialectic all our lives. They will seem to merge only to reassert their independence, but this they share: we can no more escape the one than the other.

If, by its stereotyping as well as by its proliferating and disturbing resemblances, the family reunion seems to oppose individuality, so does it also, again with its resemblances as well as with its ruthless Chronicle, oppose anonymity.

When I was a boy I looked upon these reunions with sharp skepticism. Our blood tie, I would complain, was not a sufficient reason for all of us to carry on as though we had things in common—like friends, for example. My experience of the actual occasions was usually bearable—I did have some relatives of whom I was fond—but not joyous; I disliked—perhaps even feared—the judging and reckoning, and I disliked the interminable bragging of parents about their children. They would labor the large and puff up the small accomplishment, or, in the absence of accomplishment, dwell on their children's deference and devotion. A good deal of lying would be necessary to explain away failure and to exalt the minor achievement. Fortunate the parents whose children were both successful and devoted, although seldom fortunate enough to be able to resist a bit of boastful lying themselves.

What I recall most vividly, however, is that the entity of the family, with its uncles, aunts, nephews, nieces, cousins, seemed to obliterate any claim to individuality, no matter how overweening the effort. In the midst of my boredom I thought I would never succeed in escaping or transcending this family, which would continue to multiply and wander even as I would. Even if I were to change my name and settle in Australia, I would eventually be found out by a third cousin who had also ventured to Australia, no doubt for identical reasons. And the one who had fled last could tell the one who had fled first how his departure had been set into the Chronicle, how often the family spoke of him, speculated about him, making him present in his absence. (One reason for the popularity of the movie *The Godfather* was its near sanctification of the family, which was seen to be larger than caste or class or culture or geography.)

For the family is, indeed, inescapable. You may revile it, renounce it, reject it—but you cannot resign from it; you are born into it, and *it* lives within and through you, to the end of your days. This may be inspiring, it may also be very annoying; in either case it is humbling.

Family reunions differ from one another in mood and style (a funeral will obviously not have the same tone as a wedding), and from one family to another, but on the whole I think the similarities, surprisingly, are more striking than the differences.

On the issue of resemblances, more is at stake here than literal facial structure. Families seem to have particular styles and themes that run through them in uncanny variation and repetition, making it possible, for example, immediately to spot a family connection between two remote cousins who hardly know each other and share no physical resemblance at all. And however much the composition of the family may change, and the fates of individuals may alter, this thematic behavior seems to persist, almost as though it had a life of its own. This is particularly apparent in families where power relations are a controlling concern. Reversals and retributions of extraordinary dramatic force may occur as individuals rise to and fall from positions of power, without disturbing the thematic continuity that seems to govern the particular family. On the occasion of a family reunion it is the theme that will be apparent, not the drama, whose real events—those that led to and established a changed situation among the family members—will all have occurred offstage. As I mentioned earlier, one of the first rules of a family reunion is: Nothing must move.

This can be a hard rule both to learn and to keep. At my parents' anniversary my wife was more or less on display, since she and our baby were the newest additions to the central family, and she was meeting many of the clan for the first time. I asked her whether she had, in fact, enjoyed herself as much as she seemed to. Yes, she said, she had, except for Millie and Sam.

Millie and Sam were a married couple my parents' age—they, like my parents, are no longer living—who were members of our extended family, but who had also, accidentally, so to speak, known my wife since she was a child. She had not only a long and profound affection for them, they were important figures to her all her adult life, probably more than either of them knew. She saw them only very occasionally in those years, and much had happened since the last time they met. She had been looking forward particularly to seeing them again.

"I couldn't call off the party to be with them," she said, "so I had to be with them on the party's terms. There were no quiet empty corners we could slip into and talk in any real way, and those flying hugs and kisses and catching-up clatter just don't represent our relationship at all. We pressed each others' hands a lot, and looked into each others' eyes, and so on, but what all that amounted to was just a disagreeable cheapening of what I feel for them, which is serious, and very private and quiet, and doesn't, apparently, have a convenient public form. There I stood, with these people I loved, my arms around them, longing to say something that would be true, about me, about them, about our relation—and unable to speak a sensible word. It was painful."

Ironic though it may be, a family reunion is not an occasion that offers much scope to this major human concern, *love,* either as a personal emotion, pleasurable or not, or as a sacred duty, possible or not. Affection among members of this party may be commonplace and deep; it may also be virtually absent; these conditions will be reflected in differences in the quality, but not the necessity, of the occasion. Regardless of how instrumental affection is, or is not, in determining the shape and style of this family, it has no governing purpose—and has even a restricted place—on the occasion of a reunion. Affection may be felt; it may be expressed, for that can be handled symbolically; but it must not actually be exercised, for the exercise of love between people is an event that moves lives, and on the occasion of this collective portrait nothing must move; it would blur the picture. What is praised here is not persons, or the relationships between persons, whatever the nature of those relationships, but the state, the condition, of relatedness itself. What is honored is not the chosen connectedness that characterizes our friendships, and indeed may prevail within our intimate families as well, but that connectedness whose reality lies entirely outside our inclination, and whose inescapability is, therefore, absolute.

So far as the occasion is concerned, I think some of the most deeply felt and cherished—and enjoyed—family reunions tend to occur at funerals. The pace of the event is slow, the mood reflective, intimate. People draw closer together to speak of the past, to frame that part of the story that holds the life that is gone. The young, especially, are instructed in the Chronicle, as their elders make fresh discoveries, new connections with their heritage. Death broods over the company, foretelling but also enhancing the lives of the living, whether they are harshly grieving or merely wondering at the eternal struggle between finality and endurance.

What, we are entitled to ask, does a family reunion have to tell us about ordinary life—life, and family life?

On the surface, very little, if we are looking for correspondences, references. Daily life within that irreducible unit of willed and unwilled connection that we have learned to call the "nuclear family" differs in every important way from the experience of a family reunion.

At a family reunion all is stasis; time stands still, so that an image of the structure that exists only in time may be conceived and grasped in that stilled moment. Family life, on the other hand, is all flow; living it is rather like a trip down a treacherous river in a small canoe; we spend a lot of time keeping the craft afloat, shooting the rapids. There are, of course, calmer passages as well, blessedly uneventful, unexpected havens of simple routine—and in these quieter periods perhaps we will merely rest, perhaps we will look around, get our bearings, mark changes in the current, note the altered features of the countries we are passing through.

If the family reunion offers us a primer of birth and aging and death, family life constitutes the workbook, or the lab manual, for the same course.

Family life is much concerned with the passage of time: from now to next spring and graduation; from now to someone's birthday, next month; from now to the meeting this weekend; from now to lunch; and from all the nows that came before and pointed to this one.

The flow of family life, with its turbulence and calm, is actually a double current of time and activity. Now and then one or the other may predominate, at times they seem quite out of phase, even in conflict. Time may be experienced as boredom, or anticipation, or change. Activity may be simply an inertia of exertion on a single spot, or it may be felt as significant movement. In any case, this flow, in which time is always passing and we are sometimes truly moving—not with it, but within it—and sometimes still, "marking time" it is said—this flow is very much part of our awareness of life together in a family. Events occur that punctuate and dramatize the flow itself. Children are born, they grow, they grow up, they go away from us toward their own lives, our own parents die, our friends die, it is growing late, it is years since we began.

What is it that we think of, when we think of ourselves and the time—and the times—that are gone? We want: to have lived honorably, to have mattered—to our time and to one another, to have had a meaning . . . we want, we want; meanwhile the potatoes are burning and the gas man is here to read the meter. What family life teaches us about time is that it goes—that what it brings or gives or permits, it also transforms or hardens or takes away. We learn that family life is a passionate daily traffic in perishables, and that what endures, in joy or grief, is seldom what we knew or chose.

Family life is personal life. The people within it play "roles" for one another, as we like to point out these days, but these roles are useful, flexible conventions (like everything else under the sun of course they can be abused); we can hide out inside them when we need relief, we can find a wealth of opportunity for expression and communication within them, and, we discover, we can transcend them altogether in moments when we reach one another deeply in one way or another. Family members talk a lot to one another and some of it is real talk. Family members move around and about in relation to one another, giving and taking their first—and thousandth—lessons in pride, anger, forgiveness, envy, betrayal, and love. A child growing up in a nuclear family learns that a human being is a creature who: is born into a family he did not choose, has needs and feelings and thoughts and ambitions—which are, or are not, filled, expressed, shared, and encouraged—and eventually becomes an independent individual, ready to address the world—and the family that nurtured him—on his own terms.

What endures for an individual is his individuality—his experience of his individuality—and that occurs in the now, connected, of course, to many other nows of personal consequence. An individual, inspired with subjectivity, spurred by the urgencies of personality, armed with self, single-handedly takes on time in mortal combat. Time wins, of course, but the battle may be glorious. We are all, needless to say, individuals, and most of us are the better for it.

But a human being is more than this, too. There are realities to his existence that seldom penetrate his consciousness because they are not directly perceived in experience, but may be brought to awareness through metaphor. At a family reunion a person may glimpse his own life in a way that does not belong to his ordinary perceptions.

As he looks from the oldest members at the gathering, many of whom may not be present at the next reunion, to the youngest, who were not here the last time, he can conceive an image of his own life as a trajectory in time, an arc that began at one point and will end at another, creating a tangible shape, and linking those points to a far huger but still tangible network of interconnecting arcs. That is, he sees his life as a whole, not as a series of experiences, but as a single act—a *thing,* real, objective, unique. He sees that his existence has a dimension in reality that is beyond his experience—almost, but perhaps not quite, beyond his comprehension.

He, who thought his existence was his own, belonged to him, is abruptly reeducated. His experience, which *is* his own, has taught him that living is a process of tracing on sand—that some patterns are deeper, or larger, or more beautiful than others, but that the wind and the water ultimately wash over all. Now, at this family reunion, as he beholds the great chain of generation (to which he belongs), threading its way through the present moment, linking the old to the young, the dead to the unborn, and as he sees that it contains—and is contained by—his own life, he imagines his life taking its particular place in a vast, organic, historical continuity.

In the same process by which time is constantly erasing its own surface, it is forming the deep structure that we never see—and that may be apprehended only through imagery—wherein our disappearing lives are set in stone. For, beneath the sand there is rock; the rock is shaped, is being shaped, will be shaped—by us, by our lives, by our tracings in the sand.

A human being, the family reunion teaches, is a creature who: is born into a family, lives without and within it, colors and shapes it with his being, brings to it his gifts, his acts, replenishes it with his children, and diminishes it—his final shaping—with his own death.